DIHAM

CONSUMER CREDIT ACT 2006

D0537386

Related titles by Law Society Publishing:

Data Protection Handbook
General Editor: Peter Carey

Drafting Confidentiality Agreements (2nd edition)
Mark Anderson

Execution of Documents: A Practical Guide
Mark Anderson and Victor Warner

Freedom of Information Handbook
General Editors: Peter Carey and Marcus Turle

Pensions Act 2004: A Guide to the New Law
Hammonds: Jane Marshall, Catherine McKenna and Elizabeth Graham

Titles from Law Society Publishing can be ordered from all good legal bookshops or direct from our distributors, Marston Book Services (tel. 01235 465656 or email **law.society@marston.co.uk**). For further information or a catalogue, email our editorial and marketing office at **publishing@lawsociety.org.uk**.

CONSUMER CREDIT ACT 2006

A Guide to the New Law

Julia Smith and Sandra McCalla

The Law Society

Crown copyright material is reproduced with the permission of the Controller of Her Majesty's Stationery Office

ISBN 10: 1–85328–543–9

ISBN 13: 978–1–85328–543–1

Published in 2006 by the Law Society
113 Chancery Lane, London WC2A 1PL

Typeset by J&L Composition Ltd, Filey, North Yorkshire
Printed by TJ International, Padstow, Cornwall

CONTENTS

FOREWORD

The Consumer Credit Act 2006 has made significant changes to the law relating to consumer credit. The Act of 1974 has not proved to be as effective as it should have been to protect the interests of consumers. One of the key changes is the introduction of an unfair relationship test in place of the draconian extortionate credit bargain test. Other changes include improved regulation of this important area of commercial activity.

This book is intensely practical. It describes clearly and succinctly the principal provisions of the new act. Where the Act is silent, it offers some helpful suggestions as to how it may be interpreted by the courts. For example, the Act gives no guidance as to the type of terms, actions or omissions that will make a relationship unfair beyond saying that the court is to have regard to 'all matters it thinks relevant (including matters relating to the creditor and matters relating to the debtor)'. The authors suggest how the court might approach this important and difficult question of interpretation by reference to Unfair Terms in Consumer Contracts Regulations 1999.

I commend this book to all practitioners who practise in this area. The authors are to be congratulated on providing such an accessible and useful contribution to this highly technical part of our law.

Rt Hon Lord Justice Dyson
14 July 2006

INTRODUCTION

The Consumer Credit Act 2006 (CCA 2006) is the culmination of a three-year review of consumer credit law. It is intended to reform the Consumer Credit Act 1974 (CCA 1974) so as to create a fairer and more competitive credit market.

> Millions of consumers will enjoy greater protection from unscrupulous lenders . . . The Consumer Credit Act 2006 is the biggest overhaul of consumer credit legislation since 1974. It will be a huge boost to consumer rights and redress where borrowing of money is concerned. The Act also introduces major changes to the licensing of consumer credit businesses and new powers to drive rogues out of the market (DTI press release, 30 March 2006).

The rights of debtors and hirers are to be enhanced by removing the financial limits on regulated agreements, by affording relief in respect of 'unfair relationships', and by giving access to free alternative dispute resolution. The regulation of consumer credit, consumer hire and ancillary credit businesses is to be improved and made fairer for businesses, by enabling the Office of Fair Trading (OFT) to impose more proportionate sanctions for unsatisfactory conduct.

Rogue traders are to be driven out of the market, but, in the interests of product development and differentiation, and so as not to drive lawful creditors out of the 'non-status' or 'sub-prime' markets, no ceiling is to be imposed on interest rates; no restrictions are to be imposed on the manner in which interest is to be calculated and applied to an account; and no restriction is to be imposed on a creditor's allocation of repayments between lower interest-bearing and higher interest-bearing balances.

Borrowers are to be kept informed about the state of their accounts. Notices are to be given to customers who are in arrears, together with standard information from the OFT designed to help them to avoid an escalation of financial difficulty.

More limited licences are to be made available, so as to make the licensing process simpler, fairer and more efficient, where licences are only required for businesses of limited descriptions, within the existing categories. However, in considering a person's fitness to hold a licence, the OFT will be required to look at competence and proposed practices and procedures as well as past conduct.

Indefinite licences are to become the norm, removing the need for renewal. However, businesses will be subject to periodic charges and the overall level of charges payable may be expected to increase in order to cover the additional work required of the OFT. The OFT is to have an explicit duty to monitor businesses and will have wide powers to gather information, to enter and search premises, to impose requirements, and to fine businesses.

An independent Consumer Credit Appeals Tribunal is to hear appeals against the OFT's decisions, with appeals from the tribunal on points of law to be heard by the Court of Appeal.

Legal practitioners will need to have regard to the width of relief that will be available to customers under the unfair relationship provisions: any unfair practices may have a significant impact on the value of a credit portfolio in that, for example, payments already received from debtors may become repayable and debtors may be discharged from future liabilities. When considering advertising, agreement forms, and any standard communications and procedures, account will have to be taken of the ways in which unfair relationships might be created and could be avoided.

A focused approach will be required for licensing applications, to take full advantage, for example, of entitlement to more limited licences, where fitness to hold an unlimited licence is in any doubt or an unlimited licence is unnecessary, and to ensure that appropriate practices and procedures are in place.

Practitioners should be aware of the procedures for making representations in relation to proposed sanctions, the scope of the OFT's new powers, and the new routes of appeal.

TABLE OF CASES

TABLE OF STATUTES

TABLE OF STATUTORY INSTRUMENTS AND EUROPEAN LEGISLATION

Statutory instruments

European legislation

1 REGULATED AGREEMENTS

Key changes

- Partnerships of four or more to lose the protection of the Consumer Credit Act 1974
- Financial limits to be removed
- Exemption for high net worth customers
- Exemption of agreements for business purposes where a financial limit is exceeded

1.1 LOSS OF PROTECTION FOR LARGE PARTNERSHIPS

Most of the protections and remedies provided for by the Consumer Credit Act 1974 (CCA 1974) are only provided to debtors or hirers under agreements that are 'regulated agreements'. An agreement is only a regulated agreement for the purposes of CCA 1974 when the debtor or hirer is an 'individual'. There are two types of regulated agreement, namely consumer credit agreements within the definition set out in s.8 and consumer hire agreements within the definition set out in s.15. The definition of 'consumer credit agreement' requires the debtor to be an 'individual'.[1] The definition of 'consumer hire agreement' requires the hirer to be an 'individual' (s.15(1)).

The relief available to debtors under credit agreements that are not regulated agreements, namely the remedies available in respect of extortionate credit bargains under ss.137–140, is also only available to debtors who are 'individuals' (s.137(2)). Similarly, the unfair relationship provisions, which are to replace the extortionate credit bargain provisions (see **Chapter 5**), will provide protection to individuals in respect of credit agreements (s.140C(1), to be inserted by the Consumer Credit Act 2006 (CCA 2006), s.21).

However, up until now, a partnership of an unlimited number of individuals has been treated as an 'individual' and so has been afforded the protections and remedies available under CCA 1974, as well as being subjected to what some may have found to be the inconvenience of the procedural requirements for execution of regulated agreements (CCA 1974, Part V).

Under the CCA 2006 the definition of 'individual' in CCA 1974, s.189(1) is to be amended (CCA 2006, s.1)[2] so that it is no longer to include partnerships of more than three persons. Accordingly, loans to partnerships of more than three persons will no longer be regulated by CCA 1974.

An agreement to lend to a partnership of two or three persons will be a regulated agreement, unless it falls within one of the exemptions provided for by CCA 1974, s.16 or unless all the partners are bodies corporate.[3] An agreement with an unincorporated body of persons which is not a partnership and which does not consist entirely of bodies corporate will still be a regulated agreement, regardless of the number of persons in the body, unless the agreement is exempt.

Credit agreements with partnerships of three or less will be susceptible to challenge under the new unfair relationship provisions, whether or not they are exempt, provided that the partnership does not consist entirely of bodies corporate.

The existing, broader, definition of individual will continue to apply for the purposes of the unfair relationship provisions (ss.140A–140D (see **Chapter 5**)) and the financial services ombudsman scheme (Financial Services and Markets Act 2000, s.226A (see **Chapter 8**)) in relation to agreements made before the amendment to s.189(1) comes into effect (CCA 2006, Sched.3, paras.17 and 29).

1   Currently achieved by the combination of CCA 1974, s.8(1) and (2). When CCA 2006, ss.1 and 2 are brought into force, s.8(2) is to be repealed and the definition of consumer credit agreement will be moved to s.8(1). The expression 'personal credit agreement' will no longer be used, having previously been used to cover credit agreements with an individual, regardless of the amount of credit.
2   Late in 2006, according to the DTI's timetable published in May 2006.
3   CCA 1974, s.8 (to be amended by CCA 2006, s.2) read together with the definition of 'individual' in CCA 1974, s.189(1) (to be amended by CCA 2006, s.1).

1.2   REMOVAL OF FINANCIAL LIMITS

The financial limit on regulated consumer credit agreements is to be removed, by the repeal of CCA 1974, s.8(2) (CCA 2006, s.2(1)(b)). Similarly, s.15(1)(c) is to be repealed (CCA 2006, s.2(2)) so that the definition of a regulated consumer hire agreement will no longer depend upon the hirer's being required to make payments exceeding a financial limit.[1]

The existing financial limit is £25,000 both for regulated consumer credit agreements and for regulated consumer hire agreements.

Once the financial limits have been removed, a consumer credit agreement (i.e. one where the debtor is an individual as defined by s.189(1)) will always be a regulated agreement unless it is 'exempt' (s.8(3)) and a consumer hire agreement (i.e. one where the hirer is an individual as defined by s.189(1)) will always be a regulated agreement unless it is 'exempt' (s.15(2)).

1 These amendments are intended to be brought into force on 6 April 2008 (DTI Timetable, May 2006).

1.3 EXEMPTION FOR HIGH NET WORTH CUSTOMERS

Provision is to be made for a new category of exempt agreement, with a view to preventing loss of business from wealthy borrowers to offshore financial centres, due to the formalities that will be required (CCA 1974, Part V), regardless of the size of the loan, when the financial limit for regulated agreements is removed.

By CCA 1974, s.16A (inserted by CCA 2006, s.3),[1] the Secretary of State is to have the power to create a new exemption in respect of debtors and hirers who are certified as being 'of high net worth'.[2]

The debtor or hirer must be a natural person;[3] the agreement must include a declaration made by the debtor or hirer that he agrees to forgo the protection and remedies that would be available to him if the agreement were a regulated agreement; the creditor or owner must have been provided with a copy of a 'statement of high net worth' in respect of the debtor or hirer before the agreement was made; and that statement of high net worth must be 'current', that is, made during the period of one year ending with the day on which the agreement is made (s.16A(1) and (3)(c)).

It is to be left to the Secretary of State to determine the level and type of income, as well as the value and type of assets that will be required for a person to be of high net worth: s.16A(2) defines a statement of high net worth as a statement that, in the opinion of the person making it, the person in relation to whom it is made either:

(a) received income of a specified description of at least the specified amount during the previous financial year; or
(b) had, throughout that year, net assets of a specified description with a total value of not less than the specified value.

For this purpose, 'specified' means specified in an order made under s.16A by the Secretary of State (s.16A(4)(a) and (6)).

The Secretary of State is also to determine the characteristics or qualifications of the persons who may make a statement of high net worth, which will have to be made by someone other than the debtor or hirer in relation to whom it is made, by a person of a 'specified description'.

The Secretary of State may make provision, by order, as to the form, content and signing of the statement of high net worth and of the declaration to be made by the debtor or hirer that he agrees to forgo the protection afforded in respect of regulated agreements by CCA 1974 (s.16A(4)(b)).

Where an agreement has two or more debtors or hirers, a separate statement of high net worth must have been provided to the creditor or owner in relation to each debtor or hirer (s.16A(5)).

The statement of high net worth must relate to the 'previous financial year', that is, the financial year, ending on 31 March, which immediately preceded the financial year in which the statement is made (s.16A(6) and (7)).

The high net worth exemption will only have the effect of preventing agreements to which it applies from being regulated credit agreements. The new unfair relationships provisions in CCA 1974, ss.140A–140C, as amended, will apply to agreements with debtors and hirers of high net worth that are not regulated by virtue of an order made under s.16A (CCA 1974, ss.16A(8) and 140C(1) as they are to be amended by CCA 2006, ss.3 and 21).

1   CCA 1974, s.16A came into force on 16 June 2006 (The Consumer Credit Act 2006 (Commencement No.1) Order 2006, SI 2006/1508 (Commencement Order (No.1) 2006)). However, it is intended that the Order to be made to create a high net worth exemption will come into force on 6 April 2008 (DTI Timetable, May 2006).
2   The figures that have been suggested are a gross annual income of £100,000 or net assets of £250,000. (See the debate on clause 3 of the Bill during the debate in Standing Committee on 23 June 2005.)
3   A debtor or hirer may be an individual, so making the agreement a regulated agreement, without being a natural person, because the definition of 'individual' in s.189(1) includes an unincorporated body of persons.

1.4   EXEMPTION OF BUSINESS AGREEMENTS EXCEEDING FINANCIAL LIMIT

A consumer credit agreement or consumer hire agreement that is entered into by the debtor or hirer wholly or predominantly for the purposes of a business that he carries on or intends to carry on will now be exempt, by s.16B (to be inserted by CCA 2006, s.4), if, in the case of a credit agreement, the creditor provides the debtor with credit exceeding £25,000 or, in the case of a hire agreement, the hirer is required to make payments exceeding £25,000.[1]

An agreement outside those financial limits will be presumed to be entered into predominantly for the purposes of a business carried on, or intended to be carried on, by the debtor or hirer, if it contains a declaration by the debtor or hirer to the effect that it is entered into by him wholly or predominantly for the purposes of such a business (s.16B(2)). However, the presumption will not apply if the creditor, or any one of two or more creditors (s.16B(5)), or any person who has acted on behalf of the creditor in connection with the entering into of the agreement, knew, when the agreement was entered into, or had reasonable cause to suspect, that the agreement was not entered into by the debtor or hirer wholly or predominantly for the purposes of a business carried on, or intended to be carried on, by him (s.16B(3)).

The Secretary of State may make provision, by Order, as to the form, content and signing of a declaration that an agreement is entered into by the debtor or hirer wholly or predominantly for the purposes of a business (CCA 1974, s.16B(4)).[2]

A credit agreement which is exempt by virtue of s.16B will, nonetheless, be subject to the unfair relationships provisions in ss.140A–140C (ss.16B(6) and 140C(1)).

---

1   The limit may be altered by order made by the Secretary of State, subject to the approval of each House of Parliament (CCA 1974, s.181 as it is to be amended by CCA 2006, s.5(7)).
2   CCA 1974, s.16B(4) came into force on 16 June 2006 (Commencement Order (No.1) 2006).

2 STATEMENTS

> **Key changes**
> - Periodic statements to be provided under fixed-sum credit agreements
> - More information to be prescribed for running-account credit agreement statements

2.1 FIXED-SUM CREDIT AGREEMENTS

Section 77A (to be inserted by CCA 2006, s.6) of CCA 1974 is to require creditors under regulated agreements for fixed-sum credit, other than non-commercial (see CCA 1974, s.189(1))[1] or small agreements,[2] to provide periodic statements to debtors.[3]

Once s.77A has come into force, the first statement will have to be given within the year that begins on the day after the date of the agreement (s.77A(1)(a), to be inserted by CCA 2006, s.6) or, in the case of agreements that have already been made before the section comes into force, within the year that begins with the day on which the section does come into force (CCA 2006, Sched.3, para.2).[4] Subsequent statements will have to be given at intervals of no more than one year (s.77A(1)(b), to be inserted by CCA 2006, s.6).

The statements may be delivered, posted or, provided that the debtor has agreed that they may be delivered to him by being transmitted to a particular electronic address in a particular electronic form, transmitted to that address in that form.[5]

Requirements may be imposed as to the form and content of the statements by regulations to be made by the Secretary of State (s.77A(2), inserted by CCA 2006, s.6, read together with the definition of 'regulations' in s.189(1)). Requisite content is likely to include reminders of rights under CCA 1974: applicable interest rates; movements on the account; and opening, running and closing balances.[6]

The obligation continues until no sum is, will or may become payable under the agreement (s.77A(4), to be inserted by CCA 2006, s.6). Accordingly, if the loan is to be repaid and is in fact repaid, or is settled, within one year, the creditor need not give any statement under s.77A.

The debtor is to have no liability to pay any sum in connection with the preparation or the giving to him of a statement under s.77A (s.77A(3), to be inserted by CCA 2006, s.6).

If the creditor fails to comply with the obligation to give statements under s.77A, he will not be entitled to enforce the agreement during 'the period of non-compliance'; the debtor will have no liability to pay any interest calculated by reference to the period of non-compliance or any part of it; and the debtor will have no liability to pay any default sum which would otherwise be payable during the period of non-compliance or after that period in connection with a breach of the agreement occurring during the period of non-compliance, whether or not the breach continues after the end of that period (s.77A(5) and (6), to be inserted by CCA 2006, s.6).

Where interest has been pre-computed at the outset, it would seem that a period of non-compliance with the requirement to provide annual statements will necessitate a recalculation of the interest. No provision is made for interest already paid in respect of a period of non-compliance (because payable in advance) to be refunded. It would seem that, if the agreement provided for the interest to be included in payments that fell due before a period of non-compliance, the debtor will have been liable to pay that interest at the time of the payments made.[7] On the other hand, where such interest should have been paid in advance but has not in fact been paid before the period of non-compliance, because the debtor is in arrears, it will no longer be recoverable and, to that extent, the arrears will need to be recalculated.

The period of non-compliance in relation to the first statement would begin immediately after the end of the year which commences on the day after the day when the agreement is made, so that, for example, if an agreement was made on 1 May 2008 (and CCA 2006, s.6 had commenced by then), the period of non-compliance in relation to the first statement would begin on 2 May 2009 (s.77A(7), read together with s.77(1)(a)). The period of non-compliance in relation to each subsequent statement would begin immediately after the period of one year after the last statement was given (s.77A(7), read together with s.77(1)(b)). Although the period within which each subsequent statement is to be given is less precisely expressed than the time limit for the first statement, it would seem that the intention is that if, for example, the first statement was given on 1 May 2009, the period of non-compliance in relation to the second statement would begin on 2 May 2010. In each case, the period of non-compliance would end at the end of the day on which the overdue statement was given or the day on which no further sum was, would or might become payable under the agreement, whichever was earlier (s.77A(7)).

---

1   A consumer credit agreement is a non-commercial agreement if it is not made by the creditor in the course of a business carried on by him (s.189(1)).

2 A small agreement is limited by amount, currently £50, and is either unsecured or secured only by guarantee or indemnity (s.17).
3 The obligation is to be imposed by s.77A(1). Section 77A(8) is to exclude small agreements and non-commercial agreements from the application of the section.
4 Apart from the power to make regulations in CCA 1974, s.77A(4), which came into force on 16 June 2006 (Commencement Order (No.1) 2006), it is intended that s.77A should come into force on 6 April 2008 (DTI Timetable, May 2006). The obligation to provide statements will not arise until s.77A(1) comes into force. The first statement must be given in relation to existing agreements within one year after s.77A(1) comes into force.
5 The creditor is to 'give' each statement, which, by virtue of s.189(1), means 'deliver or send by an appropriate method', an 'appropriate method' meaning, again by virtue of s.189(1), post or transmission in the form of an electronic communication in accordance with s.176A(1). An electronic transmission must be in the form of an electronic communication that is capable of being stored for future reference in such a way that the information in it may be reproduced without change (s.176A(1)).
6 See the agenda for the DTI IT Discussion Group meeting on 3 May 2006.
7 It is possible that licensing sanctions, or the unfair relationship provisions, could be used to deter or reverse the charging of interest in advance. However, it should be noted that the Government resisted attempts to include any provision in the Bill to restrict the methods that may be adopted in the application of interest, because that would remove 'an important element of product differentiation' (see the debate in the House of Lords on Amendment No. 18 in Grand Committee, 8 November 2005).

2.2   RUNNING-ACCOUNT CREDIT AGREEMENTS

Creditors are already required to provide periodic statements to debtors under regulated agreements for running-account credit, showing the state of the account at regular intervals of not more than 12 months (s.78(4)(a)). Where the agreement provides for the making of payments by the debtor, or the charging of interest or any sum, in relation to specified periods, each statement must show the state of the account at the end of any of those periods during which there is a movement in the account (s.78(4)(b)).

Each statement must be given within a certain period after the end of the period to which the statement relates (s.78(5)). If the statement includes a demand for payment, it must be given within one month after the end of the period to which it relates; if it does not include a demand for payment and it indicates that there is no credit or debit balance at the end of the period to which it relates, it must be given within 12 months of the end of the period; if there has been no credit or debit balance on the account at any time during the period to which it relates, the statement is only required to be given within 12 months after the date of the first credit or debit balance on the account following the end of the period to which the statement relates; and, in any other case, the statement must be given within six months from the end of the period to which it relates. These periods are prescribed by regulations made by the Secretary of State (Consumer Credit (Running-Account Credit Information) Regulations 1983, SI 1983/1570, reg. 3, made under CCA 1974, s.78(5)).

The statements may be delivered, posted or, provided that the debtor has agreed that they may be delivered to him by being transmitted to a particular electronic address in a particular electronic form, transmitted to that address in that form.[1]

There is already power for the Secretary of State to make regulations as to the form and content of the periodic statements to be served in respect of running-account credit agreements (s.78(4)). The existing regulations require each statement to be in legible writing and to contain the following information:

(1) the opening and closing balances at the beginning and end of the period to which the statement relates;
(2) the date of any movement on the account that is shown on the statement;
(3) the date of the end of the period to which the statement relates;
(4) the amount of any payment credited to the account;
(5) the amount of any drawing, with sufficient information to enable the debtor to identify it;
(6) the amount of any interest or other charges payable by the debtor and applied to the account during the period to which the statement relates; and
(7) where the statement shows that interest has been applied to the account during the period to which it relates, sufficient information to enable the debtor to check the calculation of the interest, or the rate(s) of interest applied and, if more than one rate, the time during which each rate applied, or a statement that the rate, or each rate, of interest that has been used in the calculation of the interest will be provided on request, together with a clear explanation of the manner in which the interest has been calculated (Consumer Credit (Running-Account Credit Information) Regulations 1983, reg. 2 and Sched.).

A new subsection, s.78(4A) (inserted by CCA 2006, s.7(1)),[2] makes explicit provision for the Secretary of State to make regulations that require a periodic statement in respect of a regulated running-account credit agreement to contain information, in whatever terms which may be prescribed by the regulations, about the consequences of the debtor's failing to make payments as required by the agreement or only making payments of a description prescribed by the regulations in circumstances prescribed by the regulations. The regulations may apply in relation to agreements regardless of when they were made (CCA 2006, Sched.3, para.3).

It is envisaged that the statements will be required to contain warnings such as:

> Paying only your minimum repayment will substantially increase the amount that you must repay and the time that it takes to pay it. You may also incur additional charges, which may be added to your balance

and

> Failure to make your minimum repayment can mean that you are in breach of this credit agreement and could result in the creditor bringing legal proceedings against you. This could have a detrimental effect on your credit rating and affect your ability to borrow in future.[3]

A warning might also be required that payments will be applied first in repayment of that part of the outstanding balance which bears the lowest rate of interest, such as balances transferred from other credit card accounts,[4] leaving unpaid that part, or those parts, of the balance on which interest will be charged at a higher rate, or higher rates.[5]

1 The creditor is to 'give' each statement, which, by virtue of s.189(1), means 'deliver or send by an appropriate method', an 'appropriate method' meaning, again by virtue of s.189(1), post or transmission in the form of an electronic communication in accordance with s.176A(1). An electronic transmission must be in the form of an electronic communication that is capable of being stored for future reference in such a way that the information in it may be reproduced without change (s.176A(1)).
2 With effect from 16 June 2006 (Commencement Order (No.1) 2006).
3 See the debate on clause 7 of the Bill during the first sitting of the Standing Committee on 23 June 2005.
4 In response to advertisements for low interest, or no interest, on balance transfers.
5 See the debate on clause 7 of the Bill in Grand Committee in the House of Lords on 8 November 2005, and the debate on Amendment No. 7 at the Report Stage on 18 January 2006.

2.3   STATEMENTS TO JOINT DEBTORS

Where there are two or more debtors under a regulated agreement, the general rule is that anything that the creditor is required to do to the debtor, or in relation to the debtor, by or under CCA 1974, must be done to or in relation to each of the debtors (s.185(1)(a)).

Section 185(2) provides that, where there are two or more debtors, any debtor may authorise the creditor, by a notice signed by the debtor, a 'dispensing notice', not to comply with the requirement to provide that debtor with periodical statements under s.78(4). This provision is to be amended (by CCA 2006, s.7(3), the existing s.185(2) being replaced by s.185(2), (2A), (2B), (2C) and (2D)), so as to apply also in respect of the statements that a creditor will be required to give under s.77A in relation to fixed-sum credit agreements. The proviso currently contained in s.185(2)(a) is to be moved to s.185(2B) and clarified, so as to make it clear that no dispensing notice will take effect if its effect would be to make dispensing notices operative in relation to all of the debtors to whom credit is provided. For example, where there are three debtors, two may serve dispensing notices, with the result that the creditor need only provide statements to the third debtor. However, if all three were to serve dispensing notices, the notice that was served last would be of no effect.

3 PROTECTION FOR CUSTOMERS IN DEFAULT

Key changes

- Customers to receive notices when in arrears
- No interest on default charges before notice
- No compound interest on default charges
- Notice required for interest after judgment

3.1 INFORMATION

3.1.1 Information sheets

The Government are committed to ensuring that all consumers receive clear, concise, independent information about debt management options, including debt advice.[1]

The OFT will be required to prepare an arrears information sheet and a default information sheet (CCA 1974, s.86A(1), to be inserted by CCA 2006, s.8), and to publish them by general notice, as soon as practicable after s.86A comes into force (CCA 2006, Sched.3, para.5).[2]

Each information sheet will take effect at the end of the period of three months beginning with the day on which general notice of it is given (s.86A(5)). Any revised information sheet will take effect at the end of the period of three months beginning with the day on which general notice of the revised information sheet is given (s.86A(6) and (7)).

The arrears information sheet is to include information to help debtors and hirers who receive 'notices of sums in arrears' (arrears notices) (s.86A(2)). Arrears notices will have to be given to debtors and hirers, under s.86B in respect of fixed-sum credit agreements and hire agreements, and under s.86C in respect of running-account credit agreements (ss.86B and 86C, to be inserted by CCA 2006, ss.9 and 10 (see below)). A copy of the current arrears information sheet will have to be sent to the debtor or hirer with each arrears notice (ss.86B(6) and 86C(3)).

The default information sheet is to include information to help debtors who receive default notices (s.86A(3)). A default notice must be served under s.87(1) before the creditor or owner under a regulated agreement can become entitled, by reason of any breach by the debtor or hirer, to terminate the agreement, or to demand earlier payment of any sum, or to recover possession of any goods or land, or to treat any right conferred on the debtor or hirer by the agreement as terminated, restricted or deferred, or to enforce any security. A copy of the current default information sheet will have to be sent to the debtor or hirer with each default notice (s.88(4A), to be inserted by CCA 2006, s.14).

Regulations may be made by the Secretary of State, to make provision about the information to be included in an information sheet (s.86A(4), to be inserted by CCA 2006, s.8).

3.1.2   Arrears notices under fixed-sum credit and hire agreements

Creditors will have to give periodic notices to customers who are in arrears under regulated fixed-sum credit agreements and regulated consumer hire agreements (s.86B). The obligation will not apply in respect of non-commercial agreements or small agreements (s.86B(12)(b), to be inserted by CCA 2006, s.9).[3]

Under s.86B, notice will have to be given to the customer, unless there is a judgment debt, or part of a judgment debt, outstanding from him in relation to the agreement (s.86B(1)(e)), whenever:

(a)   at least two payments have fallen due under the agreement (s.86B(1)(a)), or, in the case of an agreement requiring weekly or more frequent payments, at least four payments have fallen due (s.86B(1)(a) and (9)); and

(b)   the amount of the customer's arrears equate to, or exceed, the sum of the most recent two payments to have fallen due (s.86B(1)(b) and (c)), or, in the case of an agreement requiring weekly or more frequent payments, the sum of the most recent four payments to have fallen due (s.86B(1)(b), (c) and (9)).

Within 14 days, beginning with the day on which the above conditions are satisfied, the creditor or owner must give the customer a notice under s.86B (CCA 1974, s.86B(2)(a)), unless he is already giving periodic notices under s.86B, as a result of those conditions having been satisfied previously (s.86B(2)(a) read together with s.86(1)(d)). He must then give further notices under s.86B at intervals of not more than six months (s.86B(2)(b)) until the debtor or hirer ceases to be in arrears or a judgment is given in relation to the agreement, requiring payment of a sum by the debtor or hirer (s.86B(3), (4)(a) and (b)).

For this purpose, the debtor or hirer will cease to be in arrears when:

(a) he has paid any sums that he has failed to pay on time;
(b) he has paid any default sum that has become payable in connection with his failure to pay any sum on time;[4]
(c) he has paid any interest that has become payable in connection with such a default sum; and
(d) he has paid any other interest that has become payable in connection with his failure to pay any sum on time (s.86B(5)).

If the debtor or hirer ceases to be in arrears during the 14 days within which the first arrears notice is to be given, the creditor or owner must still give him that notice (s.86B(3)).

The notices may be delivered or posted.

No requirement is to be specified in CCA 1974 as to the form or content of the arrears notices to be given under s.86B, but each notice must include a copy of the current OFT arrears information sheet (s.86B(6))[5] and the Secretary of State may make regulations as to the form and content (s.86B(8)). It is likely that the regulations will require arrears notices to be on paper and not in electronic form.[6]

The debtor or hirer is to have no liability to pay any sum in connection with the preparation or giving to him of an arrears notice under s.86B (s.86B(7)).

In the case of an agreement which requires payments at weekly or more frequent intervals and which was made more than 20 weeks before the day on which the most recent payment fell due, the obligation to give the first of a series of arrears notices under s.86B will only arise in respect of arrears of payments falling due within that 20-week period (s.86B(10), which must be read together with s.86(9) and (11)).

Section 86B will apply in relation to agreements made before s.86B comes into force (on the commencement of CCA 2006, s.9), but the obligation to give the first notice will not arise until at least two payments have fallen after the section has come into force and the arrears equate to or exceed the sum of the last two payments that the debtor or hirer has been required to pay (CCA 2006, Sched.3, para.6(1) and (2)).[7] Where payments are required to be made weekly or more frequently, the obligation to give the first notice will not arise until at least four payments have fallen due after the section has come into force and the arrears equate to or exceed the sum of the last four payments required (CCA 2006, Sched.3, para.6(3)).

3.1.3   Arrears notices under running-account credit agreements

Creditors will also have to give notices to debtors who are in arrears under regulated agreements for running-account credit (s.86C(1), read together with the definition of 'applicable agreement' in s.86C(7), both to be inserted by CCA 2006, s.10), other than non-commercial or small agreements (s.86B(12)(b), to be inserted by CCA 2006, s.9).[8]

Under s.86C, a notice will have to be given to the debtor, unless there is a judgment debt, or part of a judgment debt, outstanding from him in relation to the agreement (s.86C(1)(d)), whenever:

(a) at least two payments have fallen due under the agreement (s.86C(1)(a));
(b) the last two payments to have fallen due have not been made (s.86C(1)(b)); and
(c) the creditor has not already become obliged to give a notice under s.86C in relation to either of those two payments (s.86C(1)(c)).

The notice must be given no later than the end of the period within which the creditor is next required to give a periodic statement in relation to the agreement under s.78(4) (s.86C(2)).

Again, no requirement is to be specified in CCA 1974 as to the form or content of the notice, but it will have to include a copy of the current OFT arrears information sheet (s.86C(3)) and the Secretary of State is empowered to make regulations as to the form and content (s.86C(6)).

The notice may be incorporated in the next periodic statement required to be given under s.78(4) or in any other statement or notice that the creditor gives the debtor in relation to the agreement by virtue of any other provision of CCA 1974 (s.86C(4)).

The notice may be delivered, posted or, provided that the debtor or hirer has agreed that it may be delivered to him by being transmitted to a particular electronic address in a particular electronic form, transmitted to that address in that form.[9]

The debtor or hirer is to have no liability to pay any sum in connection with the preparation or giving to him of an arrears notice under s.86C (s.86C(5)).

Section 86C will apply to agreements made before it comes into force, but the obligation to provide a notice will not arise until at least two payments have fallen due after the section has come into force and the last two payments have not been made (CCA 2006, Sched.3, para.7).

Apart from the power to make regulations under s.86C(6), which came into force on 16 June 2006,[10] s.86C is intended to come into force on 6 April 2008.[11] References here to the section coming into force should be read as references to s.86C(1) and (2).

3.1.4 Consequences of failure to give arrears notices

If a creditor or owner fails to give an arrears notice that he is required to give under s.86B or s.86C, the agreement will be unenforceable against the debtor or hirer during the 'period of non-compliance' (s.86D(1), (2) and (3), to be inserted by CCA 2006, s.11).

Moreover, the debtor or hirer will be released from the following liabilities:

(a) to pay any interest calculated by reference to a period of non-compliance or to any part of the period of non-compliance;
(b) to pay any default sum that would otherwise have become payable during the period of non-compliance;
(c) to pay any default sum that would have become payable after the end of the period of non-compliance in connection with a breach occurring during the period of non-compliance (whether or not the breach continues after the end of the period of non-compliance) (s.86D(4)).

For these purposes, a period of non-compliance will begin on the day after the period within which any arrears notice should have been given under s.86B or s.86C (s.86D(5)) and it will end:

(a) in the case of the first notice to be given when a debtor under a regulated fixed-sum credit agreement or a hirer under a regulated consumer hire agreement falls into arrears, on the day that notice is given (s.86D(5)(b) and (6)(a));
(b) in the case of the second or any subsequent notice to be given when a debtor under a fixed-sum credit agreement or a hirer under a regulated consumer hire agreement is in arrears, the day on which the notice is given or, if earlier, the day on which the debtor or hirer ceases to be in arrears (s.86D(5)(b) and (6)(b));[12] and
(c) in the case of a notice to be given when a debtor under a regulated running-account credit agreement is in arrears, at the end of the day on which the notice is given (s.86D(5)(b) and (6)(c)).

---

1 The Parliamentary Under-Secretary of State for Trade and Industry, introducing clause 8 of the Bill during the first sitting of the Standing Committee on 23 June 2005.
2 It is intended that CCA 1974, s.86A should come into force 6 April 2008 (DTI Timetable, May 2006).
3 A consumer credit or consumer hire agreement is a non-commercial agreement if it is not made by the creditor or owner in the course of a business carried on by him (s.189(1)). A small agreement is limited by amount, currently £50, and is either unsecured or secured only by guarantee or indemnity (s.17).
4 It would seem that the debtor will not be in arrears for the purposes of s.86B by reason of his owing a 'default sum' in respect of a breach other than non-payment. 'Default sum' is defined in a new s.187A, inserted by s.18 of CCA 2006 with effect from 16 June 2006 (Commencement Order (No.1) 2006).
5 The arrears information sheet is to be published by general notice under s.86A.
6 See the agenda for the DTI IT Discussion Group meeting on 3 May 2006.
7 Apart from the power to make form and content regulations in CCA 1974, s.86B(8), which came into force 16 June 2006 (Commencement Order (No.1) 2006), s.86B is intended to come into force 6 April 2008 (DTI Timetable, May 2006). References here to the section coming into force should be read as relevant to s.86B(1) coming into force.
8 See ss.17 and 189(1) for the definitions of small and non-commercial agreements. A consumer credit agreement is a non-commercial agreement if it is not made by the creditor in the course of a business carried on by him (s.189(1)). A small agreement is limited by amount, currently £50, and is either unsecured or secured only by guarantee or indemnity.

9   The creditor is to 'give' each notice, which, by virtue of s.189(1), means 'deliver or send by an appropriate method', an 'appropriate method' meaning, again by virtue of s.189(1), post or transmission in the form of an electronic communication in accordance with s.176A(1). An electronic transmission must be in the form of an electronic communication that is capable of being stored for future reference in such a way that the information in it may be reproduced without change (s.176A(1)).
10   CCA 1974, s.86C(6) brought into force by Commencement Order (No.1) 2006.
11   According to the DTI Timetable, May 2006.
12   The debtor or hirer may cease to be in arrears for this purpose, notwithstanding that a default sum payable in respect of a breach other than non-payment remains outstanding (s.86B(5), to be inserted by CCA 2006, s.9).

3.2   DEFAULT SUMS

3.2.1   Default sums defined

The new CCA 1974 s.187A (inserted by CCA 2006, s.18) defines the meaning of the expression 'default sum' when it is used in relation to the debtor or hirer under a regulated agreement. It is any sum other than interest which is payable by the debtor or hirer in connection with a breach of the agreement by him (s.187A(1)). A sum is not a default sum simply because the obligation to pay it is accelerated as a consequence of a breach of the agreement (s.187A(2)).

The expression is intended to include the cost of legal proceedings and court costs,[1] although it may not always be clear whether such costs are costs payable in connection with a breach of the agreement by the debtor or hirer.[2]

3.2.2   Notice of default sums

Creditors and owners are to be required, by a new s.86E (to be inserted by CCA 2006, s.12), to give debtors and hirers notice of any default sums that become payable under regulated credit and regulated consumer hire agreements, other than non-commercial agreements and small agreements.[3]

The period within which notice is to be given is to be prescribed by regulations made by the Secretary of State (s.86E(2)). The current proposal is that regulations should require notice to be given within 28 days after the sum of any default sums 'applied to the account' exceeds a specified amount (probably around £50 to £100).[4] Whatever period is prescribed, it will not be permissible to apply a default sum to an account and to charge interest on it until the notice has been given (see 3.2.3 below). Regulations may also make provision about the form and content of the notice and may provide that the obligation is not to apply in relation to a default sum which is less than such amount as the regulations may prescribe (s.86E(7)).

The notice may be incorporated in any statement or other notice that the creditor or owner gives the debtor or hirer in relation to the same agreement by virtue of another provision of CCA 1974 (s.86E(3)). Subject to any requirement of regulations as to the form of the notice, it may be delivered, posted or, provided that the debtor or hirer has agreed that it be delivered to him by being transmitted to a particular electronic address in a particular electronic form, transmitted to that address in that form.[5] However, it does not appear to have been the Government's intention that such notices should be sent by e-mail,[6] and, accordingly, regulations as to the form of the notices (to be made under s.86E(7)) may require that they are provided on paper and not in an electronic form.

The debtor or hirer is to have no liability to pay any sum in connection with the preparation or the giving to him of the notice (s.86E(6)).

Section 86E is to apply in relation to agreements made before it comes into force, but only in relation to default sums which become payable after it comes into force (CCA 2006, Sched.3, para.8). Apart from the power to make regulations under CCA 1974, ss.86E(2) and 86E(7), which came into force on 16 June 2006 (Commencement Order (No.1) 2006) it is intended that s.86E should come into force on 6 April 2008 (DTI Timetable, May 2006). It is submitted that s.86E will only apply to default sums which become payable after s.86E comes into force fully.

3.2.3   Interest on default sums

No compound interest

The debtor or hirer will only be liable to pay simple interest in connection with a default sum (s.86F, to be inserted by CCA 2006, s.13). Accordingly, any additional interest that is charged by the creditor or hirer as a result of compounding interest on a default sum will not be recoverable.

This restriction will apply to agreements whenever made, but only in relation to default sums which become payable after s.86F comes into force (CCA 2006, Sched.3, para.9(1)). A contractual right to compound interest in respect of a default sum payable after s.86F comes into force, in an agreement made before it comes into force, will be treated as a right to simple interest (CCA 2006, Sched.3, para.9(2)). It is intended that CCA 1974, s.86F will come into force on 6 April 2008 (DTI Timetable, May 2006).

The enactment of this provision is largely the result of extensive comment in the press about small loans escalating into unmanageable debts due to the compounding of interest in the event of default. Press interest was fuelled by a case in which a county court judge expressed the view that a term providing for compound interest on arrears, costs and charges, combined with relatively high interest rates and other charges, could make a credit agreement an extortionate credit bargain[7] or could constitute an unenforceable penalty.[8] The question whether or not the agreement was an extortionate credit bargain did not actually arise for decision because the agreement was held to be altogether unenforceable by reason of the creditor's failure to include an accurate statement of the amount of credit in the agreement form.[9]

No interest before notice of default sum

No interest at all will be recoverable on a default sum in respect of any period before:

(a) the debtor or hirer has been given notice in accordance with s.86E and the regulations to be made under that section; and
(b) a further 28 days have elapsed (s.86E(4)).

This will give the debtor or hirer four weeks in which to pay the default sum before interest may be charged upon it.

3.2.4   Failure to give notice of default sum to make agreement unenforceable

If the creditor or owner fails to give notice of a default sum within such period as may be prescribed by regulations, the agreement itself will become unenforceable against the debtor or hirer until the notice is given (s.86E(5)).

1 See the debate on a proposed amendment to clause 6 of the Bill during the first sitting of the Standing Committee on 23 June 2005.
2 Where, for example, a debtor issues proceedings for relief under CCA 1974 and the creditor incurs costs attributable both to defending the claim and to counter-claiming for arrears.
3 Non-commercial agreements and small agreements are excluded from this requirement to give notice by s.86E(8).
4 See the agenda for the DTI IT Group Discussion meeting on 3 May 2006.
5 The creditor or owner is to 'give' the notice, which, by virtue of s.189(1), means 'deliver or send by an appropriate method', an 'appropriate method' meaning, again by virtue of s.189(1), post or transmission in the form of an electronic communication in accordance with s.176A(1). An electronic transmission must be in the form of an electronic communication that is capable of being stored for future reference in such a way that the information in it may be reproduced without change (s.176A(1)).
6 See the debate on clause 12 during the second sitting of the Standing Committee on 23 June 2005.
7 Sections 137–140 of CCA 1974, which are to be repealed by s.22(3) of CCA 2006, permit the court to re-open an extortionate credit bargain and to re-write it so as to rectify injustice to the debtor (see **Chapter 5**).
8 The common law doctrine of penalties is set out in *Dunlop Pneumatic Tyre Company Limited* v. *New Garage and Motor Company Limited* [1915] AC 79.
9 *London North Securities Limited* v. *Meadows*, unreported; upheld by the Court of Appeal on the ground that the agreement was unenforceable for failure to include a statement of the prescribed term of the amount of credit ([2005] EWCA Civ 956; CCA 1974, ss.9(4), 61, 65 and 127(3); Consumer Credit (Agreements) Regulations 1983, SI 1983/1553, reg.6 and Sched.6).

3.3   DEFAULT NOTICES

The new requirement for notice of default sums is to be distinguished from the existing provisions of CCA 1974, ss.87 and 88, by which a creditor or owner must give a default notice before becoming entitled, by reason of any breach of a regulated agreement by a debtor or hirer, to terminate the agreement, to demand earlier payment of any sum, to recover possession of any goods or land, or to treat any right conferred on the debtor or hirer by the agreement as terminated, restricted or deferred.

However, s.88 is to be amended, so as to increase the minimum length of a default notice from seven to 14 days.[1] This will apply to any default notice that is served after the amendment takes effect, regardless of when the breach to which the notice relates occurred or when the agreement was made (CCA 2006, Sched.3, para.10).

The Secretary of State's power to make regulations as to the information to be contained in default notices about the consequences of failure to comply with them is extended so that regulations may also prescribe any other matters relating to the agreement that must be contained in a default notice.[2] It is intended that regulations will require the inclusion of information about whether the agreement gives the creditor or owner the right to interest after judgment (see **para.3.5**) and a reminder, in the case of regulated hire-purchase or conditional sale agreements, that the debtor has a right, under CCA 1974, ss.99 and 100, to terminate the agreement without incurring liability to pay more than one half of the total price.[3]

A default notice will also have to include a copy of the current default information sheet (s.88(4A), to be inserted by CCA 2006, s.14(3)).

---

1   This is to be achieved by the amendment of s.88(2) and (3) by CCA 2006, s.14(1), with effect from 1 October 2006 (Commencement Order (No.1) 2006).
2   This is the effect of the amendment of s.88(4) by CCA 2006, s.14(2), which took effect from 16 June 2006 (Commencement Order (No.1) 2006).
3   See the debate on clause 14 in the second sitting of the Standing Committee on 23 June 2005.

3.4   PRE-EMPTIVE RIGHT TO APPLY FOR A TIME ORDER

A time order is an order that may be made by the court under CCA 1974, s.129, giving the debtor or hirer more time to pay any sum already owed under a regulated agreement or under a security for a regulated agreement, or more time to remedy any breach of a regulated agreement other than the non-payment of money. The court may, as a consequence of a time order, vary the agreement (s.136) by, for example, reducing the rate at which interest may accrue on any sum owed, or by extending the repayment term.[1]

Under the existing provisions, the court can make a time order either:

(a) of its own motion, when the creditor or owner is applying for an enforcement order (under s.127) or bringing an action to enforce a regulated agreement or any security, or to recover possession of any goods or land to which a regulated agreement relates (s.129(1)(a) and (c)); or
(b) on an application made by a debtor or hirer after service on him of:

(i)   a default notice under s.76 (a notice required before a creditor or owner can rely on a term of a regulated agreement to demand earlier payment of any sum, recover possession of any goods or land, or treat any right conferred on the debtor or hirer by the agreement as terminated, restricted or deferred);

(ii) s.87 (a default notice); or

(iii) s.98 (a termination notice) (s.129(1)(b)).

Section 129 is to be amended so as to enable a debtor or hirer to apply for a time order before the creditor or owner takes any steps to enforce the agreement, even before the creditor has taken the step of giving a notice under s.76, s.87 or s.98. In future, a debtor or hirer will be able to apply for a time order when he has been served with an arrears notice under s.86B or s.86C (s.129(1)(ba), to be inserted by CCA 2006, s.16(1)).[2] This will be so, regardless of when the agreement was made (CCA 2006, Sched.3, para.12). However, before he can apply for a time order in reliance on the service of an arrears notice, he must give the creditor or owner at least 14 days' notice that he intends to make an application for a time order, giving details of a payment proposal (s.129A(1) and (2) to be inserted by CCA 2006, s.16(2)).

---

1 See *Southern and District Finance plc* v. *Barnes* [1995] CCLR 62, where the sum owed, in relation to which the court was held entitled to vary the rate of interest, included the full amount of credit not yet repaid. This sum was owed because the obligation to pay the full amount of capital lent had been accelerated, the bringing of an action for possession having constituted a demand for the debt.

2 This amendment is intended to take effect on 6 April 2008, to coincide with the introduction of the requirements for arrears notices (DTI Timetable, May 2006).

3.5   NOTICES TO BE REQUIRED FOR INTEREST AFTER JUDGMENT

Under the common law, a contract may provide for interest to be payable on a sum for which judgment has been obtained, in respect of any further period for which the sum remains outstanding after the judgment is given, provided that a separate covenant is made for such interest from the covenant for payment of the sum itself.[1]

In 1999, the OFT attempted to establish that a term providing for interest after judgment under a regulated consumer credit agreement was unfair and so not binding on the debtor by virtue of the Unfair Terms in Consumer Contracts Regulations 1994, SI 1994/3159 (now revoked and replaced by the Unfair Terms in Consumer Contracts Regulations 1999, SI 1999/2083). In *Director General of Fair Trading* v. *First National Bank Plc* [2000] QB 672 at 688, the Court of Appeal held that the term was unfair in such an agreement by reason of the fact that a court might give judgment for a sum owed under the agreement and order the judgment to be paid by instalments under County Courts Act 1984, s.71, without considering the exercise of its powers (under CCA 1974, ss.129 and 136 (see para.3.4)) to make a time order and, in consequence, to reduce the rate of interest that would accrue on the judgment while the instalments were being paid off.[2] The House of Lords held ([2001] UKHL 52) that the term providing for interest after judgment, which was in common use and would have been unlikely to have been considered unfair by the customer, or any lawyer who might have advised him on the question, had he addressed his mind to it at the date of the contract (see the analysis of Lord Millett in paras. 54 and 55), was not unfair. However, the case identified real cause for complaint in the failure of either CCA 1974 and the regulations made under it or the county court procedure to alert debtors to the fact that, while they were paying off a judgment by instalments, in accordance with a court order, interest would continue to build up on their account unless they had obtained an order under CCA 1974, ss.129 and 136, reducing that interest.

It is to be expected that the OFT will include information about time orders and interest after judgment in the arrears information sheets and default information sheets that they are to prepare and publish under s.86A.

Section 130A of CCA 1974 (to be inserted by CCA 2006, s.17) will be a further step towards ameliorating the mischief identified in *Director General of Fair Trading v. First National Bank Plc*, in that it will:

(a) require creditors and owners to give debtors and hirers periodic notices of any post-judgment debt interest that they wish to recover (s.130A(1)); and
(b) enable regulations to be made prescribing the form and content of the notices (s.130A(6)).

The regulations may be expected to require the inclusion of reminders about the court's powers under CCA 1974, ss.129 and 136.

If a creditor or owner under a regulated agreement, other than a non-commercial agreement or a small agreement,[3] wants to be able to recover interest on a sum for which judgment is given, in respect of any period after the judgment is given, he will have to give notices to the debtor or hirer at intervals of no more than six months (s.130A(1) and (9), subs.(9) defining 'post-judgment interest' for the purposes of the section). There is no time limit specified for service of the first notice, but it is to be given after the judgment is given (s.130A(1)(a)) and the debtor or hirer will have no liability to pay interest in respect of the period between the giving of the judgment and the giving of the first notice (s.130A(2)).

If the creditor or hirer fails to give a second or subsequent notice of post-judgment interest within the period of six months immediately following the day on which the last post-judgment interest notice was given, the debtor or hirer will have no liability to pay interest on the judgment debt in respect of the period beginning immediately after the end of the period of six months following the day on which the previous notice was given and ending at the end of the day on which the late notice is given (s.130A(3)).

The notices may be delivered, posted or, provided that the debtor or hirer has agreed that they may be delivered to him by being transmitted to a particular electronic address in a particular electronic form, transmitted to that address in that form.[4]

The debtor or hirer is to have no liability to make any payment in connection with the preparation or giving to him of a notice of post-judgment debt interest under s.130A (s.130A(4)).

Any notice required by s.130A may be incorporated in a statement or other notice which the creditor or owner gives to the debtor or hirer in relation to the agreement by virtue of another provision of CCA 1974 (s.130A(5)).

The obligation to serve notices of post-judgment interest does not arise in relation to interest payable under the County Courts Act 1984, s.74, the Administration of Justice (Scotland) Act 1972, s.4, or the Judgments Enforcement (Northern Ireland) Order 1981 (SI 1981/226 (NI 6)), art. 127 (s.130A(7)).

Section 130A will apply to agreements made before it comes into force, but only in relation to sums payable under judgments that are given after it comes into force (CCA 2006, Sched.3, para.13). It is intended that CCA 1974, s.130A will come fully into force on 6 April 2008 (DTI Timetable, May 2006) although the power to make regulations as to the form and content of notices under s.130A(6) came into force on 16 June 2006. It is submitted that the section will not apply in relation to sums payable under judgments given before it comes fully into force.

1   *Economic Assurance Society v. Usborne* [1902] AC 147, thus avoiding the merger of the right to interest in the judgment (see *In re Sneyd, ex p. Fewings* (1883) 25 Ch D 338).
2   It was accepted that, in practice, the courts frequently did make instalment orders without considering their powers to reduce future interest on the judgment debt.
3   Non-commercial and small agreements are to be excluded from the requirement for notice of post-judgment debt interest by s.130A(8).
4   The creditor or owner is to 'give' each notice, which, by virtue of s.189(1), means 'deliver or send by an appropriate method', an 'appropriate method' meaning, again by virtue of s.189(1), post or transmission in the form of an electronic communication in accordance with s.176A(1). An electronic transmission must be in the form of an electronic communication that is capable of being stored for future reference in such a way that the information in it may be reproduced without change (s.176A(1)).

4 ENFORCEMENT OF AGREEMENTS

Key changes

- Repeal of provisions making agreements irredeemably unenforceable
- Only licensed businesses to enforce agreements

4.1 DEFECTIVE AGREEMENTS NOT TO BE AUTOMATICALLY UNENFORCEABLE

Regulated agreements will no longer be automatically and irredeemably unenforceable against the debtor or hirer in the event of the failure to include accurate statements in the agreement forms of all the applicable prescribed terms.[1] Cancellable agreements (defined in CCA 1974, s.67) will no longer be automatically unenforceable against the debtor or hirer where the creditor or owner has failed to provide the correct cancellation notices.[2]

Where a regulated agreement is improperly executed, in that the creditor or owner has failed to comply with all the requirements of CCA 1974 and the regulations made under it as to form and content, signing and the provision of copies, it cannot be enforced by the creditor or owner without an order of the court (s.65(1)). At present, where an agreement does not contain, for example, an accurate statement of the amount of credit in a fixed-sum credit agreement, and there is no document signed by the debtor which contains an accurate statement of the amount of credit as well as any of the other prescribed terms that apply to the agreement, the court is prevented, by s.127(3), from making an enforcement order. Similarly, cancellable agreements are automatically unenforceable, by virtue of s.127(4), in the event of a failure to meet the cancellation notice requirements of s.64(1), for example, where a creditor has inserted the incorrect cancellation notice in the copy of the agreement given or sent to the debtor at the same time as the agreement itself was given or sent to him, as required by ss.62 and 64(1)(a), the court cannot make an enforcement order.

Section 127(3) and (4) are to cease to have effect, but only in relation to agreements that are made after the subsections have been repealed (CCA 2006, s.15 and Sched.3, para.11). The present intention is that they should be repealed on 6 April 2007 (DTI Timetable, May 2006).

Section 127(5), which gives the court express power to direct that an agreement is to have effect as if it did not include a term omitted from the document signed by the debtor or hirer, is also to be repealed.[3]

The repeal of s.127(3) and (4) follows the indication given by the House of Lords in *Wilson* v. *First County Trust Ltd* [2003] UKHL 40; [2004] 1 AC 816 that a provision making a credit agreement automatically unenforceable due to a technical defect, regardless of whether or not the defect was culpable or caused prejudice to the party who would benefit from its being unenforceable, might be contrary to the human rights of the creditor (under Art. 6(1) of the Convention for the Protection of Human Rights and Fundamental Freedoms and Art. 1 of the First Protocol to the Convention) if it was to apply to agreements for more than £25,000. It is to be reasonably expected that the repeal will take effect no later than the coming into force of the amendments to CCA 1974, ss.8 and 15 (on the commencement of CCA 2006, s.2), by which the financial limits on regulated agreements are to be removed.

It will then always be a matter for the court's discretion whether or not to make an enforcement order in respect of an improperly executed agreement and the court will, in all cases, be obliged (by CCA 1974, s.127(1)) to make an enforcement order, unless it considers it just to dismiss the application for the order, having regard to:

(a) prejudice caused to any person by the contravention which has caused the agreement to be improperly executed;
(b) the degree of culpability for it; and
(c) the court's powers,
     (i)   to reduce or discharge any sum payable so as to compensate for prejudice suffered (under s.127(2));
     (ii) to make the order conditional on the doing of specified acts by any party to the proceedings or to suspend the operation of any term of the order (under s.135); and
     (iii) to amend any term of any agreement or security as a consequence of making the order (under s.136).

---

1 The prescribed terms are prescribed under CCA 1974, s.61(1)(a) by the Consumer Credit (Agreements) Regulations 1983, SI 1983/1553, reg. 6 and Sched.6.
2 The cancellation notices to be provided under CCA 1974, s.64(1) are prescribed by the Consumer Credit (Cancellation Notices and Copies of Documents) Regulations 1983, SI 1983/1557.
3 If the court considers that the agreement has given rise to an unfair relationship, it will be able to make an equivalent order under the new unfair relationship provisions (CCA 1974, ss.140A and 140B, to be amended by CCA 2006, ss.19 and 20 (see **Chapter 5**)).

4.2   AGREEMENTS WITH UNLICENSED TRADERS

Where a person carries on a consumer credit business or a consumer hire business without a licence to do so, the regulated agreements that he makes will be unenforceable unless or until he, or his successor in title, obtains an order, commonly referred to as a 'validation order', under CCA 1974, s.40(2).

Section 40 is to be amended[1] so as to make it clear that no agreement may be enforced by an entity that does not have an appropriate licence, at the time of enforcement (s.40(1), to be inserted by CCA 2006, s.26(1)). The section is also to be amended to reflect the fact that it will be possible for a licence to be limited to specified descriptions of business, within the previously recognised types (see **Chapter 6**). In order to enforce an agreement that was made by an unlicensed trader, it will be necessary both:

(a) for the enforcing party itself to be currently licensed to carry on a business of a description which covers the enforcement of the agreement (s.40(1), inserted by CCA 2006, s.26(1)); and

(b) for a validation order to have been made under s.40(2) (to be amended by CCA 2006, s.26(1)).

Where a trader's licence is limited to the carrying on of a certain description, or descriptions, of consumer credit or consumer hire business, any agreements that he makes that do not fall within that description, or those descriptions, will be unenforceable unless or until he, or his successor in title, is licensed to carry on a business of a description which covers the enforcement of those agreements and a validation order has been made under s.40(2) to the effect that those agreements are to be treated as if the trader who made them was licensed to carry on a business of a description which included the making of those agreements.

The expression 'unlicensed' is no longer to be used in s.40, with the result, it seems, that there will be no doubt that agreements made by a trader under a different name from the name(s) in which he is authorised to carry on a consumer credit or consumer hire business, as the case may be, will be unenforceable unless or until a validation order is obtained (see s.24 and the definitions of 'licensed' and 'unlicensed' in CCA 1974, s.189(1)). It was previously arguable that s.40(1) rendered agreements made by an 'unlicensed' trader unenforceable, but not agreements made by a trader who had a licence to carry on business of the type covering the agreements, notwithstanding that they were made in a name other than the name(s) in which he was authorised to carry on the business.

A local authority does not require a licence in order to carry on a consumer credit, consumer hire or ancillary credit business and a body corporate does not require a licence in order to carry on a business which it is empowered to carry on by a public general Act naming the body (CCA 1974, s.21(2) and (3)). Agreements entered into by a local authority will not be unenforceable by reason of the local authority's not having been licensed when the agreements were made and nor will agreements entered into by such a body corporate in the course of a business for which it did not require a licence. The local authority may also enforce its agreements without obtaining a licence, as may the body corporate provided that the business which it is empowered to carry on by public general Act covers the enforcement of the agreements (s.40(1) and (8), inserted by CCA 2006, s.26). If any entity other than the local authority or body corporate that made such agreements is to enforce them and that entity is acting in the course of a consumer credit business or consumer hire business, it must have a licence to carry on business of a description which covers the enforcement of such agreements (s.40(9), to be inserted by CCA 2006, s.26), but it need not obtain a validation order under s.40(2) (s.40(8), to be inserted by CCA 2006, s.26).

1   This amendment is intended to come into force on 6 April 2008 (DTI Timetable, May 2006).

4.3   AGREEMENTS UNENFORCEABLE WHILE CREDITOR OR OWNER FAILS TO GIVE NOTICE OF ARREARS OR DEFAULT SUM

Regulated agreements will be unenforceable by the creditor or owner during any period of non-compliance with the obligations to give arrears notices under ss.86B and 86C (CCA 1974, s.86D(3) to be inserted by CCA 2006, s.11). For the arrears notices requirements, see **Chapter 3** at **paras.3.1.2** and **3.1.3**.

If the creditor or owner fails to give the debtor or hirer notice of a default sum within such period as may be prescribed by regulations under s.86E(2), the agreement will be unenforceable until the notice is given (s.86E(5) to be inserted by CCA 2006, s.12). For the requirement to give notices of default sums, see **Chapter 3** at **para.3.2**.

5 UNFAIR RELATIONSHIPS

5.1 COURT'S POWERS TO RE-WRITE AGREEMENTS

The court's powers to re-open extortionate credit bargains are to be replaced by extensive new powers to assist a debtor when the court determines that the relationship between the creditor and the debtor is unfair to the debtor. The extortionate credit provisions in CCA 1974, ss.137–140 are to be repealed (CCA 2006, s.22(3)) and the unfair relationship provisions are to be introduced by new CCA 1974, ss.140A–140C (to be inserted by CCA 2006, ss.19–21).[1]

---

1 These amendments are intended to be brought into force on 6 April 2007 (DTI Timetable, May 2006).

5.2 FACTORS THAT MAY MAKE A RELATIONSHIP UNFAIR

The relationship in question will be the relationship between a creditor and a debtor[1] arising out of a credit agreement or the credit agreement taken with any related agreement, a related agreement being one that has been refinanced by the credit agreement, a linked transaction or a security (s.140A(1)). (See **para.5.3** for a full explanation of what is meant here by a 'related' agreement).

The court's powers under s.140B will arise where it determines that such a relationship is unfair to the debtor by reason of any one or more of the following:

(a) any of the terms of the credit agreement or of any related agreement;
(b) the way in which the creditor has exercised or enforced any of his rights under the agreement or any related agreement;

(c) any other thing done or not done by or on behalf of the creditor, whether
     before or after the making of the agreement or any related agreement
     (s.140A(1)).

There need not be culpability on the part of the creditor: conduct of, or in relation to, an associate or former associate of the creditor may give rise to a finding
of an unfair relationship, as the court is required to treat any act or omission on
the part of an associate or former associate, or its agent, and any act or omission
in relation to an associate or former associate of the creditor as if done or, in the
case of an omission, not done by, or on behalf of, or in relation to, the creditor
(s.140A(3)).

No guidance is given as to the type of terms, actions or omissions that will make
a relationship unfair. The court is to have regard to 'all matters it thinks relevant
(including matters relating to the creditor and matters relating to the debtor)'
(s.140A(2)).

Attempts were made, during the passage of the Consumer Credit Bill through
Parliament, to introduce amendments by which an 'unfair relationship' would be
defined, or by which provision might have been made for regulations to set out
illustrative lists of practices that might be considered to be unfair. However, the
Government resisted any such definition or provision for an illustrative list, fear-
ing that they might result in a narrow construction of 'unfair relationship' and
undue restriction of the protection that the new provisions are intended to afford:

> The new test . . . does not exist in a vacuum – Parliament and Ministers have already
> specified in other legislation those terms and practices that are unfair when consid-
> ered alone. The new test is broader and is directed at looking at the substance of the
> relationship between the debtor and the creditor . . . It is not possible to define an
> unfair relationship as being certain things, or combinations of specific types of con-
> duct, without limiting it in some way. That would serve to reduce the effectiveness
> of the test and the ability of the court to tackle unfair relationships – whatever form
> they take . . . The test means that lenders have to look beyond simply complying
> with procedural rules, to ensuring that the substance of the relationship is not unfair
> . . . Lenders do not need another list of specific practices as those are already made
> clear in other legislation, although complying with all of them will not necessarily
> mean that a relationship is fair.[2]

It would seem from this that it is intended that the court may draw some assistance from existing law, such as the definition of 'unfair' in the Unfair Terms in
Consumer Contracts Regulations 1999, SI 1999/2083, reg.5, in relation to contractual terms, and the indicative but non-exhaustive list, in Sched.2 to those
Regulations, of terms that may be unfair. However, the court is to look beyond the
fairness of the contractual terms, at the way in which agreements are introduced
and negotiated, the way in which they are administered, and any other aspect of
the relationship that the court considers relevant.

Moreover, a finding that a practice has caused or contributed to an unfair relationship with one customer may have little relevance to the question of whether
or not relationships with other customers are unfair. It was also said, in defence

of the decision not to include a list of practices that may be unfair in CCA 2006, or in regulations, that:

> Such an approach would have the consequence of unjustifiably stigmatising conduct that may be perfectly fair and reasonable in some cases but not in others.[3]

The provisions are not intended to increase the existing regulatory burden on businesses, but to afford better protection to consumers in circumstances where businesses fail to meet their existing responsibilities.[4] However, it was suggested by those promoting the Bill that lenders' responsibilities might extend to ascertaining and recording the particular circumstances of individual debtors, from the outset of any relationship, so as to be in a position to deal with them fairly, according to their particular abilities and weaknesses:

> We are saying that the lender has to give as much information as possible to the borrower on the form of the agreement. For the lender to lend responsibly he will have to know the borrower's position. For example, within the qualification of the content of the form of the agreement, I would expect the lender to know about the person's individual circumstances . . . In respect of consumer friendly language, there is no reason why the lender could not put the notice in the first language of the individual concerned.[5]

The Consumer Credit Act 2006 does not introduce, or codify, any duty for lenders to act responsibly[6] towards debtors or any requirements as to the form in which an agreement is to be made,[7] although the OFT will be required, when considering the exercise of its powers under the licensing regime, to have regard to practices that it considers to be irresponsible lending.[8]

The courts may well decide that there is no justification for considering Hansard when construing the unfair relationship provisions.[9] Having regard to the absence of any positive duty in CCA 1974, as it is to be amended, for creditors to ascertain any peculiar disabilities or weaknesses of debtors, and having regard to existing legislation on unfair terms and unfair practices, it may be that, provided credit agreements are advertised and introduced honestly and creditors keep their customers well informed, the resulting relationships will not be unfair, however unwise customers may be to enter the relationships and however imbalanced the parties' respective rights and obligations.

If the approach of the Unfair Terms in Consumer Contracts Regulations 1999 (UTCCR) was to be adopted, a relationship would not be unfair solely by reason of a high, or even an extortionate (in the sense of grossly excessive), rate of interest, provided that the rate and the manner in which it was to be calculated and applied to the account were stated in plain intelligible language.[10] When looking at any conduct on the part of the creditor or an associate of the creditor, before or after the making of the agreement, key factors, as with the UTCCR, are likely to be a lack of candour on the part of the creditor or his associates and inability of the debtor to make informed choices. Those terms that may be challenged under the UTCCR will be unfair[11] if, contrary to the requirement of good faith, they cause a significant imbalance in the rights of the parties, to the detriment of the consumer. Good faith involves fair and open dealing, openness requiring full and clear expression, with no concealed pitfalls or traps, and fair dealing that advantage is not taken, even unconsciously, of the consumer's necessity, indigence, lack of experience, unfamiliarity with the subject-matter of the contract, or weak bargaining position.[12]

The EU Unfair Commercial Practices Directive (2005/29/EC) prohibits unfair commercial practices and provides that a commercial practice will be unfair if:

(a) it is contrary to the requirement of good faith or does not meet the standard of skill and care commensurate with honest market practice; and

(b) it appreciably impairs the consumer's ability to make an informed decision, causing him to take a decision that he would not otherwise have taken as to whether, how and on what terms to make a purchase or a payment, retain or dispose of a product, or exercise a contractual right (Art. 5, read together with the definitions in Art. 2(e), (h) and (k)).

The Directive imposes a requirement of maximum harmonisation in relation to business to consumer commercial practices, although permitting more restrictive or prescriptive requirements to be imposed by Member States in relation to financial services (Art. 3(9)).

If decisions on unfair relationships are to be consistent with the UTCCR and the Unfair Commercial Practices Directive, the test may be whether conduct on the part of the creditor or any associate, which is contrary to good faith or generally accepted standards of honest market practice, has appreciably impaired the debtor's ability to make an informed decision, with the result that he has made a decision which he would not otherwise have made and which has affected his relationship with the creditor, to his detriment.[13] Failure to meet statutory obligations not to use certain expressions in advertising, to allow certain cooling-off periods, and to provide certain information before and after entering into an agreement, would be relevant. Moreover, if the creditor was aware that some particular characteristic of the debtor, such as illiteracy, made him peculiarly unable to make informed decisions on the basis of standard communications, the creditor might be at risk of an unfair relationship unless it took steps to ensure that that particular debtor understood his options. However, as no positive duty is to be imposed on creditors to behave responsibly by, for example, not entering into agreements with customers who may be acting unwisely, it is doubtful that a relationship would be unfair simply by reason of the creditor's agreeing to lend money without first, for example, satisfying itself of the debtor's ability to afford the repayments.

---

1   Including any assignee of the debtor or the creditor (s.140C(2)).

2   The Parliamentary Under-Secretary of State for Trade and Industry, responding to suggested amendments in Grand Committee on 8 November 2005. See also the debate on clause 19 during the second sitting of the Standing Committee on 23 June 2005.

3   The Parliamentary Under-Secretary of State for Trade and Industry responding to pro-
    posed amendments to clause 19 of the Bill during the Report Stage in the House of
    Lords, Official Report, 18 January 2006, col. 725.
4   According to the Parliamentary Under-Secretary of State for Trade and Industry dur-
    ing debate on the application of the provisions to exempt agreements in Grand
    Committee on 8 November 2005.
5   The Parliamentary Under-Secretary of State for Trade and Industry, in the context of
    a question as to the form in which a creditor or owner must give notice of a default
    sum and how he is to know whether the customer is partially sighted or has learning
    difficulties in the debate on clause 12 of the Bill during the second sitting of the
    Standing Committee on 23 June 2005.
6   An amendment moved but withdrawn in the House of Lords would have introduced
    an express duty to ascertain the ability of an intended debtor to make the repayments
    and would have set out specific steps that could be taken in order for it to be deemed
    in the creditor's favour that the duty was discharged. Failure to meet the duty would
    have led to a presumption that the relationship was unfair.
7   The form and content requirements have already been amended, since publication
    of the White Paper 'Fair, Clear and Competitive, the Consumer Credit Market in
    the 21st Century' (8 December 2003), by the Consumer Credit (Agreements)
    (Amendment) Regulations 2004, SI 2004/1482. The new requirements under the
    Consumer Credit (Agreements) Regulations 1983, SI 1983/1553 which result from
    the amendments made by the 2004 regulations are unlikely to assist a person whose
    first language is not English and may be thought to be of limited assistance to anyone
    who is not both (a) naturally inclined and (b) able to read detailed forms carefully and
    in full before signing them.
8   See s.25(2B) to be inserted by CCA 2006, s.29(2).
9   As the provisions may be thought not to be ambiguous or obscure or to lead to
    absurdity (see *Pepper v. Hart* [1993] AC 593).
10 This is because interest is the price or remuneration for the credit (see *DGOFT v. First
    National Bank Plc* [2002] 1 AC 481) and reg. 6(2) provides that, insofar as it is in plain
    intelligible language, the assessment of fairness of a term shall not relate to the
    adequacy of the price or remuneration for the services supplied.
11 Leaving aside the exemption relating to the adequacy of a clearly expressed price.
12 *DGOFT v. First National Bank Plc* [2002] 1 AC 481.
13 Although not separately mentioned in the UTCCR, the likely impairment of the
    consumer's ability to make an informed decision would seem to be an aspect of a
    term's being contrary to the requirement of good faith in the sense in which that
    requirement has been construed (see *DGOFT v. First National Bank Plc* [2002] 1 AC
    481). Significant imbalance between the parties' rights and obligations, caused by the
    term, is an additional requirement for unfairness in the UTCCR.

5.3   THE AGREEMENTS THAT MAY BE RE-WRITTEN

The unfair relationship provisions are to apply to any credit agreement between a
creditor and an individual (defined by s.189(1) as it is to be amended by CCA
2006, s.1), whether or not it is a regulated agreement (the combined effect of
ss.140A(1) and 140C(1), to be inserted by CCA 2006, ss.19 and 21), apart from
an agreement secured by a first mortgage over residential land that falls within
the category of exempt agreement provided for by CCA 1974, s.16(6C) (CCA
1974, ss.140A(5) and 16(7A), to be inserted by CCA 2006, ss.19 and 22(2)
respectively).

The court's new powers may arise by reason of the terms of an agreement related to a credit agreement (s.140A(1)(a)), rather than the credit agreement itself, or as a result of actions or omissions in connection with such a related agreement (s.140A(1)(b) and (c)), and the powers may also be exercised in respect of such a related agreement (s.140B(1)). For the purposes of the unfair relationship provisions, an agreement is related to a credit agreement if it is:

(a) 'consolidated' by the (main) credit agreement;
(b) a linked transaction[1] in relation to the credit agreement or to an earlier agreement consolidated by the credit agreement; or
(c) a security[2] provided in relation to:
  (i)   the credit agreement;
  (ii) a credit agreement consolidated by the main credit agreement; or
  (iii) a linked transaction in relation either to the main credit agreement or in relation to a credit agreement consolidated by the main credit agreement (s.140C(4)).

The word 'consolidated' is to be given a wide meaning. An earlier credit agreement will have been consolidated by a later credit agreement if the later credit agreement is entered into by the debtor wholly or partly 'for purposes connected with debts owed by virtue of the earlier agreement' and at any time before the later agreement is entered into the parties to the earlier agreement included the debtor under the later agreement and the creditor under the later agreement or an associate or former associate of the creditor (s.140(7)). If a consolidating agreement is itself consolidated by another credit agreement, then the first consolidated agreement is also consolidated by the second consolidating agreement, so that all agreements in a series of consolidating agreements will be 'related' agreements to the subsisting credit agreement that re-financed the most recent consolidated agreement (s.140(8)).

The court may exercise the powers to be conferred by s.140B even after the relationship in question has ended (s.140A(1) and (4)). This would seem to mean that the powers may be exercised in relation to a credit agreement or any related agreement even after the credit agreement has come to an end and when neither party has any further obligation to the other.

---

1 As defined in s.19. Where the credit agreement is not regulated, a transaction is to be treated as a linked transaction in relation to that agreement if it would have been a linked transaction had the credit agreement been a regulated agreement (s.140C(5)).
2 For the purpose of these provisions, the definition of security in s.189(1) is to apply in respect of a credit agreement which is not a consumer credit agreement and in respect of a linked transaction, as it applies in respect of consumer credit agreements (s.140C(6)).

5.4   THE ONUS OF PROOF OF AN UNFAIR RELATIONSHIP

If the debtor or a surety alleges that the relationship between the creditor and the debtor is unfair to the debtor, it is for the creditor to prove that it is not (s.140B(9)). The DTI's original proposal was that the onus would shift to the debtor if the terms of the agreement were clear and the consumer had not been misled. However, it would seem that that would have placed more importance upon the terms of the agreement, in relation to the question of whether or not a relationship was fair, than was ultimately intended by CCA 2006.[1] The intention would appear to be that a creditor will have to adduce more evidence than a clearly worded agreement, and probably more evidence than written terms that appear to be fair, in order to rebut the presumption that the relationship is unfair.

1   See the comments of the Parliamentary Under-Secretary of State for Trade and Industry, responding to tabled Amendment No. 22 in Grand Committee on 8 November 2005.

5.5   WHAT THE COURT MAY DO TO REDRESS THE UNFAIRNESS

The court may:

(a)   require the creditor, or any associate or former associate of the creditor, to repay any sum paid by the debtor or by a surety[1] by virtue of the credit agreement or any related agreement (see **para.5.3** for a full explanation of what is meant here by a related agreement), regardless of whether the sum was originally paid to the creditor or to any other person (s.140B(1)(a) and (3));

(b)   require the creditor, or any associate or former associate of the creditor to do, not to do, or to cease doing anything specified in the order in connection with the credit agreement or any related agreement (s.140B(1)(b));

(c)   reduce or discharge any sum payable by the debtor or by a surety by virtue of the credit agreement or any related agreement (s.140B(1)(c));

(d)   direct that any property provided by a surety for the purposes of a security[2] be returned to the surety (s.140B(1)(d));

(e)   set aside, in whole or in part, any duty imposed on the debtor or on a surety by virtue of the credit agreement or any related agreement (s.140B(1)(e));

(f)   alter the terms of the credit agreement or of any related agreement (s.140B(1)(f));

(g)   direct accounts to be taken, or in Scotland an accounting to be made, between any persons (s.140B(1)(g)).

1   For the purpose of these provisions, the definition of surety in s.189(1) is to apply in respect of a credit agreement which is not a consumer credit agreement and in respect of a linked transaction, as it applies in respect of consumer credit agreements (s.140C(6)).

2   For the purpose of these provisions, the definition of security in s.189(1) is to apply in respect of a credit agreement which is not a consumer credit agreement and in respect of a linked transaction, as it applies in respect of consumer credit agreements (s.140C(6)).

5.6   PROCEDURE

An order will only be able to be made under s.140B at the instance of the debtor or a surety:

(a) on an application made by the debtor or by a surety to the county court in England and Wales, the sheriff court in Scotland, or the High Court in Northern Ireland;[1] or

(b) in any proceedings in any court to enforce a credit agreement or any related agreement, if the debtor and the creditor are both parties (s.140B(2)(b)); or

(c) in any other proceedings in any court where the amount paid or payable under the credit agreement or any related agreement is relevant (s.140B(2)(c)).[2]

A party to any such proceedings is to be entitled, in accordance with rules of court, to have any person who might be made the subject of an order under s.140B made a party to the proceedings (s.140B(8)).

---

1 Section 140B(2)(a). Application may be made to the county court in Northern Ireland if the credit agreement is for fixed-sum credit not exceeding £15,000 or for running-account credit on which the credit limit does not exceed £15,000 (s.140B(6)). In Scotland, the application may be made in the sheriff court for the district in which the debtor or surety resides or carries on business (s.140B(5)).

2 A creditor, its associate or its former associate, may be made a party to the proceedings solely for this purpose (s.140B(8)).

5.7   TRANSITIONAL ARRANGEMENTS

5.7.1   Retrospective effect

The court will be able to provide relief in relation to an unfair relationship arising from an agreement that has been made before the new provisions come into force,[1] unless the debt is repaid or settled before the end of the year following the date when the provisions come into force. No application for relief may be entertained in connection with such an agreement before the end of that transitional year. However, after the end of that year, it will be open to the court:

(a) to find that a relationship is unfair by reason of conduct or events that have occurred at any time before the provisions come into force; and

(b) to order the repayment of payments made before the provisions come into force,

save to the extent, if at all, that the Secretary of State, by order (under s.69(2) and (3) of CCA 2006), limits the court's powers in respect of existing matters or past actions.[2]

The court will not have any powers in respect of an unfair relationship under s.140B in connection with a credit agreement which has been made before s.140B is brought into effect (by the commencement of s.20 of CCA 2006) if it has either become a 'completed agreement' before s.140B is brought into effect or become a completed agreement during 'the transitional period' of one year beginning with the day on which s.140B is brought into effect (CCA 2006, Sched.3, para.14(2), 'transitional period' being defined in para.14(4)). An agreement will become a completed agreement once no sum remains payable, or will or may become payable, under the agreement (CCA 2006, Sched.3, para.1(2)).

The court may exercise its powers to redress unfair relationships in connection with other credit agreements that are made before s.140B comes into effect (and not completed before the end of the following year), though only:

(a) on an application made by the debtor or a surety after the end of the transitional period; or

(b) at the instance of the debtor or a surety, in any proceedings which have been commenced after the end of the transitional period and which are either proceedings to enforce the agreement, or any related agreement, or proceedings in which the amount paid or payable under the agreement is relevant (CCA 2006, Sched.3, para.14(1)).

When the court makes an order under s.140B during the transitional period of one year beginning with the day on which s.140C (interpretation of ss.140A and 140B) is brought into effect (by the commencement of CCA 2006, s.21), the court will not be able to exercise its powers under s.140B(1) in respect of related agreements (see **para.5.3** for a full explanation of what is meant here by a 'related' agreement) or securities that have been made or provided before s.140C is brought into effect if they have ceased to have any operation before the order is made (CCA 2006, Sched.3, para.16(2) and (3)). In making such an order after the end of that transitional period, the court will not be able to exercise its powers in respect of related agreements or securities that have been made or provided before s.140C is brought into effect if they have ceased to have any operation before the end of the transitional period (CCA 2006, Sched.3 para.16(4) and (5)).

5.7.2   Phasing out of extortionate credit bargain provisions

The repeal of the extortionate credit bargain provisions will not affect the court's power to re-open an agreement which is made before the repeal is brought into effect (by the commencement of CCA 2006, s.22(3)) and which becomes a completed agreement before the end of 'the transitional period' of one year beginning with the day on which the repeal is brought into effect (CCA 2006, Sched.3, para.15(1),with 'transitional period' being defined in para.15(7)). The court will also be able to re-open an agreement which is made before the repeal takes effect:

(a) on an application made by the debtor or any surety before the end of the transitional period; or

(b) at the instance of the debtor or surety in any proceedings which are commenced before the end of the transitional period, to enforce the credit agreement, any security or any linked transaction, and to which the debtor and creditors are parties, or in other proceedings commenced before the end of the transitional period where the amount paid or payable under the credit agreement is relevant (CCA 2006, Sched.3, para. 15(3)).

As this extension of the extortionate credit bargain provisions would appear to be intended to cover agreements that are to be excluded from the unfair relationship provisions, it is not clear why the transitional period for the introduction of the unfair relationship provisions and the transitional period for the repeal of the extortionate credit bargain provisions are defined in such a way that they may not necessarily be the same. However, it would seem likely that these transitional periods, and also the transitional period for the application of s.140B to related agreements, will be made the same, by ensuring that ss.20, 21 and 22(3) commence on the same date, expected to be 6 April 2007 (DTI Timetable, May 2006).

5.7.3   Powers of the Secretary of State

The Secretary of State may, by order under CCA 2006, s.69, extend the transitional periods of:

(a) one year from the date when the court's powers under s.140B, to redress unfair relationships, are brought into force;

(b) one year from the date when the provisions of s.140C, for the interpretation of ss.140A and 140B, are brought into force; and

(c) one year from the date when the repeal of the extortionate credit bargain provisions, by s.22(3), takes effect (CCA 2006, Sched.3, paras. 14(5), 15(8) and 16(8)).[3]

The Secretary of State's powers under s.69 would appear to be broad enough to enable the transitional periods to be extended for different periods in relation to different types or descriptions of business or in relation to different categories or descriptions of agreement. Moreover, there is power, by order, to place a transitional or transitory restriction upon a provision's application to things already in existence or things done before the coming into force of the provision (in CCA 2006, s.69(3)). This would enable the court's powers under s.140B to be restricted in respect of agreements already in existence when the section comes into force or in respect of unfair conduct occurring, or payments made, before it comes into force.

---

1   Subject to such orders as may be made by the Secretary of State under s.69.

2   The DTI policy statement of February 2004 indicated that the new provisions would only apply to 'payments demanded or sums charged after the Bill becomes law'.

3   Section 69 permits the Secretary of State to make such transitional or transitory provisions and savings as he thinks fit in connection with the coming into force of any provision of CCA 2006.

5.8   ROLE OF THE OFFICE OF FAIR TRADING

The new powers of the OFT, to obtain information and access to premises, to impose requirements and to fine licensees for non-compliance with such requirements (see **Chapter 7**), should improve the OFT's ability to prevent or deter practices that are likely to result in unfair relationships between creditors and debtors. CCA 1974 does not, and will not, impose a duty on creditors not to enter into unfair relationships and, accordingly, the OFT will have no direct power or authority either to prohibit lenders from entering into unfair relationships or to punish them for doing so. However, it would seem to be intended that the OFT will be entitled to use its powers not just to put an end to practices that directly contravene the statutory requirements imposed by and under CCA 1974, but also to stop other practices that have the potential to make a person unfit to hold a licence.[1] As the OFT is required, when considering whether to renew, vary, suspend or revoke a creditor's licence, to take into account any business practices that the OFT considers to be unfair (see CCA 1974, s.25(2A), to be amended by CCA 2006, s.29, and the existing s.25(2)), its new powers are likely to be construed as being available for the purpose of deterring or preventing any unfair business practices, whether or not they amount to a contravention of the statutory requirements.

A court ruling that a creditor has an unfair relationship with a debtor may be a factor that weighs against the renewal of the creditor's licence, if it is of fixed duration, or in favour of the variation, suspension or revocation of the licence, depending upon the nature of the facts giving rise to the unfairness of the relationship.

It is possible that the OFT may seek to put a stop to practices that cause relationships to be unfair by obtaining undertakings or orders prohibiting those practices under Part 8 of the Enterprise Act 2002 (EA 2002) (see EA 2002, ss.211, 215 and 219). The OFT will be required to indicate, in the advice and information that it publishes under EA 2002, s.229, 'how the OFT expects' the unfair relationship provisions of CCA 1974, as it is to be amended, 'to interact with Part 8' of EA 2002 Act (CCA 1974, s.140D inserted by CCA 2006, s.22(1)). That advice and information, must:

(a) explain the provisions of Part 8 to persons who are likely to be affected by them; and
(b) indicate how the OFT expects the provisions of Part 8 to operate (EA 2002, s.229(1)),

and should indicate the extent to which, and the manner in which, if at all, the OFT considers that it, or other enforcement authorities, will be able, or will intend, to use EA 2002, Part 8 in relation to unfair relationships. It is possible that it might also provide examples of acts or omissions that the OFT would consider to give rise to unfair relationships in such a way as to cause harm to the collective interests of consumers in the UK, so as to justify action under the EA 2002.[2]

However, the OFT's guidance will not define what an unfair relationship is. The obligation of the OFT to give advice and information under EA 2002, s.229 explaining how Part 8 will interact with the unfair relationship provisions does not confer any power on the OFT to define what practices or other circumstances should be considered by the court as giving rise, or as likely to give rise, to unfair relationships. It will be for the court to determine, in each case, whether an unfair relationship has arisen, by reference to such circumstances as the court considers relevant.

The OFT's guidance on the criteria for fitness to hold a consumer credit licence contains a non-exhaustive list of business practices that the OFT considers to be unfair (*Consumer Credit Licences, Guidance for Holders and Applicants*, March 2006).

---

1   See the debate on Amendment No. 10 during the Report Stage of the Bill in the House of Lords, 18 January 2006, Official Report, cols. 747 and 748.
2   The OFT's draft guidance in its consultation document, published June 2006, indicates that it is the OFT's view that Part 8 action might be appropriate where a lender's behaviour has the potential to give rise to a nunber of unfair relationships (see para. 3.27).

6 LICENSING

6.1 BUSINESSES REQUIRING A LICENCE

6.1.1 Trading without a licence

Where a person carries on a business involving activities for which a licence is required under CCA 1974, he commits an offence by engaging in those activities without the requisite licence (s.39(1)). Regulated credit agreements and regulated hire agreements that are made when the creditor or owner does not have a licence to make such agreements will be unenforceable unless or until a validation order is obtained from the OFT (s.40(1) (see **Chapter 4**)).

6.1.2 Consumer credit and consumer hire

The main businesses requiring a licence under CCA 1974 are consumer credit and consumer hire businesses.

The definition of consumer credit business is to be clarified or, arguably, extended, so as to make it clear that a licence to carry on a consumer credit business is required not only by a person who is himself in the business of providing credit, but also by a person whose business otherwise comprises or relates to his being a creditor, in either case under regulated consumer credit agreements (s.189(1), to be amended by CCA 2006, s.23(a)).[1]

Similarly, the definition of consumer hire business is to be clarified or, arguably, extended, so as to make it clear that a licence to carry on a consumer hire business is required not only by a person who is himself in the business of the bailment or hiring of goods but also a person whose business otherwise comprises or relates to his being an owner, in either case under regulated consumer hire agreements (s.189(1), to be amended by CCA 2006, s.23(b)).[2]

The intention behind the amendment to these definitions is to ensure that 'purchasers' of portfolios of agreements will require a licence to administer and enforce the agreements.[3]

However, in order for a person carrying on a business to be caught by the new limb of the definitions, he must himself be a 'creditor' or 'owner'. Section 189(1) defines 'creditor' as:

> the person providing credit under a consumer credit agreement or the person to whom his rights and duties under the agreement have passed by assignment or operation of law . . .

and 'owner' as:

> a person who bails or (in Scotland) hires out goods under a consumer hire agreement or the person to whom his rights and duties under the agreement have passed by assignment or operation of law . . .

The use of 'and' between 'rights' and 'duties' would appear to exclude contractual assignees, who take the creditor's benefits, but not his duties, from the scope of the definition. At common law, the creditor's duties cannot pass by assignment but only by operation of law.[4] Accordingly, it may be that 'rights and duties' in the s.189(1) definitions of creditor and owner is intended to mean 'rights or duties'.[5] Alternatively, it may be that the word 'assignment' is used in the definitions to mean a transfer or novation.[6] The 'purchase' of a portfolio of agreements will very often be effected by an assignment of the creditor's benefits under the agreement, rather than a novation by which his duties are also transferred, and, upon an assignment, the duties will remain with the original creditor. There is, therefore, some doubt as to whether or not an assignee of the benefit of a portfolio of agreements is a 'creditor' or 'owner' for the purposes of CCA 1974.

It is perhaps unfortunate that CCA 2006 does not amend the definitions of 'creditor' or 'owner', but imports the uncertainty created by those definitions into the definitions of consumer credit and consumer hire businesses. Arguably, the existing definitions of those businesses suffice to include businesses carried on by assignees of the benefits of consumer credit or consumer hire agreements, since the existing definitions extend to businesses that comprise or relate to the provision of credit and businesses that comprise or relate to the bailment or hiring of goods, without the requirement now included in the first limb of the new definitions ('the provision of credit by him' and 'the bailment or . . . hiring of goods by him'), that the provision of credit, bailment or hiring is, or was, by the person carrying on the business in question.

6.1.3   Ancillary credit businesses

A licence is also required for the carrying on of any of the ancillary credit businesses of credit brokerage, debt adjusting, debt counselling, debt collecting, or the operation of a credit reference agency[7] and will be required, by CCA 2006, for the carrying on of either of two further types of ancillary credit business: debt administration (CCA 1974, s.145(da), to be inserted by CCA 2006, s.24(1)) and the provision of credit information services (CCA 1974, s.145(db), to be inserted by CCA 2006, s.25(1)). Although the provisions defining debt administration and credit information services have already come into force,[8] these businesses are not presently intended to be brought within the licensing regime until 1 October 2008 (DTI Timetable, May 2006).

6.1.4   Debt administration

Debt administration is defined as the taking of steps, other than debt-collecting and other than as a creditor or owner:

(a) to perform duties under a consumer credit agreement or a consumer hire agreement on behalf of the creditor or owner; or
(b) to exercise or to enforce rights under such an agreement on behalf of the creditor or owner (s.145(7A), inserted by CCA 2006, s.24(2)).

Under the existing provisions, a third party's administration of an agreement on behalf of the creditor or owner is authorised by the licence of the creditor or owner (s.23(1)). The intention behind a separate requirement for a licence to carry on the business of debt administration is that CCA 1974 and the OFT should have direct control over businesses that administer regulated agreements on behalf of creditors or owners.

It has been indicated that debt administration is intended to cover not only businesses whose sole purpose is to administer agreements on behalf of the creditors or owners, for remuneration other than entitlement to the receivables, but also those who 'purchase portfolios of existing loans and administer them'.[9] As the definition of debt administration only covers the administration of agreements other than as creditor or owner, the intended inclusion of 'purchasers' would suggest that the new category of licensed business may be intended to include assignees of the creditors' or owners' benefits under the loans who then administer the loans, carrying out the creditors' or owners' duties on behalf of the creditors or owners, but who are themselves entitled to receive the payments to be made under the agreements. That would be consistent with the interpretation of the terms 'creditor' and 'owner' as not including such assignees, but only persons to whom both the rights and the duties of the creditor have passed.[10]

It should be noted that it will only be persons carrying on a business of debt administration who will be required to have a licence (under CCA 1974, s.21, as it is to be amended). No licence will be required by a retailer merely because he is authorised to accept credit cards and may, from time to time, be required by the card issuing creditor to retain such cards.[11] Such retailers would not be carrying on the business of debt administration.

6.1.5   Credit information services

The extension of the licensing requirements to cover the provision of credit information services is intended to bring credit repair businesses within the control of CCA 1974 and the OFT. The particular mischief that is sought to be addressed is the practice of misleading desperate or otherwise vulnerable consumers into believing that, for a fee, they can have their credit records cleaned, by the removal of adverse entries whether or not the entries are valid.[12]

The provision of credit information services is defined as the taking of any steps, or giving an individual advice in relation to the taking of any steps, with a view to:

(a) ascertaining whether a credit information agency holds information relevant to the financial standing of an individual;
(b) ascertaining the contents of such information;
(c) having such information corrected or modified;
(d) stopping such an agency from holding such information or from providing it to another person (s.145(7B) and (7C) of CCA 1974, inserted by CCA 2006, s.25(2)).

A credit information agency is defined for this purpose as:

(a) a person carrying on any of the activities for which a licence is required other than the activity of providing credit information services (CCA 1974, s.145(7D)(a) and (b), inserted by CCA 2006, s.25(2));
(b) a person carrying on a business which would be a consumer credit business except that it comprises or relates to consumer credit agreements that are exempt agreements, otherwise than by virtue of s.16(5)(a);[13]
(c) a person carrying on a business which would be a consumer hire business except that it comprises or relates to consumer hire agreements that are exempt, otherwise than by virtue of s.16(6).[14]

---

1   This amendment is intended to come into force on 6 April 2008 (DTI Timetable, May 2006).
2   This amendment is intended to come into force on 6 April 2008 (DTI Timetable, May 2006).
3   See the debate on clause 23 of the Bill during the third sitting of the Standing Committee on 28 June 2005.
4   *Linden Gardens Ltd* v. *Lenesta Ltd* [1994] 1 AC 85.
5   This view is expressed in *Goode's Consumer Credit Law and Practice* at IC [23.21].
6   See *Linden Gardens Ltd* v. *Lenesta Ltd* [1994] 1 AC 85 at 103 for judicial criticism of the common misuse of the word 'assignment' to describe a novation, by which one contracting party, with the consent of the other contracting party, transfers his duties as well as his rights to a third party.
7   Sections 21, 145(1) and 147(1) of CCA 1974; s.21(1), to be amended by s.33(1) of CCA 2006 so as to achieve, by the express inclusion of 'an ancillary credit business', the

requirement for such a business to be licensed, which is achieved by the application
of Part III to ancillary credit businesses by s.147(1).

8   Provisions came into force on 16 June 2006 (Commencement Order (No.1) 2006).

9   See the Parliamentary Under-Secretary of State for Trade and Industry's explanation of
clause 24 of the Bill during the third sitting of the Standing Committee on 28 June
2005.

10 See s.189(1) and the discussion of 'creditor' and 'owner' in the context of the new
definitions of consumer credit business and consumer hire business at **para.6.1.2**.

11 A fear raised during the passage of the Bill through Parliament: see the debate on
clause 24 of the Bill during the third sitting of the Standing Committee on 28 June
2005.

12 See the Parliamentary Under-Secretary of State for Trade and Industry's explanation of
clause 25 of the Bill during the third sitting of the Standing Committee on 28 June
2005.

13 Section 145(7D)(c) of CCA 1974, to be inserted by CCA 2006, s.25(2); agreements
exempt by virtue of s.16(5)(a) are exempt by reference to the number of payments
made, under the Consumer Credit (Exempt Agreements) Order 1989, art. 3.

14 Section 145(7D)(d) of CCA 1974, to be inserted by CCA 2006, s.25(2); s.16(6)
enables the Secretary of State to provide by order that specified hire agreements may
be exempt where the owner is an authorised utility supplier or a provider of a public
electronic communications service.

6.2   LIMITED LICENCES

6.2.1   Specified activities

The OFT has always had the power, under CCA 1974, s.23(2), to limit the activities covered by a licence, whether by only authorising the licensee to enter into
certain types of agreement, or in any other way. One particular activity, namely
the canvassing off trade premises of debtor-creditor-supplier agreements and regulated consumer hire agreements is only covered by a licence if, and to the extent
that, the licence specifically provides; and no such provision may be included in
a group licence (s.23(3)). Up until now, there has been power for the Secretary of
State, by regulations, to specify other activities that must not be engaged in by the
licensee unless covered by an express term in his licence (s.23(4)). This power
is now to be given to the OFT, so that it may, by general notice, specify such
activities (s.23(4), to be amended by CCA 2006, s.33(4)).[1]

Separate provision is now to be made for the OFT to limit the activities covered
by a group licence in any way the OFT thinks fit (s.22(5A), to be inserted by CCA
2006, s.33(2)), although it would seem that the OFT is already entitled to do so
under the existing provisions (s.23(2)).

6.2.2   Types and description of business

A new s.24A defines, as 'types of business', the recognised categories of business
for which licences are granted and also the new categories of debt administration
and credit information services:

(a)   a consumer credit business;

(b) a consumer hire business;

(c) a business so far as it comprises or relates to credit brokerage;

(d) a business so far as it comprises or relates to debt-adjusting;

(e) a business so far as it comprises or relates to debt-counselling;

(f) a business so far as it comprises or relates to debt-collecting;

(g) a business so far as it comprises or relates to debt-administration;

(h) a business so far as it comprises or relates to the provision of credit information services;

(i) a business so far as it comprises or relates to the operation of a credit reference agency (s.24A, to be inserted by CCA 2006, s.28).

In future, an applicant for a standard licence may state in his application that he is applying for the licence to cover the carrying on of one or more of these types of business without limitation (s.24A(1)(a) to be inserted by CCA 2006, s.28). Alternatively, he may state, in relation to any of the types of business for which the licence is sought, that he is applying for the licence to cover the carrying on of that type of business only in so far as it falls within one or more descriptions of business (s.24A(1)(b), to be inserted by CCA 2006, s.28).

The OFT is to specify, by general notice, the descriptions of business to which a standard licence may be limited (s.24A(5)(a), inserted by CCA 2006, s.28). The OFT may also stipulate, by general notice, that applications cannot be made for licences limited by description of business in relation to one or more types of ancillary credit business (s.24A(5)(b), to be inserted by CCA 2006, s.28). Different provision may be made, in such general notices, for different cases or different classes of case (s.24A(6), to be inserted by CCA 2006, s.28).

The powers of the OFT to specify descriptions of businesses by general notice came into force on 16 June 2006.[2] The right to apply for a limited licence is not expected to come into force until 6 April 2008.[3]

---

1   This amendment is intended to come into force on 6 April 2008 (DTI Timetable, May 2006).

2   Brought into force by the Commencement Order (No.1) 2006.

3   According to the DTI Timetable, May 2006.

6.3   FITNESS TO HOLD A LICENCE

6.3.1   Entitlement to a licence

An applicant must, in all cases, satisfy the OFT that any name under which he is to be licensed is not misleading or otherwise undesirable.[1] Beyond that, all that is required is that he is a fit person to carry on the type and description of business for which the licence is sought.

Section 25 is to be amended so that a person who applies for a licence to carry on a type of business without limitation will be entitled to be issued with a licence to carry on that type of business without limitation provided that he satisfies the

OFT that he is a fit person to do so (s.25(1) to be amended by CCA 2006, s.29(1)).[2] Currently, the OFT is obliged to issue a licence to a person who satisfies the OFT that he is a fit person to engage in activities covered by the licence and any name under which he applies to be licensed is not misleading or otherwise undesirable (s.25(1)), but, arguably, the OFT has more freedom either to restrict the activities covered by the licence, or to refuse a licence when the application is for a licence that will authorise activities for which the applicant is not fit as well as activities for which he is fit.

In future, it is clear that a person who applies for a licence to carry on a type of business only in so far as it falls within a description, or descriptions, of business set out in the application, will be entitled to such a licence provided that he satisfies the OFT that he is a fit person to carry on business within the stated description, or descriptions.[3]

The OFT will also be obliged to issue a licence that is more limited than the licence for which the application is made, being limited to one or more of the descriptions of business that the applicant would have been entitled to apply for, and within the description(s) and type(s) of business that he did apply for, if, but only if:

(a)   in the case of a person who has applied to carry on a type of business without limitation, the OFT is not satisfied that he is a fit person to carry on that type of business without limitation; or
(b)   in the case of a person who has applied to carry on a limited description, or limited descriptions, of a type of business, the OFT is not satisfied that he is fit to carry on the description, or descriptions, of business that he applied for,

but the OFT is satisfied that he is a fit person to carry on a business of the description, or descriptions for which the licence is to be granted (s.25(1AB), to be inserted by CCA 2006, s.29(1)).

6.3.2   Criteria for fitness

The Consumer Credit Act 2006 is intended to create a more demanding test of fitness to hold a licence, by requiring applicants to demonstrate that they have prepared adequate practices and procedures to ensure that the proposed business will be carried on competently:

> The new broader fitness test gives the OFT explicit power to require evidence of future competence to provide credit. For example, it may require an applicant to give evidence to show how he would ensure that his employees understood what was required of them. Evidence might also show that the employees understand their credit products and can explain them to consumers. The OFT will not require evidence of expertise to demonstrate fitness. Applicants will be required to demonstrate a base line of competence.[4]

A new CCA 1974, s.25(2) (to be inserted by CCA 2006, s.29(2)) is expressly to include in the matters to which the OFT is to have regard, the applicant's skills, knowledge and experience in relation to consumer credit, consumer hire or ancillary credit business; such skills, knowledge and experience of other persons whom the applicant proposes should participate in any business that would be carried on under the licence; and practices and procedures that the applicant proposes to implement in connection with any such business.

The requirements of the existing s.25(2) are to be retained in a new s.25(2A), namely for the OFT to have regard to any evidence tending to show that the applicant, his employees, agents or associates, or, in the case of a body corporate, anyone appearing to the OFT to be a controller of the body or an associate of such a person, has:

(a) committed an offence involving fraud, other dishonesty or violence;
(b) contravened any provision of or made under CCA 1974 or any other enactment regulating the provision of credit to, or other transactions with individuals;
(c) contravened any corresponding provisions in force in an EEA State;
(d) practised discrimination in, or in connection with, the carrying on of a business; or
(e) engaged in business practices appearing to the OFT to be deceitful or oppressive or otherwise unfair or improper (s.25(2A), to be inserted by CCA 2006, s.29(2)).

The OFT is also to have regard to evidence that any such person has contravened any money award, direction or other provision made by or under the consumer credit jurisdiction of the Financial Services Ombudsman Scheme (s.25(2A)(b)(ii)), a jurisdiction that is to be created by CCA 2006 (see **Chapter 8**).

Relevant discrimination now expressly includes discrimination on grounds of national origins, as well as grounds of sex, colour, race or ethnic origins in connection with the carrying on of any business (s.25(2A)(d), to be inserted by CCA 2006, s.29(2)).

The significance of irresponsible lending is highlighted by a new s.25(2B) (to be inserted by CCA 2006, s.29(2)), which will state that the business practices which the OFT may consider to be deceitful or oppressive or otherwise unfair or improper include practices in the carrying on of a consumer credit business that appear to the OFT to involve irresponsible lending. The expression 'irresponsible lending' is not to be defined, in keeping with the Government's determination not to include definitions of practices that are to be curbed because there is a perceived risk that the courts may construe such definitions unduly narrowly. However, the expression is generally taken to mean lending without first taking any, or adequate, steps to ascertain whether or not the borrower will be able to afford to make the proposed repayments; but it may also be constituted by a lack of transparency on the part of the lender in the ways in which the terms and implications of agreements are set out in the agreement forms themselves and otherwise presented to borrowers.[5]

The amendments relating to the criteria to be applied when assessing fitness to hold a licence are expected to come into force on 6 April 2008 (DTI Timetable, May 2006).

6.3.3   Guidance on fitness criteria

The OFT will be required to prepare and publish guidance, under a new s.25A (to be inserted by CCA 2006, s.30), as to how it determines, or proposes to determine, whether a person is a fit person to hold the licence for which he has applied, or a more limited licence (s.25A(1)), and, in carrying out its functions under Part III of CCA 1974 as it is to be amended, the OFT will be under a duty to have regard to the guidance as most recently published (s.25A(5)). In preparing or revising the guidance, the OFT is to consult such persons as it thinks fit (s.25A(4)).

The guidance is to be published as soon as practicable after s.25A is brought into force, but the consultation may be started, or even completed, earlier (CCA 2006, Sched.3, para.19).

The guidance, and any revision of it, must be published in such manner as the OFT thinks fit for the purpose of bringing it to the attention of those likely to be affected by it (s.25A(2) and (3)).

---

1 Section 25(1AD), to be inserted by CCA 2006, s.29(1) replacing wording to the same effect that was previously in s.25(1)(b).
2 This amendment is intended to come into force on 6 April 2008 (DTI Timetable, May 2006).
3 Section 25(1AA), to be inserted by CCA 2006, s.29(1). The description of business applied for must be one specified by the OFT in general notice under s.24A(5) (s.25(1AD), to be inserted by CCA 2006, s.29(1)).
4 See the Parliamentary Under-Secretary of State for Trade and Industry's explanation of clause 29 of the Bill during the third sitting of the Standing Committee on 28 June 2005.
5 See the debate, during the third sitting of the Standing Committee on 28 June 2005, on a proposed amendment that was not carried, which was directed at the imposition of a duty on lenders to lend responsibly.

6.4   TRANSITIONAL AUTHORITY FOR TRANSFER OR WINDING-UP

At present, the OFT may give directions, when refusing to renew a standard or group licence, or when suspending or revoking any licence, authorising a licensee to carry into effect agreements that he has made before the revocation or suspension (CCA 1974, ss.29(5) and 32(5)). This power is to be repealed by CCA 2006 (ss.29(5) and 32(5) are to be repealed by CCA 2006, s.32(3) and (6)).

In future, the OFT will, instead, have the power, in relation to standard licences, to authorise the licensee, or other persons, to carry on specified activities for specified periods, for the purpose of enabling the licensee's business, or any part of his business to be transferred or wound up. This change is expected to be brought into force on 6 April 2008 (DTI Timetable, May 2006).

When the OFT refuses to renew a standard licence, or decides to renew it in different terms from those applied for, or when it makes a compulsory variation to a standard licence under s.31, or suspends or revokes a standard licence, it may, if it thinks fit, as part of the same determination, authorise the licensee (s.34A(1) and (2), to be inserted by CCA 2006, s.32), or other persons (s.34A(3)(b), to be inserted by CCA 2006, s.32), to carry on specified activities, or activities of specified descriptions, for a specified period beyond the determination, if the determination will cause the licensee to cease to be licensed to carry on those activities. The power can only be exercised for the purposes of enabling the transfer or winding-up of the whole or part of the licensee's business (s.34A(1), to be inserted by CCA 2006, s.32).

Activities carried on under such an authorisation will be treated, for the purposes of ss.39(1), 40, 148 and 149, as if carried on under a standard licence (s.34A(5) to be inserted by CCA 2006, s.32).

Different periods of authorisation may be specified for different activities or activities of different descriptions (s.34A(3)(a), to be inserted by CCA 2006, s.32).

The authorisation may be made subject to the authorised person's compliance with specified requirements in relation to the activities that he is authorised to carry on and, if he fails to comply with those requirements, the OFT may, by notice to the person, terminate his authorisation, in whole or in part, from a specified date (s.34A(3)(c), to be inserted by CCA 2006, s.32(1)). In particular, the OFT may impose requirements which have the effect of:

(a) preventing a named person from being an employee of a person carrying on activities under the authorisation, or restricting the activities that a person may engage in as an employee of such a person;

(b) preventing a named person from doing something, or restricting his doing something, in connection with activities being carried on by a person under the authorisation;

(c) securing that access to premises is given to officers of the OFT for the purpose of enabling them to inspect documents or to observe the carrying on of activities (s.34A(4), to be inserted by CCA 2006, s.32(1)).

Where the OFT is minded to refuse an application for a licence to be renewed, or to renew a licence in different terms from those applied for, the notice that it is minded to do so, which it must give to the applicant (under s.27(1), applied to an application for a renewal by s.29(3)), must invite the applicant to make representations in accordance with s.34 about the provision, if any, that should be included in the proposed determination refusing renewal or renewing the licence in different terms from those applied for, so as to authorise the licensee or any other person to carry on specified activities for specified periods, for the purpose of the transfer or winding-up of the business.[1]

Similarly, where the OFT is minded to make a compulsory variation in a licence under s.31 or to suspend or revoke a licence under s.32, the notice that it is minded to do so, which it must give to the licensee,[2] must invite the applicant to submit representations in accordance with CCA 1974, s.34 about the provision, if any, that should be included in the proposed determination that the licence be varied, suspended or revoked, as the case may be, so as to authorise the licensee or any other person to carry on specified activities for specified periods, for the purpose of the transfer or winding-up of the business.[3]

---

1 As well as inviting him to submit representations in support of his application (CCA 1974, s.29(3A), to be inserted by CCA 2006, s.32(2)).
2 Under CCA 1974, s.31(2) in relation to compulsory variation and s.32(2) in relation to suspension or revocation.
3 As well as inviting him to submit representations about the proposed variation, suspension or revocation, as the case may be (CCA 1974, s.31(2) to be amended by CCA 2006, s.32(4) in relation to compulsory variation and CCA 1974, s.32(2) to be amended by CCA 2006, s.32(5) in relation to suspension or revocation).

6.5   DURATION OF LICENCES

Up until now, standard licences have been of a limited duration, prescribed by regulations made by the Secretary of State (CCA 1974, ss.22(1)(a) and 189(1)). The current duration of a standard licence is five years (Consumer Credit (Period of Standard Licences) (Amendment) Regulations 1991, SI 1991/817, reg.3), subject to any prior suspension or revocation under s.32 or termination under s.37. Group licences, on the other hand, have been of such limited duration as the OFT thinks fit, or, if the OFT thinks fit, of indefinite duration (s.22(1)(b) to be amended by CCA 2006, s.34(1)).

In the future, any standard licence will be of indefinite duration, unless the original application is for a licence of limited duration or the OFT thinks there is a good reason why it should have effect for a limited period only (s.22(1C), to be inserted by CCA 2006, s.34(2)). A group licence is to be of limited duration unless the OFT thinks there is a good reason why it should have effect indefinitely (s.22(1D), to be inserted by CCA 2006, s.34(2)).

The Secretary of State is to prescribe, by regulations, the maximum duration of a licence that is to be of limited duration (s.22(1B), to be inserted by CCA 2006, s.34(2)). Subject to that maximum, a licence of limited duration will be for such period as the OFT thinks fit (s.22(1B), to be inserted by CCA 2006, s.34(2)). Where an indefinite licence is varied so as to make it a licence of limited duration, its duration, from the date of the variation, must not exceed the maximum duration prescribed for a licence of limited duration by regulations (s.22(1E), to be inserted by CCA 2006, s.34(2)). Subject to that maximum, the variation will provide for it to have such duration as the applicant, in the case of an application for a variation under s.30, has applied for, or, in the case of compulsory variation under s.31, such duration as the OFT thinks fit (s.22(1E)).

The terms of a licence must specify whether it has effect indefinitely or for a limited period and, if for a limited period, specify the period (s.22(1A), to be inserted by CCA 2006, s.34(2)).

Section 29, which deals with the renewal of licences, is to be amended, so as only to apply to licences of limited duration (s.29(1) to be amended by CCA 2006, s.34(3)(a)).

These changes are expected to come into force on 6 April 2008 (DTI Timetable, May 2006).

6.6   CHARGES

6.6.1   Charge payable on application

Applicants for licences, or for the renewal of a licence, will have to pay a charge under a new s.6A (to be inserted by CCA 2006, s.27), towards the costs of the OFT's carrying out its functions under CCA 1974. The amount of the charge will be determined in accordance with provision to be made by the OFT in general notice (s.6A(2)), which may make different provision in relation to persons of different descriptions and may make provision for no charge at all to be payable by persons of specified descriptions (s.6A(3)). However, the OFT will not be able to prescribe a charge by general notice under s.6A without the approval of the Secretary of State and the Treasury (s.6A(4)).

Any application for a licence, or for the renewal of a licence, will have to be accompanied by payment of the charge (s.6(2A)).

Under the existing provisions, the 'specified fee', if any, must accompany any application to the OFT (s.6(2)). Fees are specified, for this purpose, by General Notice 50, under the power given to the OFT by CCA 1974, s.2(4) and (5). As with the new charge, a specified fee must be approved by the Secretary of State and the Treasury. The OFT is permitted to specify that reduced fees, or no fees, are to be paid by persons of a specified description, for certain of its services or facilities (s.6(5)). The 'specified fee' remains payable in respect of all applications other than original applications for licences and applications for renewals (s.6(2A)(b), to be inserted by CCA 2006, s.27(2)). There would not appear to be any difference between the OFT's existing powers to charge specified fees for original applications and applications for renewals and its new powers to specify charges payable for such applications, save to the extent that the new powers are expressly limited to imposing charges 'towards the costs of [the OFT's] carrying out its functions under [the 1974] Act' (s.6A(1), to be inserted by CCA 2006, s.27(1)). The charges are to be paid by the OFT into the Consolidated Fund, as are specified fees (CCA 1974, s.190(2), to be amended by CCA 2006, s.65). It is envisaged that the OFT will require higher charges than currently required as specified fees, in order to fund more effective monitoring of licensees.[1]

The OFT's power to make provision, by general notice, for the determination of the amount of a charge that will be payable on application under s.6A(1) came into force on 16 June 2006.[2] The obligation to pay a charge under s.6A(1) is not expected to come into force until 6 April 2008.[3]

6.6.2   Additional charges for indefinite licences

Periodic charges

Regulations are to be made by the Secretary of State to provide for the determination of 'payment periods' for licensees under indefinite standard licences and for original applicants for indefinite group licences (CCA 1974, s.28A(6), to be inserted by CCA 2006, s.35). A licensee under an indefinite standard licence will have to pay the OFT a charge before the end of each of his payment periods (s.28A(1), to be inserted by CCA 2006, s.35). Similarly, the original applicant for an indefinite group will have to pay the OFT a charge before the end of each of his payment periods (s.28A(2), to be inserted by CCA 2006, s.35). It is envisaged that these periodic charges will probably have to be paid every five years.[4]

The OFT will specify the amount of the periodic charges to be payable in respect of indefinite licences by general notice (s.28A(3)(a), to be inserted by CCA 2006, s.35) and may make different provision in relation to persons of different descriptions, different provision in relation to persons whose payment periods end at different times, and provision for no charge at all to be payable by persons of specified descriptions (s.28A(4), to be inserted by CCA 2006, s.35). The approval of the Secretary of State and the Treasury will be required for a general notice specifying what periodic charges are to be payable, or, as may be the case in relation to certain descriptions of person, not payable (s.28A(5), to be inserted by CCA 2006, s.35). Regulations made by the Secretary of State will make provision for the determination of the date when the amount of a charge specified by general notice will become current (s.28A(3)(b), to be inserted by CCA 2006, s.35).

Extension of time to pay

A person who is required to pay a periodic charge in respect of an indefinite licence may make one application to the OFT for an extension of the time in which it has to be paid (s.28B(1), to be inserted by CCA 2006, s.36). The OFT may grant an extension if it is satisfied that there is a good reason why the applicant has not paid the charge and why he cannot pay it in time (s.28B(3), to be inserted by CCA 2006, s.36). The extension will be granted by notice and it will be for such period as the OFT thinks fit having regard to the reason for the applicant's inability to pay within the original time limit (s.28B(3), to be inserted by CCA 2006, s.36).

The OFT is to make provision, by general notice, as to the day by which any application for an extension must be made (s.28B(2), to be inserted by CCA 2006, s.36). However, its power to grant an extension may be exercised even though the period within which the charge was originally required to have been paid has ended (s.28B(4)(b), to be inserted by CCA 2006, s.36).

Time for payment may be extended in relation to only a part of the charge (s.28B(4)(a)).

Termination of licence on failure to pay

If a licensee under an indefinite standard licence fails to pay a periodic charge within the time originally stipulated for its payment, or, if an extension has been granted by the OFT, within the period of that extension, his licence will automatically terminate (s.28C(1) and (3), to be inserted by CCA 2006, s.36). Where an extension has been granted in respect of part of the payment and he fails to pay the other part of the charge within the original time limit or he fails to pay the part to which the extension applies within the period of the extension, his licence will be terminated (s.28C(2) and (3)).

A licence will not terminate under this provision while an application for an extension is pending, nor will it terminate if an extension is granted after the date by which the charge should originally have been paid, provided that the charge is paid within the period of the extension (s.28C(4)).

Particulars of the termination of an indefinite standard licence on the failure of the licensee to pay the periodic charge must be kept in the register maintained by the OFT under CCA 1974, s.35 (s.28C(5)).

---

1 See the debate on clause 27 of the Bill during the third sitting of the Standing Committee on 28 June 2005.

2 This amendment was brought into force by Commencement Order (No.1) 2006.

3. According to DTI Timetable, May 2006.

4 See the Parliamentary Under-Secretary of State for Trade and Industry's introduction of clause 35 of the Bill during the third sitting of the Standing Committee on 28 June 2005.

7 THE DUTIES AND POWERS OF THE OFFICE OF FAIR TRADING

> **Key changes**
>
> - Office of Fair Trading actively to monitor businesses
> - More powers to obtain information
> - Wider powers of entry and search
> - Alternative sanctions, including financial penalties

7.1 DUTIES

The Office of Fair Trading (OFT) is given the following duties in relation to credit and hire by CCA 1974, s.1(1):

(a) to administer the licensing system set up by CCA 1974;

(b) to exercise the adjudicating functions conferred upon it by CCA 1974, in particular those conferred by Part III in relation to the issue, renewal, variation, suspension and revocation of licences to carry on consumer credit, consumer hire and ancillary credit businesses;

(c) to superintend the working and enforcement of CCA 1974 and regulations made under it; and

(d) where necessary or expedient, to take steps to enforce CCA 1974 and regulations made under it.

The OFT is also required by CCA 1974, s.1(2) so far as appears to it to be practicable and having regard both to the national interest and the interests of persons carrying on businesses to which CCA 1974 applies and their customers, to keep under review and from time to time advise the Secretary of State about:

(a) social and commercial developments in the UK and elsewhere relating to the provision of credit or the hiring of goods to individuals, and related activities; and

(b) the working and enforcement of CCA 1974 and orders and regulations made under it.

Section 1(1) of CCA 1974 is to be amended so that it expressly states that the OFT has a duty 'to monitor, as it sees fit, businesses being carried on under licences' (s.1(1)(ba), to be inserted by CCA 2006, s.62). This will oblige the OFT to keep businesses under what it considers to be an appropriate level of surveillance, rather than merely taking action in response to customer complaints.

The OFT is to be assisted in the performance of its duties by extensive new powers to obtain information, to gain access to premises, to impose requirements and to fine businesses (see **paras.7.2–7.8**).

At present, the OFT may seek court orders prohibiting behaviour that contravenes CCA 1974, either under CCA 1974, s.1(d) or the Enterprise Act 2002 (EA 2002), Part 8. However, the only sanctions that may be directly imposed by the OFT, in the event of a licensee's failure to conduct his business satisfactorily in accordance with the requirements of CCA 1974, are the extreme sanctions of varying, suspending or revoking his licence under s.31 or s.32, or varying a group licence so as to exclude him from the group under s.31(5). In order to impose such sanctions, the OFT has to be satisfied, in the case of compulsory variation, that the licensee is not fit to carry on business under the licence in its existing terms, or, in the case of suspension or revocation, that he is not fit to carry on the activities covered by the licence at all (this is the effect of ss.31(1) and 32(1) read together with ss.25(1) and 29(3)).

CCA 2006 is to provide the OFT with broad powers to impose intermediate sanctions, in the form of 'requirements' under ss.33A (to be inserted by CCA 2006, s.38) and 33B (to be inserted by CCA 2006, s.39), and to impose financial penalties under s.39A (to be inserted by CCA 2006, s.52) for failure to meet such requirements. These powers are seen by the Government as:

A vital new tool for the OFT to ensure a targeted and proportionate licensing regime.[1]

The changes discussed in this chapter are likely to come into force on 6 April 2008 (DTI Timetable, May 2006).

---

1   The Parliamentary Under-Secretary of State for Trade and Industry introducing clause 38 of the Bill during the third sitting of the Standing Committee on 28 June 2005.

7.2   POWERS TO OBTAIN INFORMATION

7.2.1   Existing powers

The OFT is currently only entitled to obtain information:

(a) under s.6(2) and (3), from people who are making applications to it under CCA 1974; or

(b) under s.162(1)(b), (c) and (d), when there is reasonable cause to suspect a breach of any provision of or under CCA 1974, for the limited purposes of ascertaining whether there has been such a breach or providing evidence in proceedings for an offence under CCA 1974.

7.2.2   Information and documents to be provided by applicants

Section 6 of CCA 1974 is to be amended (by CCA 2006, s.44) so that the OFT will be able, by general notice, to require documents as well as information to be provided with any application for a licence or for a variation or renewal of a licence (s.6(2) as it is to be amended). For the purposes of CCA 1974, as amended, 'documents' will include information recorded in any form (s.189(1) as it is to be amended by CCA 2006, s.51(6)).

The OFT will also be able, at any time after receiving an application up until making its determination on the application, to require the applicant to provide it with further information and documents relevant to the application (s.6(3) as it is to be amended by CCA 2006, s.44(2)).

Whenever the OFT publishes a new general notice specifying the information and documents that are to be provided with applications, it will be able, by that notice, to require applicants under pending applications to provide it with such of the information and documents specified in the notice as were not required, in each case, at the date the application was made, unless they have already been provided. The general notice must specify the period within which such further information and documents are to be provided (s.6(5) and (6), to be inserted by CCA 2006, s.44(3)).

Each applicant will be placed under an obligation to notify the OFT if any information or document provided in relation to the application in accordance with a general notice or in accordance with a notice addressed directly to the applicant, is to any extent superseded or affected by a change in circumstances,[1] or if the applicant becomes aware of an error in or omission from any such information or document, other than a clerical error or omission not affecting the substance of the information or document (s.6(7) and (9), to be inserted by CCA 2006, s.44(3)). He must do this within the period of 28 days beginning with the day on which the information or document is superseded, the day on which the change in circumstance occurs, or the day he becomes aware of the error or omission, as the case may be (s.6(8), to be inserted by CCA 2006, s.44(3)).

None of the new obligations to provide information or produce documents that may be imposed upon applicants as a result of the amendments to s.6 will apply in respect of applications made before the amendments take effect (CCA 2006, Sched.3, para.23(1)).[2]

7.2.3   Information and documents to be provided by existing licensees

As required by general notice

By s.36A of CCA 1974 (to be inserted by CCA 2006, s.45), whenever the OFT publishes a new general notice specifying the information and documents that are to be provided with applications, it will be able, by that notice (see s.36A(2)(b)), to require existing licensees under standard licences and original applicants for existing group licences to provide it with that information and those documents[3] in relation to each application for a licence or for its renewal or variation[4] which each standard licence holder or original applicant for a group licence has made and which was determined before the new general notice came into effect (s.36A(1) and (2)). The general notice will specify the period within which such further information and documents are to be provided (s.36A(2) and (3)).

In the event of information or documents previously provided in the course of an application under s.6, or by an existing licensee or original applicant for a group licence under s.36A, being superseded or otherwise affected by a change in circumstances,[5] the licensee under a standard licence or the original applicant for a group licence will only have to notify the OFT if the matter falls within a description of matters specified by the OFT in general notice (s.36A(5) and (6)). The OFT may only specify a description of matters for this purpose if it is satisfied that matters which would fall within that description would be relevant to the question of whether, having regard to s.25(2), a person is a fit person to carry on a business under a standard licence, or whether the public interest is better served by a group licence remaining in effect than by obliging the licensees under it to apply separately for standard licences (s.36A(7)).

If, after an application for a licence or for the variation or renewal of a licence has been determined, a licensee under a standard licence or an original applicant for a group licence, becomes aware of any error in, or omission from, any information or document that he has provided under s.6 or s.36A,[6] he must notify the OFT unless it is a clerical error or omission not affecting the substance of the information or document (s.36A(8) and (10)).

Any notification that is required to be given under s.36A, of a change affecting information or a document, or of an error or omission, must be given within 28 days beginning with the day on which the information or document is superseded, on which the change in circumstances occurs, or on which the licensee under a standard licence or the original applicant for a group licence becomes aware of the error or omission (s.36A(9)).

None of the new obligations to provide information, produce documents or notify changes that may be imposed upon licensees or original applicants for group licenses under s.36A will apply in respect of applications made before s.36A comes into force (CCA 2006, Sched.3, para 23(3)).[7]

As required by individual notice

By s.36B (to be inserted by CCA 2006, s.46), the OFT will be able, by notice to a licensee under a standard licence or to the original applicant for a group licence, to require him to provide such information or to produce such documents as is or are specified or described in the notice. The only prerequisite for service of such a notice will be that the OFT reasonably requires that information or those documents, as the case may be, for purposes connected with its functions under CCA 1974 (s.36B(1) and (4)).

The OFT may, by notice, require any person other than a licensee under a standard licence or the original applicant for a group licence, to provide such information or to produce such documents as is or are specified or described in the notice, if the OFT reasonably requires such information or documents for purposes connected with the taking of steps under Part III of CCA 1974 or for the consideration of whether to take such steps, as a consequence of an act or omission which has occurred, or which the OFT has reason to suspect has occurred, and which:

(a) casts doubt on whether, having regard to s.25(2), a person is a fit person to carry on a business under a standard licence;
(b) casts doubt on whether the public interest is better served by a group licence remaining in effect, or being issued, than by obliging the persons who are licensees under it, or who would be licensees under it, to apply separately for standard licences;
(c) gives rise, or is likely to give rise, to dissatisfaction for the purposes of s.33A(1) or s.33B(1) (the OFT's powers to impose requirements when it is dissatisfied); or
(d) constitutes or gives rise to a failure to comply with a requirement imposed by s.33A, s.33B or s.36A (s.36B(1), (5) and (6)).[8]

A notice given by the OFT under s.36B, whether given to a licensee, to an original applicant for a group licence, or to another person, must set out the reasons why the OFT requires the information or documents (s.36B(2)).

The recipient of the notice must provide the information and/or produce the documents required within such reasonable period of time as is specified in the notice and at the place specified in the notice (s.36B(3)).

1 Other than a change in particulars entered in the register which must be notified to the OFT under s.36 (s.6(9)(a)).
2 The relevant amendments will take effect on the commencement of CCA 2006, s.44.
3 Unless they have already been provided in relation to the application (s.36A(4)).
4 See the definition of 'relevant application' in s.36A(11).
5 Other than a change in particulars entered in the register which must be notified to the OFT under s.36 (s.36A(10)(a)).
6 Other than a change in particulars entered in the register which must be notified to the OFT under s.36 (s.36A(10)(a)).
7 Section 36A will come into force on the commencement of CCA 2006, s.45.
8 For civil penalties see s.39A(1), to be inserted by CCA 2006, s.52 (see **para.7.8**).

7.3   POWERS OF ENTRY AND SEARCH

7.3.1   Existing powers

A duly authorised officer of an enforcement authority may, at all reasonable hours and on production, if required, of his credentials, enter premises, other than premises used only as a dwelling, for the limited purpose of ascertaining whether there has been a breach of a provision of or under CCA 1974 (s.162(1)(a)).

An enforcement authority is an authority which has a duty under s.161 of CCA 1974 to enforce the Act and regulations made under it. The enforcement authorities are the OFT itself and local weights and measures authorities, that is, the trading standards offices or consumer protection departments of local authorities, and, in Northern Ireland, the Department of Commerce (s.161(1)).

7.3.2   Warrants for surprise raids

Section 36D of CCA 1974 (to be inserted by CCA 2006, s.48) will enable the OFT to obtain a warrant for an officer of an enforcement authority to enter and search premises without notice when there are reasonable grounds for believing:

(a) that information or documents which the OFT could require a person to provide or produce by notice under s.36B (see 'As required by individual notice' at para.7.2.3) are on specified premises; and
(b) that if such a notice was to be served, it would not be complied with, or the information or documents would be tampered with (s.36D(1) and (2)).

A warrant may be issued by a justice of the peace, if he is satisfied, on information given on oath on behalf of the OFT, that there are reasonable grounds for believing that those conditions are met.[1]

The warrant will authorise an officer of an enforcement authority:

(a) to enter the premises specified in the warrant;
(b) to search the premises and to seize and detain any information or documents appearing to be information or documents specified in the warrant or information or documents of a description specified in the warrant;
(c) to take any other steps which may appear to be reasonably necessary for preserving such information or documents or to prevent interference with them; and
(d) to use such force as may be reasonably necessary (s.36D(3)).

When an officer enters premises under a warrant issued under s.36D, he will be able to take such persons and equipment with him as he thinks necessary (s.36D(4)).

7.3.3   Entry without warrant

By s.36C of CCA 1974 (to be inserted by CCA 2006, s.47), the OFT will have power, by notice, to require a licensee or an original applicant for a group licence to give access to premises to an officer of an enforcement authority, so that he may:

(a) observe a business being carried on under a licence by the licensee on whom the notice is served; or

(b) observe activities that are being carried on by an original applicant for a group licence on whom the notice is served for the purpose of regulating or otherwise supervising licensees under the group licence in connection with the carrying on of businesses under that licence; or

(c) to inspect documents of the licensee relating to a business that he is carrying on under the licence or documents of the original applicant for a group licence relating to such activities as are mentioned in (b) (s.36C(1)).

This power will arise in relation to licensees under standard licences and original applicants for group licences whenever such observation or inspection is reasonably required for purposes connected with the OFT's functions under CCA 1974 (s.36C(1), (8) and (10)).

The power will arise in relation to licensees other than licensees under standard licences and original applicants for group licences[2] whenever the observation of a business carried on by the licensee or inspection of his documents is reasonably required for purposes connected with the taking of steps by the OFT under Part III of CCA 1974 or its consideration of whether to take such steps, as a consequence of an act or omission which has occurred, or which the OFT has reason to suspect has occurred, and which:

(a) casts doubt on whether, having regard to s.25(2), a person is a fit person to carry on a business under a standard licence;

(b) casts doubt on whether the public interest is better served by a group licence remaining in effect, or being issued, than by obliging the persons who are licensees under it, or who would be licensees under it, to apply separately for standard licences;

(c) gives rise, or is likely to give rise, to dissatisfaction for the purposes of s.33A(1) or s.33B(1) (the OFT's powers to impose requirements when it is dissatisfied); or

(d) constitutes or gives rise to a failure to comply with a requirement imposed by s.33A, s.33B or s.36A (s.36C(1) and (9)) (s.39A(1), to be inserted by CCA 2006, s.52, gives the OFT power to impose civil penalties for such failures (see **para.7.8**)).

The OFT must give notice to the licensee, or to the original applicant for a group licence, of the requirement to give access and the notice must specify or describe any documents that are to be inspected (s.36C(1)). The notice must set out the reasons why access is required (s.36C(2)).

The premises to which access may be gained in this way are not to include premises which are used only as a dwelling, but may include premises which are not premises of the licensee if they are premises from which he carries on activities in connection with a business that he carries on under the licence (s.36C(3)), or, in the case of an original applicant for a group licence, premises from which he carries on activities for the purpose of regulating or otherwise supervising licensees under that group licence (see s.36C(10)).

The OFT is required to give reasonable notice of the times at which access is required to be given (s.36C(5)) and the licensee will only be required to ensure that access is given at those times if it is reasonable for the OFT to require access to be given at those times (s.36C(4)).

Once the officer is on the premises, it is the licensee's obligation to ensure that persons on the premises give the officer such information or assistance as he may reasonably require in connection with his observation of the business or his inspection of documents (s.36C(6)), including assistance by giving an explanation of a document that is being inspected (s.36C(7)).

7.3.4   Entry and search by other enforcement authorities

An officer of an enforcement authority other than the OFT will only be able to exercise the powers to gain access to premises, with or without a warrant, that are conferred by ss.36C and 36D of CCA 1974 as amended, if the enforcement authority of which he is an officer has made arrangements for its exercise of such powers with the OFT (s.36F(1), to be inserted by CCA 2006, s.50).

The OFT will bear responsibility for any act or omission by an officer of another enforcement authority in the exercise or purported exercise of a power under s.36C or s.36D, in that the act or omission will be treated as having been that of an officer of the OFT (s.36F(2)), save for the purposes of any criminal proceedings (s.36F(3)).

Where an officer of an enforcement authority other than the OFT obtains information by the exercise of a power under s.36C or s.36D, he must not disclose it to any person other than the OFT unless he has the approval of the OFT to do so or he is under a duty to do so (s.36F(4)).

---

1   In Scotland, the warrant may be issued by a sheriff and 'evidence', rather than information, on oath will be required (s.36D(5)).

2   On a literal reading of s.36C(1), access can only be required by notice to a licensee and, therefore, this narrower power would appear to apply in respect of licensees under group licences who are not original applicants. However, the intention may perhaps have been for this narrower power to apply in respect of persons other than licensees.

7.4 FORM OF INFORMATION AND COPIES

When an enforcement authority or an officer of an enforcement authority is entitled, by virtue of any power conferred by or under CCA 1974 to require the provision or production of information or documents,[1] the authority or the officer may require that information which is recorded otherwise than in a legible form be provided in a legible form.[2] They may take copies of, or extracts from,[3] any documents produced (s.174A(1)(b)). They may require the person who is required to provide or produce any information or document to state, to the best of his knowledge and belief, where the information or document is (s.174A(1)(c)(i)); they may require that he give an explanation of the information or document (s.174A(1)(c)(ii)); they may require him to ensure that any information provided, whether or not in a document, is verified in such manner as they may specify (s.174A(1)(c)(iii)); and they may require him to ensure that any document provided is authenticated in such manner as they may specify (s.174A(1)(c)(iv)).

When an enforcement authority or an officer of an enforcement authority is entitled, by virtue of any power conferred by or under CCA 1974, to inspect or to seize documents at any premises,[4] they may take copies of, or extracts from,[5] any documents inspected or seized by virtue of the power (s.174A(2), to be inserted by CCA 2006, s.51(2)).

---

1 This entitlement will arise under s.6, as it is to be amended by CCA 2006, s.44 (see **para.7.2.2** above), and each of the new ss.36A, 36B, 36C (by virtue of subs.(6)) and 36D (by virtue of subs.(3)(b)).
2 Section 174(1)(a) of CCA 1974, to be inserted by s.51(5) of CCA 2006, replacing, in effect, the former wording of s.162(1)(b)(ii).
3 The literal meaning of the provision would appear to be that they may remove extracts from original documents, but the intention is presumably that they may take copies of extracts of original documents.
4 This entitlement exists under s.162 and will also arise under ss.36C and 36D.
5 Again, the literal meaning of the provision would appear to be that they may remove extracts from original documents, but the intention is presumably that they may take copies of extracts of original documents.

7.5 LEGAL PROFESSIONAL PRIVILEGE

An enforcement authority's powers to obtain information and documents under ss.6, 36A, 36B, 36C and 36D may be resisted in relation to information and documents that would be privileged from disclosure in a High Court action on grounds of legal professional privilege, or, in Scotland, in proceedings in the Court of Session on grounds of confidentiality of communications (s.174A(3) and (4) of CCA 1974, to be inserted by CCA 2006, s.51(5)).

7.6   COURT ENFORCEMENT OF POWERS TO OBTAIN INFORMATION AND ENTRY

By s.36E of CCA 1974 (to be inserted by CCA 2006, s.49), the OFT will be able to apply to the High Court or the county court (or, in Scotland, the Court of Session or the sheriff) (s.36E(1) and (4)) for an order that a person who has failed to provide information or documents in accordance with a notice requiring him to do so under s.36B or to give access to premises in accordance with a notice requiring him to do so under s.36C either:

(a) complies with the requirement(s) set out in the notice within such period as may be specified in the order; or
(b) otherwise takes such steps to remedy the consequences of his failure as may be specified in the order (s.36E(2)).

The person against whom such an application is made is referred to in s.36E as an 'information defaulter' (s.36E(1)). Where the person is a body of persons, whether incorporated or not, the order may require any officer who is wholly or partly responsible for the failure to comply with the OFT's notice to meet such costs of the application as are specified in the order (s.36E(3)). For this purpose, 'officer' means any director, manager or secretary, or person holding a similar position, and, in the case of a partnership, unincorporated body of persons, or a body corporate whose affairs are managed by its members, any member of the body (s.36E(4) and (5)).

7.7   POWERS TO IMPOSE REQUIREMENTS

7.7.1   Individual licensees

The OFT is to have the power, under s.33A of CCA 1974 (to be inserted by s.38 of CCA 2006), to impose requirements on licensees. It will be able, by notice, to require a licensee to do, or not to do, or to cease doing 'anything specified in the notice for purposes connected with addressing' a matter with which the OFT is dissatisfied or for purposes connected with 'securing that matters of the same or a similar kind do not arise' (s.33A(2)).

The power will arise whenever the OFT is 'dissatisfied with any matter in con-nection with' a business being carried on, or a business which has previously been carried on, by a licensee or by an associate or a former associate of a licensee; or in connection with a proposal to carry on a business which has been made by a licensee or an associate or former associate of a licensee; or in connection with any other conduct of a licensee or any other conduct of an associate or former associate of a licensee (s.33A(1)). For this purpose, a business associate is 'an associate', in addition to those persons who are specified as associates in CCA 1974, s.184 (s.33A(7)).

A requirement imposed on a licensee may require the licensee to restrict the activ-ities of a named person, other than the licensee, in connection with the licensee's business (s.33A(4)). Protection is afforded to other persons whose activities may be restricted as a result of the imposition of a requirement on the licensee, to the extent that they have the right to make representations in respect of a proposed requirement, variation or revocation of a requirement, and to apply for variation or revocation of a requirement (s.33D(1), (2) and (3) read together with s.33C(4), (5) and (7) (see **para.7.7.4**)).

The matter with which the OFT is dissatisfied may be a matter that arose before or after the licensee became a licensee and before or after the OFT's power to impose the requirement came into force (CCA 1974, s.33A(5) and CCA 2006, Sched.3, para.20).

7.7.2   Group licences

The OFT will also be able to impose requirements, under CCA 1974, s.33B (to be inserted by CCA 2006, s.39), on 'a responsible person' in relation to a group licence, namely the original applicant if he has a responsibility, whether by virtue of an enactment, an agreement, or otherwise, for regulating or otherwise supervising persons who are licensees under the licence (s.33B(6)).

Where the OFT is dissatisfied with the way in which a responsible person in relation to a group licence is regulating or otherwise supervising persons who are licensees under that licence, or the way in which that person is proposing to regulate or otherwise supervise them, the OFT will have power to require the supervisory body to do or not to do, or to cease doing, anything with a view to addressing the matters giving rise to the OFT's dissatisfaction or with a view to securing that matters of the same or a similar kind do not arise (s.33B(1) and (2)).

The matters giving rise to the OFT's dissatisfaction may be matters that arose before or after the issue of the group licence and before or after the OFT's power to impose the requirement came into force (CCA 1974, s.33B(4) and CCA 2006, Sched.3, para 21).

7.7.3   Limits on discretion to impose requirements

The power to impose requirements on a licensee will be limited in that the requirements are only to relate to a business which the licensee is currently carrying on, or to a business which the licensee is proposing to carry on, under his licence (s.33A(3)). Similarly, the power to impose requirements on responsible bodies in respect of group licences will be limited in that the requirements are only to relate to practices and procedures for regulating or otherwise supervising licensees under the licence in connection with their carrying on of businesses under the licence (s.33B(3)). The only other express limitation that is to be placed upon the powers is that the OFT will not be able to require the licensee or supervisory body to compensate another person, or otherwise to make amends to another person (s.33C(3), to be inserted by CCA 2006, s.40).

Unlike the new powers to obtain information by notice to existing licensees (see 'As required by individual notice' at **para.7.2.3**) and to gain access to premises (see **para.7.3.3**), the power to impose requirements is not to be expressed as limited to taking action that is reasonably required for purposes connected with the OFT's functions under CCA 1974. Nonetheless, it would seem that the powers to impose requirements will inevitably be limited to the extent that the OFT will only be entitled to use them in the course of the duties conferred upon it by CCA 1974 in relation to businesses requiring a licence and only upon grounds of public interest which fall within the objectives of CCA 1974.[1]

It would seem to be intended that the OFT will be entitled to impose requirements not just to deter or put an end to practices that directly contravene the statutory requirements imposed by and under CCA 1974, but also to stop other practices that have the potential to make a licensee unfit to hold a licence.[2] A note provided by the OFT on requirements, during the passage of the Consumer Credit Bill through Parliament, stated that:

> The OFT will normally be dissatisfied with a licensee or applicant's conduct if the OFT has evidence that the conduct causes or could cause consumer detriment and is directly linked to the activities covered by the licence or the licence applied for.

A report of the Joint Committee on Human Rights (*Scrutiny: Seventh Progress Report, Fifteenth Report of Session 2004–05*) concluded that the power to impose requirements was expressed in such broad terms as to give rise to a significant risk of incompatibility with the right to peaceful enjoyment of possessions in Art. 1 of the First Protocol to the European Convention on Human Rights.

The OFT will no doubt have regard to the intention that these requirements should be used as less draconian and more proportionate regulatory sanctions than the refusal, compulsory variation, suspension or revocation of a licence.[3] It is also likely only to impose requirements that are necessary and proportionate, in accordance with the Cabinet Office Enforcement Concordat, the principles of which the OFT accepts.

7.7.4 Procedure

Before deciding to impose a requirement under s.33A or s.33B, the OFT will have to give notice that it is minded to do so (s.33D(1) and (2), to be inserted by CCA 2006, s.41). Notice will have to be given to the licensee or supervisory body in question. It will also have to be given to any other person who is to be named in the requirement if the requirement will prevent him from being an employee of the licensee on whom the requirement is imposed or restrict the activities that he may engage in as an employee of the licensee, or otherwise prevent him from doing something, or restrict his doing something, in connection with the licensee's business (s.33D(3), read together with s.33C(7)).

The notice must inform the recipient that the OFT is minded to impose a requirement; it must give reasons; and it must invite the recipient to submit representations to the OFT under s.34 of CCA 1974 (s.33D(2)).

The licensee, supervisory body or other person who is to be named in the requirement and prevented or restricted in his activities in connection with the licensee's business may, within 21 days, or such longer period as the OFT may allow, make written representations and may give notice to the OFT that he wishes to make oral representations (s.34(1)).

The OFT must take into account any such written or oral representations in deciding whether or not to impose a requirement (s.34(2)).

Once the OFT has decided to impose a requirement, it does so by further notice to the licensee or supervisory body upon which the requirement is to be imposed (s.33A(2) and s.33B(2)). Notice must also be given to any employee or other person named in the requirement where it has the effect of preventing him from doing something, or of restricting his doing something, in connection with the licensee's business (s.34(3), read together with s.33C(7) and s.33D(3)).

A notice imposing a requirement may specify the time at or by which, or the period during which, the requirement is to be complied with (s.33C(1)). A requirement will not have effect after the licence in question has ceased to have effect (s.33C(2)).

7.7.5   Variation or revocation

The OFT may vary or revoke a requirement of its own motion. It may also do so on the application of the licensee or supervisory body on whom the requirement has been imposed, or on the application of a person, such as an employee, who is named in the requirement and has been prevented by the requirement from doing something, or restricted by it in doing something, in connection with the licensee's business (s.33C(4), (5), (6) and (7), to be inserted by CCA 2006, s.40).

Before varying or revoking a requirement or refusing an application to vary or revoke a requirement, the OFT must give notice that it is minded to do so to the licensee or supervisory body in question and to any other person who is, or is to be, named in the requirement and has been, or is to be, prevented from doing something, or restricted in doing something, in connection with the licensee's business (s.33D(1), (2) and (3), read together with s.33C(7)), unless it proposes to vary or revoke the requirement in a way proposed by that person (whether as part of an application for variation or revocation or otherwise) (s.33D(4), to be inserted by CCA 2006, s.41). The notice must give reasons and invite representations under s.34 (s.33D(2)), which must be taken into account by the OFT in deciding whether or not to proceed with the variation or revocation (s.34(2)).

If the OFT does decide to vary or revoke a requirement, it does so by notice to the person on whom the requirement was imposed, with effect from such date as is specified in the notice (s.33C(4)). Notice will also have to be given to any employee or other person previously named in the requirement or named in the requirement as a result of the variation, where the requirement had or has the effect of preventing him from doing something, or of restricting his doing something, in connection with the licensee's business (s.34(3), read together with ss.33C(7) and 33D(3)).

7.7.6   Negotiation and voluntary submission

The new provisions will enable negotiations to take place, prior to the imposition of a requirement, or in relation to its variation or revocation, with a view to agreement being reached between the OFT, the licensee and any other person whose activities in connection with the licensee's business may be affected, as to the terms of a requirement or its variation or revocation.

It will be permissible for a requirement to be imposed, by notice under s.33A(2) or s.33B(2), or varied or revoked, by notice under s.33C(4), without the licensee or other person affected being given the opportunity to make formal representations under ss.33D and 34, if the requirement, variation or revocation is in the same terms as a proposal made to the OFT by the person who would otherwise have been entitled to the opportunity to make representations (s.33D(4), to be inserted by CCA 2006, s.41).

This would appear to provide an opportunity for resolving disputes between the OFT and licensees or other persons who may be affected by the OFT's intended action, equivalent to the way in which licensing issues may currently be resolved by the giving and acceptance of undertakings. When conduct is challenged by the OFT informally, or when notice is given that the OFT is minded to impose a requirement, a business might itself propose a requirement which would be less damaging to the business or easier to comply with than the requirement proposed by the OFT, but nonetheless meet the OFT's objectives. Under the existing system, the OFT may agree to renew, or agree not to revoke, suspend or vary a licence upon undertakings being given that a business will or will not take certain action or continue certain practices. However, whereas breach of an undertaking results in no direct sanctions, although it may be regarded as evidence that a person is not fit to hold a licence, breach of a requirement imposed by agreement may result in a financial penalty under s.39A (to be inserted by CCA 2006, s.52 (see **para.7.8**)). The person who proposes a requirement which is then imposed in the terms of his proposal will not be able to appeal against the imposition of the requirement (see table to s.41, as it is to be amended by CCA 2006, s.43(2)).

7.7.7   Record of requirements to be kept in the register

The OFT is to include particulars of all requirements imposed, with details of any variations, in the public register maintained under CCA 1974, s.35(1) (s.35(1)(ba), to be inserted by CCA 2006, s.43(1)).

---

1   The OFT's duties are set out in CCA 1974, s.1 as it is to be amended by CCA 2006, s.62 (see para.7.1). The lawful scope of an ostensibly wide discretion is ultimately a matter of law, to be determined by the court, in the context of the court's construction of the policy and objects of the enactment which confers the discretion (*Padfield* v. *Minister of Agriculture, Fisheries and Food* [1968] AC 997).
2   See the debate on Amendment No. 10 during the Report Stage of the Bill in the House of Lords, 18 January 2006, Official Report, cols. 747 and 748.
3   See, for example, the introduction of clause 38 of the Bill by the Parliamentary Under-Secretary of State for Trade and Industry during the third sitting of the Standing Committee on 28 June 2005.

7.8   CIVIL PENALTIES

Section 39A of CCA 1974 (to be inserted by CCA 2006, s.52) will enable the OFT to serve a penalty notice, imposing a financial penalty of up to £50,000, on any person who has failed or is failing to comply with a requirement imposed on him under:

(a) s.33A (OFT's power to impose requirements when it is dissatisfied with any conduct of a licensee or of an associate or former associate of a licensee);
(b) s.33B (OFT's power to impose requirements on any responsible person when dissatisfied with the way in which he is regulating or otherwise supervising licensees under a group licence); or
(c) s.36A (requirement in a new general notice under s.6(2) that existing licensees and original applicants for group licences provide the OFT with further information or documents) (s.39A(1) and (3)).

The OFT must itself be 'satisfied' that the person in question is failing or has failed to comply with a relevant requirement (s.39A(1)).

The limit of £50,000 has been set with a view to avoiding a challenge to the new provisions under the Human Rights Act 1998, as being in contravention of the European Convention on Human Rights, and with the intention that the penalty actually imposed will, in each case, be proportionate to the gravity of the matter to which the contravened requirement relates and to the means of the licensee.[1] The limit may be reduced or increased by order of the Secretary of State, subject to approval by each House of Parliament (CCA 1974, s.181(1) and (2) as it is to be amended by CCA 2006, s.53(3)).

The penalty notice must specify the amount of the penalty; set out the OFT's reasons for imposing the penalty and for specifying that amount; specify how the penalty may be paid to the OFT; and specify the period within which it is to be paid (s.39A(2)).

Before imposing a penalty on a person, the OFT must give him notice informing him that it is minded to impose a penalty on him, stating the proposed amount, setting out its reasons both for imposing the penalty and for the proposed amount, setting out the proposed period for payment of the penalty, and inviting him to submit representations to it under s.34 (s.39B(1), to be inserted by CCA 2006, s.53(1)). He will then have the opportunity to make written and oral representations to the OFT and the OFT will be required to take those representations into account in deciding whether or not to impose a penalty and, if so, the amount of the penalty (s.34(2)).

The OFT will not be permitted to impose a penalty under s.39A in relation to any failure occurring before it has published a statement of policy as to how it proposes to exercise its powers under the section (s.39C(7), to be inserted by CCA 2006, s.54). The statement of policy must be published in such manner as the OFT thinks fit for the purpose of bringing it to the attention of those likely to be affected by it (s.39C(4)) and any revision of the policy must be similarly published (s.39C(2)). In preparing or revising the statement of policy, the OFT is to consult such persons as it thinks fit (s.39C(5)). However, no statement of policy is to be published without the approval of the Secretary of State (s.39C(3)). The first statement is to be published as soon as practicable after the OFT's obligation to publish it is brought into effect (by the commencement of CCA 2006, s.54), but the consultation may start, or be concluded, earlier (CCA 2006, Sched.3, para 25).

In determining whether and how to exercise its powers to impose a penalty, the OFT will be required to have regard to the statement of policy as most recently published at the time of the failure to which the proposed penalty relates (s.39C(6), to be inserted by CCA 2006, s.54). The OFT will also have to have regard to any penalty or fine that has been imposed on that person by another body in relation to the conduct giving rise to the failure and any other steps that the OFT has taken or might take under Part III of CCA 1974 in relation to that conduct (s.39B(2), to be inserted by CCA 2006, s.53(1)).

Where a penalty is imposed on a person who is a responsible person in relation to a group licence, general notice is to be given of its imposition (s.39B(3), to be inserted by CCA 2006, s.53(1)). The general notice will have to state the amount of the penalty, the reasons why the OFT imposed the penalty, and its reasons for specifying that amount (s.39B(4), to be inserted by CCA 2006, s.53(1)).

If the penalty is not paid within the period specified, the OFT may recover the amount of the penalty and interest on the penalty, or any unpaid part of it, at the rate for the time being specified in s.17 of the Judgments Act 1838 (s.39A(5)), currently 8 per cent (Judgment Debts (Rate of Interest) Order 1993, SI 1993/564).

---

1   See the debate on clause 52 of the Bill during the fourth sitting of the Standing Committee on 28 June 2005.

7.9   APPEALS AGAINST REQUIREMENTS AND PENALTIES

The licensee or supervisory body on whom a requirement is imposed under s.33A or s.33B and any other person named in a requirement whose activities in connection with the licensee's business are prevented or restricted by the requirement, may appeal the imposition, variation or revocation of the requirement and may appeal any refusal to grant an application to vary or revoke the requirement (CCA 1974, s.41, as it is to be amended by CCA 2006, s.43(2)), unless he proposed the terms of the requirement, variation or revocation in question (s.41, read together with s.33D(4)).

The person on whom a penalty is imposed will also have a right of appeal and the time allowed for payment of the penalty must not be shorter than the period during which an appeal may be brought against the imposition of the penalty (s.39A(4)), namely such period as may be specified by rules to be made by the Lord Chancellor under s.40A(3) of CCA 1974, as it is to be amended (s.41(1) and (1D), as it is to be amended and inserted by CCA 2006, s.56(1) and (2)).

Any such appeal will be a rehearing by the Consumer Credit Appeals Tribunal, from which an appeal may be brought, on a question of law, to the Court of Appeal, or, in Scotland, to the Court of Session (see **Chapter 8**). The lawful scope of the OFT's discretionary powers will be a question of law.[1]

---

1 *Padfield v. Minister of Agriculture, Fisheries and Food* [1968] AC 997.

8 THE CONSUMER CREDIT APPEALS TRIBUNAL

Key changes

- Independent appeal tribunal
- Rules to be made by the Lord Chancellor
- Appeal on point of law from tribunal to Court of Appeal

8.1   RIGHTS OF APPEAL

The existing system of appeals from decisions of the Office of Fair Trading (OFT) to the Secretary of State for Trade and Industry (CCA 1974, s.41) is to be replaced with provision for appeals to an independent Consumer Credit Appeals Tribunal (CCA 1974, ss.40A and 41, as inserted and amended by CCA 2006, ss.55 and 56). This is expected to take place on 6 April 2008 (DTI Timetable, May 2006).

The present system is for appeals against determinations of the OFT to be heard by a person appointed from a specialist panel,[1] on behalf of the Secretary of State. The procedure for bringing appeals and for the hearing and determination of appeals is prescribed by regulations (the Consumer Credit Licensing (Appeals) Regulations 1998, SI 1998/1203).

The types of determination that can be appealed include:

(a) the refusal to issue, renew or vary a licence;
(b) the refusal to end the suspension of a licence;
(c) the exclusion of a person from a group licence;
(d) the compulsory variation, suspension or revocation of a group or standard licence;
(e) the refusal to give directions authorising a licensee to give effect to agreements made by him before the expiry of the licence in circumstances where the licence is revoked, suspended or will not be renewed;
(f) the imposition of, or refusal to withdraw, a consumer credit prohibition under the Financial Services and Markets Act 2000.[2]

Once the relevant provisions of CCA 2006 have come into force, there will also be a right of appeal against:

(a) the imposition of a requirement under s.33A or s.33B;[3]
(b) the refusal of an application under s.33C(5) for a requirement to be varied or revoked;
(c) the variation or revocation of a requirement imposed under s.33A or s.33B; and
(d) the imposition of a financial penalty under s.39A (table to s.41, as it is to be amended by CCA 2006, ss.43(2) and 49(2)).

The person on whom a requirement is imposed will have the rights of appeal set out in s.41 in relation to the requirement, as will any other person who is named in the requirement and restricted in his activities in connection with a business being carried on by the person on whom the requirement is imposed, save that no person who has proposed the terms of a requirement to the OFT will have a right of appeal against a requirement that is then imposed in those terms (table to s.41, as it is to be amended by CCA 2006, s.43(2) read together with s.33D(4), to be inserted by CCA 2006, s.41).

The imposition of a financial penalty may be appealed by the person on whom it is imposed.

CCA 2006 will remove the appellate role from the Secretary of State and create a dedicated and independent Consumer Credit Appeals Tribunal (ss.40A and 41, to be inserted and amended by CCA 2006, ss.55(1) and 56). The new tribunal will have jurisdiction in relation to all determinations which may be appealed under s.41 and which are made after the amendment creating the right of appeal to the new tribunal is brought into effect (CCA 2006, Sched.3, para.27(1)).[4]

The need for an independent appeal tribunal will be all the greater in the light of the new powers that are to be conferred on the OFT to impose requirements and financial penalties (see **Chapter 6**). The new tribunal will be called the Consumer Credit Appeals Tribunal (to be inserted as CCA 1974, s.40A(1) by CCA 2006, s.55(1)). It will be controlled by the Department for Constitutional Affairs to the extent that the Lord Chancellor is to make such rules as he thinks fit to regulate the conduct and disposal of appeals before the tribunal (s.40A(3), to be inserted by CCA 2006, s.55(1)) and he will also have the powers of appointment and dismissal of the tribunal members (see **para.7.2**).

A new Sched.A1 to CCA 1974 (to have effect under s.40A(4) and to be inserted by CCA 2006, s.55(2)) sets out the framework for the composition, powers and procedure, remuneration and staffing of the new tribunal.

The tribunal will be subject to the supervision of the Council on Tribunals under the Tribunals and Inquiries Act 1992[5] and a member of the Council or of its Scottish Committee will be entitled to attend any hearing held by the tribunal or a member of the panel of chairmen whether or not the hearing is held in public.

The Council member will also be entitled to attend any deliberations of the tribunal in relation to an appeal (Sched.A1, para.11).

1 Appointed by the Secretary of State under the Consumer Credit Licensing (Appeals) Regulations 1998, SI 1998/1203, reg 24.
2 A full list of the determinations that can be appealed is set out in the table to CCA 1974, s.41. The table also includes details of the person who has the right to appeal in relation to each type of determination.
3 The OFT's powers under ss.33A, 33B, 33C and 39A are discussed in **Chapter 6**.
4 On the commencement of CCA 2006, s.56.
5 The Consumer Credit Appeals Tribunal is to be added to Tribunals and Inquiries Act 1992, Sched.1 at para.9A, by CCA 2006, s.58(5).

8.2   COMPOSITION OF THE TRIBUNAL

The Lord Chancellor is to appoint a panel of persons for the purpose of serving as chairmen of the tribunal (the panel of chairmen) and another panel (the lay panel) of persons who appear to him to be qualified, by experience or otherwise, to sit on the hearing of appeals, with a chairman (CCA 1974, Sched.A1, para.3, to be inserted by CCA 2006, s.55(2) and Sched.1). A person may only be appointed to the panel of chairmen if he has one of the following legal qualifications:

(a) he has a seven-year general qualification within the meaning of Courts and Legal Services Act 1990, s.71;
(b) he is an advocate or solicitor in Scotland of at least seven years' standing; or
(c) he is a member of the Bar of Northern Ireland, or a solicitor of the Supreme Court of Northern Ireland, of at least seven years' standing (Sched.A1, para.3(2)).

There will be no obligation to appoint lay members who are considered to be representative of the interests of persons entitled to bring appeals under s.41, as there is under the present system (Consumer Credit Licensing (Appeals) Regulations 1998, SI 1998/1203, reg.24(2)(c)).

Members of the existing panel[1] from which persons are appointed to hear appeals on behalf of the Secretary of State will be treated as having been appointed to the new panels, for the purposes of hearing appeals as the new tribunal. Those with the requisite legal qualification will be treated as appointed to the panel of chairmen; the others will be treated as appointed to the lay panel (CCA 2006, Sched.3, para.26).

The Lord Chancellor will appoint one of the members of the panel of chairmen to be the President of the Consumer Credit Appeals Tribunal, who will preside over the discharge of the tribunal's functions (Sched.A1, para.2(1) and (2)), and another of the panel of chairmen to be the Deputy President of the Consumer Credit Appeals Tribunal (Sched.A1, para.2(3)). The Deputy President will be responsible for such functions as the President may assign to him (Sched.A1, para.2(4)). If the President is absent or otherwise unable to discharge his functions, they will be discharged by the Deputy President, or, if there is no Deputy

President or he too is absent or otherwise unable to act, the President's functions will be discharged by a person appointed for that purpose from the panel of chairmen by the Lord Chancellor (Sched.A1, para.2(6)).

Each member of the panel of chairmen and each member of the lay panel is to hold and vacate office in accordance with the terms of his appointment (Sched.A1, para.4(1)). A member's term of office will not be limited to five years, as under the present system (Consumer Credit Licensing (Appeals) Regulations 1998, SI 1998/1203, reg.24(3)(a)). The Lord Chancellor will have the power to remove any member of either panel from office on the ground of incapacity or misbehaviour (Sched.A1, para.4(2)).

If the President or the Deputy President ceases to be a member of the panel of chairmen, he will also cease to be the President or (as the case may be) the Deputy President (Sched.A1, para.2(5)).

A member of either panel may resign office by notice in writing to the Lord Chancellor, but each member remains eligible for re-appointment if he ceases to hold office (Sched.A1, para.4(3)).

For the purposes of each appeal, the members of the tribunal who are to hear the appeal will be selected from the panel of chairmen and the lay panel in accordance with arrangements to be made by the President (Sched.A1, para.7(1) and (2)). The arrangements will have to provide for at least one member who hears each appeal to be selected from the panel of chairmen (Sched.A1, para.7(3)).

Where it appears to the tribunal hearing an appeal that the appeal involves a question of fact of special difficulty, the tribunal may appoint one or more experts to provide assistance (Sched.A1, para.7(4)).

---

1   Appointed by the Secretary of State under the Consumer Credit Licensing (Appeals) Regulations 1998, SI 1998/1203, reg.24.

8.3   APPEALS TO THE TRIBUNAL

8.3.1   Manner and nature of appeal

The Consumer Credit Act 1974, as amended, is to provide that an appeal will be brought by notice of appeal (s.41(1A), to be inserted by CCA 2006, s.56(2)), setting out the grounds and including such information and documents as the rules to be made by the Lord Chancellor may specify, in such form as those rules may specify (s.41(1B) and (1D), to be inserted by CCA 2006, s.56(2)).

The appeal will be by way of a rehearing of the determination appealed against (s.41(1C), to be inserted by CCA 2006, s.56(2)), but the tribunal will be required to decide the appeal by reference to the grounds of appeal set out in the notice of appeal (Sched.A1, para.12(1)).

8.3.2   Powers of the tribunal

The powers of the tribunal will be:

(a) to confirm the determination appealed against;
(b) to quash the determination;
(c) to vary the determination;
(d) to remit the matter to the OFT for reconsideration and determination in accordance with such directions, if any, as the tribunal may give to the OFT; and
(e) to give directions to the OFT for the purpose of giving effect to the tribunal's decision (Sched.A1, para.12(2)).

The tribunal will have no power to increase the amount of a penalty, but it may extend the period within which the penalty is to be paid, whether or not that period has already ended (Sched.A1, para.12(3)). When the tribunal directs the OFT to reconsider a determination to impose a penalty, that may result in the OFT's imposing an increased penalty, although it is not clear to what extent the tribunal may direct that the penalty be increased (Sched.A1, para.12(4)).

When the tribunal remits a matter to the OFT for reconsideration and determination, the appellant's obligations, as an applicant, to provide information to the OFT under s.6(1), (3) and (9) of CCA 1974, will apply as if the application had not previously been determined (Sched.A1, para.12(6)), save that he will be allowed 28 days from the date when the application is remitted to the OFT, or such longer period as the OFT may allow, in respect of information required under s.6(6) or (7) (Sched.A1, para.12(6), (7) and (8)).

The tribunal may direct that the requirements of s.34 of CCA 1974, as to the giving of notice and an opportunity to submit written representations and make oral representations, will not apply in respect of a matter remitted to the OFT, or that they are not to apply to a specified extent, in relation to the OFT's reconsideration of the matter (Sched.A1, para.12(5)).

8.4   PROCEDURE OF THE TRIBUNAL

8.4.1   General procedure

The tribunal will sit at such times and in such places as the Lord Chancellor may direct (Sched.A1, para.8).

Rules may make provision restricting the evidence that the tribunal may consider in specified circumstances. Subject to any such rules, the tribunal may consider any evidence, on an appeal, that it thinks relevant, whether or not the evidence was available to the OFT at the time it made the determination appealed against (Sched.A1, para.9).

The procedural rules that are to be made by the Lord Chancellor are not to be restricted by CCA 1974, as amended, but may include provision as to the withdrawal of appeals; as to representation; setting time limits; conferring powers on the tribunal or a member of the panel of chairmen to extend time limits, including the time limit for serving notice of appeal; conferring powers on the tribunal or a member of the panel of chairmen to give directions to the parties to an appeal for purposes connected with the conduct and disposal of the appeal; placing restrictions on disclosure; as to the consequences of failure to comply with a requirement imposed by or under the rules; for the suspension of determinations of the OFT; and for the suspension of decisions of the tribunal (Sched.A1, para.10).

8.4.2   The hearing

It would seem likely that the basic procedure to be established by the rules and to be adopted by the tribunal will be similar to the procedure followed under the current system and will be less formal than procedures applying to court proceedings. The existing rules (under the Consumer Credit Licensing (Appeals) Regulations 1998, SI 1998/1203) confer rights upon the appellant and the OFT to attend the appeal hearing and to be represented; the right for the parties to call and to question witnesses; and the right for the parties to address the appointed person(s). Under the existing system, the appointed person(s) hearing an appeal may limit these rights if satisfied that to do so will not prevent the appeal from being decided fairly. However, it may reasonably be expected that the provision for there to be a President of the Consumer Credit Appeal Tribunal will result in a more uniform approach to the directions that may be given and to the general conduct of appeals.

8.4.3   The decision

The decision of the tribunal may be by majority of the members hearing the appeal (Sched.A1, para.13(1)). The decision will have to be recorded in a document containing a statement of the tribunal's reasons, any other information that may be required to be included by the rules, and a statement whether the decision is unanimous or by majority, signed by a member of the panel of chairmen (Sched.A1, para.13(2)). A copy of the decision will be sent to each party to the appeal and the decision will be published in such manner as the tribunal thinks fit (Sched.A1, para.13(3)). However, the rules may specify descriptions of information that is to be excluded from the publication of any decision (Sched.A1, para.13(4)).

8.5   COSTS OF TRIBUNAL HEARINGS

If the tribunal decides that the OFT was wrong to make the determination appealed against, or if, during the course of the appeal, the OFT accepts that it was wrong to make the determination, the tribunal may order the OFT to pay the whole or part of the appellant's costs (Sched.A1, para.14(1)). In determining whether to order costs against the OFT, and the terms of such an order, the tribunal will be required to have regard to whether it was unreasonable for the OFT to make the determination (Sched.A1, para.14(2)).

The tribunal will have no power to order that the appellant pay the OFT's costs unless, on the disposal or withdrawal of an appeal, it thinks that the appellant acted vexatiously, frivolously or unreasonably in bringing the appeal or otherwise in relation to the appeal. If it thinks that any party acted in that way, it may order that party to pay the whole or part of the costs incurred by the other party in relation to the appeal (Sched.A1, para.15).

A costs order made by the tribunal may be enforced as if it were an order of the county court or, in Scotland, as if it were an interlocutor of the Court of Session (Sched.A1, para.16).

8.6   APPEALS FROM THE TRIBUNAL

Appeals from a decision of the tribunal, by the appellant or the OFT (s.41A(1) and (7)), will be direct to the Court of Appeal, or, in Scotland, to the Court of Session. They may only be brought on points of law and with the leave of either the tribunal or the Court of Appeal or the Court of Session (s.41A(1) and (2), to be inserted by CCA 2006, s.57). An application for leave to appeal may be made to the Court of Appeal or the Court of Session only if the tribunal has already refused leave (s.41A(3)).

If, on appeal, the court considers that the decision of the tribunal was wrong in law, it may:

(a)   quash or vary the decision;
(b)   substitute a decision of its own; or
(c)   remit the matter to the tribunal for rehearing and determination in accordance with the directions (if any) given to it by the court (s.41A(4)).

An appeal may be brought from a decision of the Court of Appeal only if leave is given by the Court of Appeal or the House of Lords (s.41A(5)).

The rules to be made by the Lord Chancellor may make provision for regulating or prescribing any matters incidental to, or consequential on, an appeal from the tribunal to the Court of Appeal or a further appeal to the House of Lords (ss.41A(6) and 40A(3)).

9 THE FINANCIAL SERVICES OMBUDSMAN SCHEME

Key changes

- Free alternative dispute resolution service for complaints against consumer credit, consumer hire and ancillary credit business licensees
- Levy on business to fund the service

9.1 ALTERNATIVE DISPUTE RESOLUTION FOR DEBTORS AND HIRERS

The Financial Services Ombudsman Scheme has been established, under the Financial Services and Markets Act 2000 (FSMA 2000) (Part XVI, ss.225–234, and Sched.17), to provide an independent dispute resolution service for insurance and money-related matters. It is intended to be an efficient and less intimidating alternative to court proceedings:

> A scheme under which certain disputes may be resolved quickly and with minimum formality by an independent person (FSMA 2000, s.225(1)).

It is also free to complainants.[1]

The scheme is administered by a body corporate, Financial Ombudsman Service Limited (FOS), referred to in FSMA 2000 as the scheme operator (see FSMA 2000, s.225(2) and (3)).

CCA 2006 is to extend the remit of the ombudsman scheme to cover complaints brought against businesses that require a licence under CCA 1974. This is to be achieved by adding a third type of jurisdiction, namely a consumer credit jurisdiction, to the existing 'compulsory' and 'voluntary' jurisdictions of the scheme, by a new FSMA 2000, s.226A (inserted by CCA 2006, s.59).[2]

The relevant provisions of CCA 2006 were introduced with the assurance that the ombudsman scheme 'can, and no doubt will, resolve the vast majority of cases concerning consumer credit, leaving only some cases to go to court'.[3]

Before the consumer credit jurisdiction of the scheme applies to a type of business, that type of business must be specified as included in the jurisdiction by an order made by the Secretary of State (FSMA 2000, s.226A(1) and (2)(e)). The types of business that may be specified as included are the types for which a licence is required under CCA 1974, s.21 as set out in s.24A (to be inserted by CCA 2006, s.28):

(a) a consumer credit business;
(b) a consumer hire business;
(c) a business so far as it comprises or relates to credit brokerage;
(d) a business so far as it comprises or relates to debt-adjusting;
(e) a business so far as it comprises or relates to debt-counselling;
(f) a business so far as it comprises or relates to debt-collecting;
(g) a business so far as it comprises or relates to debt-administration;
(h) a business so far as it comprises or relates to the provision of credit information services;
(i) a business so far as it comprises or relates to the operation of a credit reference agency (FSMA 2000, s.226A(3)).

The rate at which businesses are to be introduced to the consumer credit jurisdiction of the scheme is to be agreed with the Treasury after consultation with FOS and the Financial Services Authority (FSA), so as to ensure that FOS is not overloaded with additional work.[4]

Once a type of business has been specified by order of the Secretary of State for the purposes of inclusion in the consumer credit jurisdiction of the scheme, it will be possible to bring a complaint to FOS in respect of an act or omission occurring in the course of a business of that type if the complaint falls within a description of complaint that has been specified in the consumer credit rules. These rules are to be made by FOS with the approval of the FSA (FSMA 2000, s.226A(7)). Financial Ombudsman Service Ltd published a draft of the proposed rules in June 2006, accompanied by an explanation and a statement that representations about the proposals may be made to FOS by 11 October 2006 (in accordance with FSMA 2000, Sched.17, para.16G(1) and (2), to be inserted by s.59 of and Sched.2 to CCA 2006). Financial Ombudsman Service Ltd must have regard to any representations made to it within the time allowed before making any consumer credit rules and it must publish a statement of any significant difference between the draft previously published and the rules made (FSMA 2000, Sched.17, para.16G(3) and (4)).

---

1   Although complainants who behave unreasonably or improperly may be penalised with costs orders (see **para.8.5**).
2   This amendment made on the 16 June 2006 by Commencement Order (No.1) 2006.
3   The Parliamentary Under-Secretary of State for Trade and Industry during debate on the new unfair relationship provisions in the second sitting of the Standing Committee on 23 June 2005.

4 See the explanation given by the Parliamentary Under-Secretary of State for Trade and Industry when introducing clause 59 of the Bill during the fourth sitting of the Standing Committee on 28 June 2005.

9.2   THE CONSUMER CREDIT JURISDICTION OF THE OMBUDSMAN SCHEME

Debtors or hirers who wish to make a complaint must be 'eligible' (FSMA 2000, s.226A(1) and (2)(a)). A complainant will be eligible under the consumer credit jurisdiction if:

(a) (i) he is an individual;[1] or
  (ii) he is a surety in relation to a security provided to the respondent in connection with a business carried on by the respondent of a type which requires a licence under CCA 1974 (FSMA 2000, s.226A(5)(b), read together with subss.2(d) and (3)); and
(b) he falls within a class of person specified in the consumer credit rules (FSMA 2000, s.226A(4)(b)).[2]

However, the complaint will only fall within the consumer credit jurisdiction of the scheme if:

(a) the complaint falls within a description of complaint specified in the consumer credit rules (FSMA 2000, s.226A(2)(b));[3]
(b) the complaint relates to an act or omission of the respondent that occurred in the course of a business being carried on by the respondent which was of a type for which a licence is required under CCA 1974 (FSMA 2000, s.226A(1) and (2)(d));
(c) at the time of the act or omission the respondent was the licensee under a standard licence or was authorised to carry on an activity for the purposes of transferring or winding-up a business under CCA 1974, s.34A (FSMA 2000, s.226A(2)(c));
(d) at the time of the act or omission, the type of business was specified in an order made by the Secretary of State (FSMA 2000, s.226A(2)(e)); and
(e) the complaint cannot be dealt with under the compulsory jurisdiction of FOS.[4]

It is proposed that the compulsory jurisdiction of FOS will be extended, by the compulsory jurisdiction rules made by the FSA, so that all complaints to FOS against businesses which carry on regulated activities under FSMA 2000 and which are therefore required to be authorised by the FSA, will come within the compulsory jurisdiction, rather than the consumer credit jurisdiction.[5]

1 As defined in CCA 1974, s.189(1) as amended (see **Chapter 1**). Expressions used in CCA 1974 are to have the same meaning in FSMA 2000, s.226A as they do in CCA 1974 (FSMA 2000, s.226A(9)).
2 The rules are to be made by FOS with the approval of the FSA (FSMA 2000, s.226A(7)).

3   The rules are to be made by FOS with the approval of the FSA (FSMA 2000, s.226A(7)).
4   FSMA 2000, s.226A(2)(f). The compulsory jurisdiction only covers activities that are specified as falling within the compulsory jurisdiction by the compulsory jurisdiction rules made by the FSA (FSMA 2000, s.226(3)).
5   See *Delivering Better Regulatory Outcomes, A Joint FSA and OFT Action Plan* (published April 2006) and FOS consultation paper (June 2006) .

9.3   HOW THE SCHEME OPERATES

9.3.1   The personnel who operate the scheme

The Chairman and the other members of the Board of FOS are appointed and are liable to be removed by the FSA, with the appointment of the Chairman being subject to the approval of the Treasury (FSMA 2000, Sched.17, para.3).

Financial Service Ombudsman Limited appoints and maintains a panel of ombudsmen, consisting of people who appear to it to have appropriate qualifications and experience (FSMA 2000, Sched.17, para.4(1)). Appointment to the panel is to be on such terms, including terms as to the duration and termination of the appointment and as to remuneration, as FOS considers consistent with the independence of the person appointed and otherwise appropriate (FSMA 2000, Sched.17, para.4(2)).

Financial Service Ombudsman Limited appoints one of the panel of ombudsmen to act as the Chief Ombudsman, again on such terms, including terms as to the duration and termination of his appointment, as FOS considers appropriate (FSMA 2000, Sched.17, para.5(1)).

9.3.2   The compulsory jurisdiction

Where the creditor under a regulated consumer credit agreement not only carries on consumer credit business but also carries on one or more regulated activities for which authorisation is required, and in relation to which the creditor is an authorised person, under FSMA 2000, the debtor may already be able to bring a complaint about his regulated consumer credit agreement under the compulsory jurisdiction of FOS.

The compulsory jurisdiction rules are made by the FSA and are set out in the *FSA Handbook*, under 'Dispute Resolution: Complaints' (DISP). Complaints may be brought against authorised persons under the compulsory jurisdiction in relation to acts or omissions occurring in the course of activities which are 'regulated activities' under FSMA 2000, s.22 but also in relation to acts or omissions by authorised persons in the course of carrying on any of the following activities:

(a) lending money secured by a charge on land;
(b) unsecured lending other than 'restricted credit';[1]

(c) making payments by credit cards; or
(d) activities that are ancillary to the activities described above (DISP 2.6.1).

Lending money under regulated consumer credit agreements is not a regulated activity and so a creditor does not have to be an authorised person in order to carry on a consumer credit business. However, if, for example, a creditor is authorised to carry on the regulated activity of entering into regulated mortgage contracts[2] and also carries on the business of lending under regulated consumer credit agreements,[3] debtors under that creditor's regulated consumer credit agreements may be able to bring a complaint to FOS under the compulsory jurisdiction.

9.3.3 Procedure under the compulsory jurisdiction rules

Financial Service Ombudsman Limited will not entertain a complaint under the compulsory jurisdiction unless the complaint has already been addressed to the person against whom it is made and he has had eight weeks in which to consider it (DISP 2.3.1 and 3.2.3) or he has already given a 'final response'. The rules set out the manner in which a business is required to respond to a complaint (DISP 1), including the provision of a final response, namely a written response which:

(a) accepts the complaint and, where appropriate, offers redress; or
(b) offers redress without accepting the complaint; or
(c) rejects the complaint and gives reasons for doing so,

and which informs the complainant that, if he remains dissatisfied with the response, he may now refer his complaint to FOS.

There are time limits for bringing a complaint to FOS:

(a) where the complainant has complained to the business and received a final response, he must bring the complaint to FOS within six months from the date when a final response is sent to him advising him that he may refer his complaint to FOS;
(b) otherwise, the complaint must be brought no more than six years after the event complained about or, if later, no more than three years from the date on which the complainant became aware, or ought reasonably to have become aware, that he had cause for complaint, unless he has referred the complaint to the business within that period and has a written acknowledgement or some other record of the complaint having been received (DISP 2.3.1(1)).

The ombudsman can consider complaints outside these time limits when, in his view, the failure to comply with the time limits was as a result of exceptional circumstances or when the business has not objected to his considering the complaint (DISP 2.3.1(2)).

The ombudsman may dismiss a complaint without consideration of its merits, once he has given the complainant an opportunity to make representations (DISP

3.2.8). There are a number of circumstances in which the ombudsman may dismiss a complaint without consideration of the merits. He may do so when:

(a) he is satisfied that the complainant has not suffered, or is unlikely to suffer, financial loss, material distress or material inconvenience;
(b) he considers the complaint to be frivolous or vexatious;
(c) he considers that the complaint clearly does not have any reasonable prospect of success;
(d) he is satisfied that the business has already made an offer of compensation that is fair and reasonable;
(e) he is satisfied that the complaint has been the subject of court proceedings which have been decided on the merits;
(f) he is satisfied that the complaint is the subject of current court proceedings unless they are stayed by agreement of all parties or order of the court in order for the matter to be considered under the ombudsman scheme;
(g) he considers that the matter would be more appropriately dealt with by a court, by arbitration or by another complaints scheme; or
(h) he is satisfied that it is a complaint about the legitimate exercise of the respondent's commercial judgment (DISP 3.3.1).

The ombudsman may also be persuaded to dismiss a complaint without considering its merits if he receives a detailed written statement from the respondent explaining how and why, in the respondent's opinion, the complaint raises an important or novel point of law with significant consequences and an undertaking in favour of the complainant that, if either party commences court proceedings against the other in respect of the complaint in any court in the UK within six months of the complaint being dismissed, the respondent will pay the complainant's reasonable costs and disbursements, to be assessed if not agreed on an indemnity basis, in connection with the proceedings, both at first instance and in any subsequent appeal brought by the respondent, and make interim payments on account of those costs if and to the extent that it appears reasonable. He will then dismiss the complaint if he considers that the complaint raises an important or novel point of law, which has important consequences and which would more suitably be dealt with by a court as a test case (DISP 3.3.1A).

The ombudsman will attempt to resolve complaints at the earliest possible stage and by whatever means appear to him to be most appropriate, including mediation or investigation (DISP 3.2.9). The parties will be informed of their right to make representations before the ombudsman makes a determination, but, if the ombudsman decides that the complaint can be fairly determined without convening a hearing, he will determine the complaint without inviting the parties to attend a hearing (DISP 3.2.12).

If the complainant or the respondent wishes to request a hearing, he must do so in writing, setting out the issues that he wishes to raise and, if he considers that the hearing should be in private, his reasons why (DISP 3.2.13). In deciding whether there should be a hearing and, if so, whether it should be in public or private, the ombudsman will have regard to the provisions of the European Convention on Human Rights (DISP 3.2.14).

An ombudsman may delegate the investigation and consideration of a complaint to members of the staff of FOS, but only an ombudsman may determine a complaint (DISP 3.7.1). The Chief Ombudsman designates which members of staff may exercise delegable powers on behalf of an ombudsman (DISP 3.7.2).

9.3.4   Procedure under the consumer credit rules

The Board of FOS will be responsible for making the consumer credit rules, subject to the approval of the FSA (FSMA 2000, s.266A(7)). It is to be expected that they will establish almost identical procedural requirements to the compulsory jurisdiction rules.[4]

The rules may, among other things:

(a) specify matters which are to be taken into account in determining whether an act or omission was fair and reasonable;
(b) provide that a complaint may, in specified circumstances, be dismissed without consideration of its merits;
(c) provide for the reference of a complaint, in specified circumstances and with the consent of the complainant, to another body with a view to its being determined by that body instead of by an ombudsman;
(d) make provision as to the evidence which may be required or admitted, the extent to which it should be oral or written and the consequences of a person's failure to produce any information or document which he has been required (under FSMA 2000, s.231 or otherwise) to produce;
(e) allow an ombudsman to fix time limits for any aspect of the proceedings and to extend a time limit;
(f) provide for certain things in relation to the reference, investigation or consideration (but not determination) of a complaint to be done by a member of the scheme operator's staff instead of by an ombudsman;
(g) make different provision in relation to different kinds of complaint.[5]

The following matters may be included in those which may be specified in the consumer credit rules as justifying the dismissal of a complaint without consideration of its merits:

(a) that the ombudsman considers the complaint to be frivolous or vexatious;
(b) that legal proceedings have been brought concerning the subject-matter of the complaint and the ombudsman considers that the complaint is best dealt with in those proceedings; or
(c) that the ombudsman is satisfied that there are other compelling reasons why it is inappropriate for the complaint to be dealt with under the ombudsman scheme.[6]

The consumer credit rules:

(a) must specify a time limit, or different time limits to be applicable in different cases, for the referral of a complaint to the FOS;

(b) may provide that an ombudsman may extend the time limit for referral of a complaint in specified circumstances;

(c) may provide that a complainant must first communicate the substance of the complaint to the respondent and give him a reasonable opportunity to deal with it before it is referred to the FOS; and

(d) may make provision about the procedure for the reference of complaints and for their investigation, consideration and determination by an ombudsman (FSMA 2000, Sched.17, para.16B(1)).

The rules may require persons carrying on a type of business to which the consumer credit jurisdiction applies to establish internal complaints procedures for the resolution of complaints which may be referred to FOS (FSMA 2000, Sched.17, Part 3A, para.16B(3) and (6), inserted by CCA 2006, s.59 and Sched.2). Different requirements for internal complaints procedures may be imposed on persons of different descriptions or in relation to complaints of different descriptions (FSMA 2000, Sched.17, Part 3A, para.16B(4)).

Financial Ombudsman Service Ltd may be given a discretionary power to vary or dispense with the application of the consumer credit rules, as it considers appropriate, in which case the rules may require FOS to be satisfied, before doing so, that certain conditions specified in the rules are met (FSMA 2000, Sched.17, Part 3A, para.16B(5)).

9.3.5   The ombudsman's ruling

An ombudsman is required to determine a complaint by reference to what is, in his opinion, fair and reasonable in all the circumstances of the case (FSMA 2000, s.228(2), which is to apply to the consumer credit jurisdiction by s.228(1), as amended by CCA 2006, s.61(3)). The compulsory jurisdiction rules require that he take into account the relevant law, regulations, regulators' rules and guidance and standards, relevant codes of practice and, where appropriate, what he considers to have been good industry practice at the relevant time (DISP 3.8.1).

The ombudsman is not required to determine complaints in accordance with legal precedent.[7] However, it is questionable whether an ombudsman could rationally decide that it was fair and reasonable to interfere with parties' contractual obligations on grounds that would be rejected by a court as grounds for a finding of an unfair relationship (see **Chapter 5**).

Financial Ombudsman Service Ltd generally attempts to resolve disputes informally by mediation or reconciliation. In more complex cases, an adjudicator, a member of FOS staff, will issue an adjudication report, setting out the details of the dispute, the adjudicator's findings and any redress that the adjudicator considers appropriate. However, if the parties remain unable to agree how the matter is to be resolved, the complaint is referred to an ombudsman for a formal determination.[8]

The ombudsman must give both the complainant and the respondent a written statement of his determination, signed by him, stating his reasons, and inviting the complainant to notify him in writing, before a date specified in the statement, whether the complainant accepts or rejects the determination (FSMA 2000, s.228(3) and (4)).

If the complainant notifies the ombudsman that he accepts the determination, it will be binding on the respondent and the complainant and it will be final (s.228(5)). If the complainant rejects the determination, the parties will not be bound by it. If the complainant has not notified the ombudsman of his acceptance or rejection of the determination within the time specified in the statement of the determination, he is to be treated as having rejected it (s.228(6)) and the parties will not be bound by it.

The ombudsman will notify the respondent of the complainant's acceptance or rejection of the determination (s.228(7)).

There is no right of appeal, but ombudsmen's decisions will be subject to judicial review.

---

1   Defined in the FSA glossary as an unsecured loan for which, as a result of an existing arrangement between a supplier and an authorised person, the customer's application to the authorised person is submitted through the supplier and the terms of the loan require that it be repaid to the supplier for goods or services supplied to the customer.
2   Regulated mortgage contracts are secured by a first legal mortgage on land (other than timeshare accommodation) in the UK, at least 40 per cent of which is used, or is intended to be used, as or in connection with a dwelling by the borrower or (in the case of credit provided to trustees) by an individual who is a beneficiary of the trust, or by a related person (Financial Services and Markets Act 2000 (Regulated Activities) Order 2001 (SI 2001/544), art. 61).
3   Regulated mortgage contracts are exempt for the purposes of CCA 1974 and so are not regulated credit agreements (CCA 1974, s.16(6)(c)).
4   See FOS consultation paper, published June 2006.
5   Schedule 17, para.14(2) applied to the consumer credit jurisdiction by para.16B(2), which is to be inserted into Sched.17 by CCA 2006, s.59 and Sched.2.
6   Schedule 17, para.14(3), applied to the consumer credit jurisdiction by para.16B(2).
7   *IFG Financial Services Ltd* v. *Financial Ombudsman Service Ltd* [2005] EWHC 1153 (Admin); [2006] 1 BCLC 534.
8   See the FOS publication, *A Guide for Complaint Handlers.*

9.4   REMEDIES AVAILABLE UNDER THE SCHEME

If an ombudsman determines a complaint in favour of the complainant, the determination may include:

(a) 'a money award' against the respondent;
(b) a direction that the respondent take such steps in relation to the complainant as the ombudsman considers just and appropriate, whether or not a court

could order those steps to be taken (FSMA 2000, s.229(2), to apply in respect of the consumer credit jurisdiction by s.229(1), as amended by CCA 2006, s.61(3)).

A money award will be of such amount as the ombudsman considers fair compensation for financial loss or for any other loss or damage of a kind specified by the compulsory jurisdiction rules for a complaint coming within that jurisdiction, or of a kind specified by the consumer credit rules for a complaint coming within that jurisdiction (FSMA 2000, s.229(3)).

For the purposes of the compulsory jurisdiction, the FSA has specified that a money award may compensate for pain and suffering, damage to reputation, or distress or inconvenience, whether or not it also compensates for financial loss and whether or not a court would award such compensation (DISP 3.9.2). The compulsory jurisdiction rules also stipulate that, for the purposes of a money award, financial loss includes consequential or prospective loss (DISP 3.9.3).

The maximum money award which the ombudsman may make under the compulsory jurisdiction is £100,000 (DISP 3.9.5; FSMA 2000, s.229(4)).

The consumer credit rules may specify a different maximum amount for a money award in respect of the consumer credit jurisdiction (FSMA 2000, s.229(4A), inserted by CCA 2006, s.61(5)). However, the current proposal is that the limit should be the same.[1]

Different monetary limits may be specified in relation to different kinds of complaint (FSMA 2000, s.229(7)) and the consumer credit rules may make different provision for different cases (FSMA 2000, s.229(12), inserted by CCA 2006, s.61(7)).

The ombudsman may recommend that the respondent pays more where he considers that the maximum amount would not be fair compensation (FSMA 2000, s.229(5) and DISP 3.9.6).

A money award may provide for the amount payable to bear interest at a rate and as from a date specified in the award (FSMA 2000, s.229(8)).

Once a money award has been registered by the ombudsman, as required under the rules, it is enforceable by the complainant through the courts (under FSMA 2000, Sched.17, paras.16 (compulsory jurisdiction) and 16D (consumer credit jurisdiction)). The complainant may also obtain an injunction, or, in Scotland, an order under the Court of Session Act 1988, s.45, to enforce a direction (FSMA 2000, s.229(9) and (10)).

---

1 See the FOS consultation paper published June 2006.

9.5   COSTS

Financial Ombudsman Service Limited may make costs rules, subject to the approval of the FSA, enabling the ombudsman to award costs against the respondent. The costs rules may not provide for costs awards to be made against the complainant in respect of the respondent's costs, but they may provide for the making of an award against the complainant in favour of FOS if the complainant's conduct was improper or unreasonable or he was responsible for an unreasonable delay (FSMA 2000, s.230(1), (2), (3) and (4), amended to apply to the consumer credit jurisdiction by CCA 2006, s.61(8)).

The compulsory jurisdiction rules provide that, when the ombudsman finds in the complainant's favour, he may award an amount which covers some or all of the costs reasonably incurred by the complainant in respect of the complaint (DISP 3.9.10). However, the rules also indicate that awards of costs should not be common, as in most cases complainants should not need to engage professional advisers (DISP 3.9.11). Awards of costs under the compulsory jurisdiction may be ordered to bear interest (DISP 3.9.12).

9.6   INFORMATION

The ombudsman has power to require the provision of information and the production of documents by the complainant and by the respondent, as he considers necessary for the determination of the complaint (under FSMA 2000, s. 231). Failure to comply with the ombudsman's requirement for the provision of information or the production of documents may be punished by the High Court, or, in Scotland, the Court of Session, in the same way as contempt of court (FMSA, s.232).

The compulsory jurisdiction rules provide that, in dealing with any information received in relation to the consideration or investigation of a complaint, FOS must have regard to the parties' rights of privacy, but that the ombudsman may disclose information, in full or in an edited version or by way of a summary or description:

(a) to the extent that he is required or authorised to do so by law; or
(b) to the parties to the complaint; or
(c) in his written determination; or
(d) at a hearing in connection with the complaint.

Provided that he has regard to the parties' rights of privacy, the ombudsman may disclose information to the FSA or to any other body exercising regulatory or statutory functions for the purpose of assisting that body or FOS (DISP 3.10.1).

The Treasury may make regulations permitting the disclosure of any information, or of information of a prescribed kind, by the FOS to the OFT for the purpose of assisting or enabling the OFT to discharge its functions under CCA 1974 (FSMA 2000, s.353(1)(c), as amended by CCA 2006, s.61(9)).

9.7   FUNDING

Financial Service Ombudsman Limited will have the power to levy contributions from licensees to meet the costs of establishing and running the consumer credit jurisdiction of the ombudsman scheme. It will, from time to time, with the approval of the FSA, determine an amount that is to be raised by way of contributions from potential respondents to complaints under the consumer credit jurisdiction. The OFT will be responsible for collecting the amount, which may include a component to cover collection costs (FSMA 2000, s.234A(1) and (2), inserted by CCA 2006, s.60).

Financial Ombudsman Service Limited will notify the OFT whenever it determines or alters the amount that it requires to be raised by levy and the OFT will, on each occasion, give general notice of that amount (FSMA 2000, s.234A(3) and (4)). The OFT may, by general notice, require contributions to be paid by licensees under standard licences authorising any type of business covered by the consumer credit jurisdiction and on applicants for such licences, or for the renewal of such licences (FSMA 2000, s.234A(5), (13) and (14)). The amount of each contribution will be specified in or determinable under the general notice and it will be required to be paid before the end of the period, or at the time, specified or determinable under the general notice (FSMA 2000, s.234A(6)). Different contributions may be required from different descriptions of licensee or applicant; some descriptions of licensee or applicant may be excluded from the requirement to pay a contribution; and provision may be made for refunds in specified circumstances (FSMA 2000, s.234A(7)). It is envisaged that the levy will be small, requiring contributions of between £10 and £20 per year.[1]

The OFT is to pay the contributions which it receives to FOS, which will pay the OFT such component of the levy as is required to cover collection costs (FSMA 2000, s.234A(8) and (9)).

The Secretary of State may, by order, provide that the OFT's functions in relation to collecting the levy are for the time being to be carried out by FOS (FSMA 2000, s.234A(11)).

Respondents to complaints under the compulsory jurisdiction may be required to pay fees (under FSMA 2000, Sched.17, para.15), currently set at £360 or, for some cases, £475, in respect of the third and any subsequent complaint brought against them in any one year (*FSA Handbook*, Fees 5, Annex 1). The consumer credit rules may require respondents to complaints under the consumer credit jurisdiction to pay similar fees (under FSMA 2000, Sched.17, para.16C).

---

1   According to the Parliamentary Under-Secretary of State for Trade and Industry during the debate on clause 60 of the Bill during the fourth sitting of the Standing Committee on 28 June 2005.

10 MISCELLANEOUS

Key changes

- Advertisements to be regulated regardless of financial limit
- Credit information services to be regulated
- Removal of hirer's right to terminate specified descriptions of hire agreement

10.1 CREDIT ADVERTISING TO BE REGULATED REGARDLESS OF AMOUNT OF CREDIT

The requirements and offences set out in CCA 1974, Part IV and the Consumer Credit (Advertisement) Regulations 2004, SI 2004/1484, apply in respect of advertisements for credit[1] if the advertiser carries on a consumer credit business, a consumer hire business, a business in the course of which he provides credit to individuals secured on land, or a business which comprises or relates to agreements that are only not regulated agreements because the law applicable to the agreements is not UK law (s.43(1)(a) and (2)). However, credit advertisements are excluded from Part IV and the ambit of the Regulations if they indicate:

(a) that the credit must exceed £25,000 and that it will not be secured upon land; or

(b) that the credit is available only to a body corporate (s.43(3)).

In line with the removal of the financial limits for regulated agreements, CCA 2006 will amend CCA 1974, s.43(3) so that a credit advertisement will not be excluded from regulation by reason of an indication that the credit will exceed £25,000 and that it will not be secured upon land (s.43(3)(a) is to be repealed by CCA 2006, s.2(3)).[2]

---

1 They also apply to consumer hire advertisements and to credit brokerage advertisements (ss.43(1)(b) and 151(1) and the definitions of credit advertisement and hire advertisement in the Consumer Credit (Advertisements) Regulations 2004, SI 2004/1484, reg.1).

2 This repeal is expected to take effect on 6 April 2008 (DTI Timetable, May 2006).

10.2   REGULATION OF CREDIT INFORMATION SERVICES

10.2.1   Advertisements

Section 151(2) of CCA 1974 is to be amended (by CCA 2006, s.25(3)(a))[1] so as to include advertisements for credit information services in the categories of advertisement that may involve the offences of advertising by a false or misleading advertisement (under CCA 1974, s.46) and of publishing, devising or procuring such an advertisement (under CCA 1974, s.47). An advertisement for credit information services may involve the commission of an offence under s.46 or s.47 even if it indicates that the advertiser is not willing to act in relation to consumer credit agreements and consumer hire agreements.[2]

Regulations may be made by the Secretary of State as to the form and content of advertisements for credit information services (s.44, applied by s.151(2), as it is to be amended by CCA 2006, s.25(3)(a)).

10.2.2   Other regulations

Regulations may be made making similar provision as to the form, content and execution of agreements for credit information services as are prescribed in relation to consumer credit and consumer hire agreements (in or under CCA 1974, ss.55, 60, 61, 62, 63, 65, 127, 179 or 180 (CCA 1974, s.156, as it is to be amended by CCA 2006, s.25(4)(c))).[3]

Regulations may also be made requiring quotations to be given by the providers of credit information services (s.52, applied by s.152(1), as it is to be amended by CCA 2006, s.25(4)(a)), imposing a duty on the providers of credit information services to display information (s.53, applied by s.152(1), as it is to be amended by CCA 2006, s.25(4)(a)), or regulating the seeking of business by the providers of credit information services (s.54, applied by s.152(1), as it is to be amended by CCA 2006, s.25(4)(a)).

10.2.3   Offence of canvassing credit information services off trade premises

It will be an offence to canvass the business of providing credit information services off trade premises (s.154, as it is to be amended by CCA 2006, s.25(4)(b)).[4] 'Canvassing off trade premises' is defined for the purposes of ancillary credit businesses as soliciting the entry of an individual (the consumer) into an agreement for the provision to the consumer of those services by making oral representations to the consumer, or any other individual, during a visit by the canvasser to any place where the consumer or other individual is, other than a place where:

(a) the ancillary credit business is carried on; or
(b) any business is carried on by the canvasser, or the person whose employee or agent the canvasser is; or

(c) any business is carried on by the consumer,

if the visit is carried out for the purpose of making such oral representations to individuals who are at that place, but not carried out in response to a request made on a previous occasion (s.153).[5]

1   This amendment, and the amendments referred to in **10.2.2** and **10.2.3**, are expected to come into force on 1 October 2008 (DTI Timetable, May 2006).
2   Whereas other advertisements are excluded from s.151(2) if they make that indication (s.151(4), as it is to be amended by CCA 2006, s.25(3)(c)).
3   At present, s.156 only applies in respect of credit brokerage, debt adjusting or debt counselling.
4   It is already an offence under s.154 to canvass credit brokerage, debt adjusting or debt counselling services off trade premises.
5   Compare the definition of canvassing a regulated consumer credit agreement off trade premises (s.48).

10.3   POWER OF THE OFFICE OF FAIR TRADING TO REMOVE HIRER'S RIGHT OF TERMINATION

Section 101 of CCA 1974 gives the hirer the right to terminate a regulated consumer hire agreement at any time after the expiry of 18 months from the date of the agreement, subject to the hirer's giving the minimum notice.

The OFT has previously only had power, under s.101(8), to direct that the section shall not apply to consumer hire agreements made by an applicant for such a direction, if it appears to the OFT that that would be in the interest of hirers. The direction is to be given by notice to the applicant and may be subject to such conditions, if any, as the OFT may specify.

The OFT now has an additional power, under s.101(8A) (inserted by CCA 2006, s.63(1)),[1] to direct by general notice that, subject to such conditions, if any, as it may specify, s.101 shall not apply to consumer hire agreements falling within a specified description. The power is only to be exercised if it appears to the OFT that it would be in the interests of hirers for consumer hire agreements of the description in question to be excluded from the application of s.101.

1   CCA 2006, s.63 came into force 16 June 2006 (Commencement Order (No.1) 2006).

Appendix 1
CONSUMER CREDIT ACT 2006 (CONDENSED)

CONTENTS

Final provisions

66   Financial provision
67   Interpretation
68   Consequential amendments
69   Transitional provision and savings
70   Repeals
71   Short title, commencement and extent

SCHEDULE 1 – Schedule A1 to the 1974 Act

SCHEDULE 2 – Part 3A of Schedule 17 to the 2000 Act

SCHEDULE 3 – Transitional Provision and Savings

SCHEDULE 4 – Repeals

CONSUMER CREDIT ACT 2006

2006 CHAPTER 14

An Act to amend the Consumer Credit Act 1974; to extend the ombudsman scheme under the Financial Services and Markets Act 2000 to cover licensees under the Consumer Credit Act 1974; and for connected purposes. [30th March 2006]

BE IT ENACTED by the Queen's most Excellent Majesty, by and with the advice and consent of the Lords Spiritual and Temporal, and Commons, in this present Parliament assembled, and by the authority of the same, as follows: –

Agreements regulated under the 1974 Act etc.

1 Definition of 'individual'
[*Amends s.189(1) of the 1974 Act*]

2 Removal of financial limits etc.
(1)   [*Amends s.8(1) and repeals s.8(2) of the 1974 Act*]
(2)   [*Repeals s.15(1)(c) of the 1974 Act*]
(3)   [*Repeals s.43(3)(a) of the 1974 Act*]

3 Exemption relating to high net worth debtors and hirers
[*Inserts new s.16A into the 1974 Act*]

4 Exemption relating to businesses
[*Inserts new s.16B into the 1974 Act*]

5 Consequential amendments relating to ss. 1 to 4
(1)   [*Amends s.8(3) of the 1974 Act*]
(2)   [*Amends s.10(1) and (3) of the 1974 Act*]
(3)   [*Amends s.17(2) of the 1974 Act*]
(4)   [*Inserts new s.145(4)(aa) into the 1974 Act*]
(5)   [*Substitutes s.158(1)(a) into the 1974 Act*]
(6)   [*Inserts new s.158(4A) into the 1974 Act*]
(7)   [*Amends s.181(1) and (2) of the 1974 Act*]

(8) [*Amends s.185(5) of the 1974 Act*]
(9) [*Amends s.185(6) of the 1974 Act*]
(10) [*Amends s.189(1) of the 1974 Act*]

Statements to be provided in relation to regulated credit agreements

6 Statements to be provided in relation to fixed-sum credit agreements
[*Inserts new s.77A into the 1974 Act*]

7 Further provision relating to statements
(1) [*Inserts new s.78(4A) into the 1974 Act*]
(2) [*Amends s.78(7) of the 1974 Act*]
(3) [*Substitutes new s.185(2)–(2D) into the 1974 Act*]

Default under regulated agreements

8 OFT to prepare information sheets on arrears and default
[*Inserts new s.86A into the 1974 Act*]

9 Notice of sums in arrears under fixed-sum credit agreements etc.
[*Inserts new s.86B into the 1974 Act*]

10 Notice of sums in arrears under running-account credit agreements
[*Inserts new s.86C into the 1974 Act*]

11 Failure to give notice of sums in arrears
[*Inserts new s.86D into the 1974 Act*]

12 Notice of default sums
[*Inserts new s.86E into the 1974 Act*]

13 Interest on default sums
[*Inserts new s.86F into the 1974 Act*]

14 Default notices
(1) [*Amends s.88(2) and (3) of the 1974 Act*]
(2) [*Amends s.88(4) of the 1974 Act*]
(3) [*Inserts new s.88(4A) into the 1974 Act*]

15 Enforceability of regulated agreements
[*Repeals s.127(3)–(5) of the 1974 Act*]

16 Time orders
(1) [*Inserts new s.129(1)(ba) into the 1974 Act*]
(2) [*Inserts new s.129A into the 1974 Act*]
(3) [*Amends s.143(b) of the 1974 Act*]
(4) In section 32(1) of the Sheriff Courts (Scotland) Act 1971 (c. 58) (regulation of civil procedure in sheriff court) after paragraph (l) insert –

'(m) permitting the debtor or hirer in proceedings for –

    (i)   a time order under section 129 of the Consumer Credit Act 1974 (time orders), or

    (ii)   variation or revocation, under section 130(6) of that Act (variation and revocation of time orders), of a time order made under section 129, to be represented by a person who is neither an advocate nor a solicitor.'

(5) In section 32(2B) of the Solicitors (Scotland) Act 1980 (c. 46) (offence for unqualified persons to prepare certain documents) –

  (a) after 'represent' insert '– (a)';

  (b) after 'cause' insert –

    '(b) a debtor or hirer in proceedings for –

       (i)   a time order under section 129 of the Consumer Credit Act 1974 (time orders); or

       (ii)   variation or revocation, under section 130(6) of that Act (variation and revocation of time orders), of a time order made under section 129'.

17 Interest payable on judgment debts etc.

[*Inserts new s.130A into the 1974 Act*]

18 Definition of 'default sum'

(1) [*Inserts new s.187A into the 1974 Act*]

(2) [*Amends s.189(1) of the 1974 Act*]

Unfair relationships

19 Unfair relationships between creditors and debtors

[*Inserts new s.140A into the 1974 Act*]

20 Powers of court in relation to unfair relationships

[*Inserts new s.140B into the 1974 Act*]

21 Interpretation of ss. 140A and 140B of the 1974 Act

[*Inserts new s.140C into the 1974 Act*]

22 Further provision relating to unfair relationships

(1) [*Inserts new s.140D into the 1974 Act*]

(2) [*Inserts new s.16(7A) into the 1974 Act*]

(3) [*Repeals ss.137–140 of the 1974 Act*]

(4) [*Amends s.181(1) and (2) of the 1974 Act*]

Businesses requiring a licence and consequences of not being licensed

23 Definitions of 'consumer credit business' and 'consumer hire business'

[*Amends s.189(1) of the 1974 Act*]

24 Debt administration etc.

(1) [*Inserts new s.145(1)(da) into the 1974 Act*]

(2) [*Inserts new s.145(7A) into the 1974 Act*]

(3) [*Amends s.146(6) of the 1974 Act*]

(4) [*Inserts new s.146(7) into the 1974 Act*]

(5) [*Amends s.177(3) of the 1974 Act*]

(6) [*Amends s.189(1) of the 1974 Act*]

25 Credit information services

(1) [*Inserts new s.145(1)(db) into the 1974 Act*]
(2) [*Inserts new s.145(7B)–(7D) into the 1974 Act*]
(3) [*Amends s.151(2)–(4) of the 1974 Act*]
(4) [*Amends ss.152(1), 154 and 156 of the 1974 Act*]
(5) [*Amends s.189(1) of the 1974 Act*]

26 Enforcement of agreements by unlicensed trader etc.

(1) [*Substitutes new s.40(1), (1A) and (2) into the 1974 Act*]
(2) [*Amends s.40(4) of the 1974 Act*]
(3) [*Amends s.40(6) of the 1974 Act*]
(4) [*Inserts new s.40(7)–(9) into the 1974 Act*]

Applications for licences and fitness to hold a licence etc.

27 Charge on applicants for licences etc.

(1) [*Inserts new s.6A into the 1974 Act*]
(2) [*Inserts new s.6(2A) into the 1974 Act*]
(3) [*Inserts new s.189(1A) into the 1974 Act*]
(4) [*Amends s.191(1)(a) of the 1974 Act*]

28 Applications for standard licences

[*Inserts new s.24A into the 1974 Act*]

29 Issue of standard licences

(1) [*Substitutes s.25(1) and inserts new s.25(1AA)–(1AD) into the 1974 Act*]
(2) [*Substitutes s.25(2) and inserts new s.25(2A)–(2B) into the 1974 Act*]

30 Guidance on fitness test

[*Inserts new s.25A into the 1974 Act*]

31 Variation of standard licences etc.

(1) [*Substitutes s.30(1) and inserts new s.30(1A)–(1B) into the 1974 Act*]
(2) [*Amends s.31(1) of the 1974 Act*]
(3) [*Inserts new s.31(1A) into the 1974 Act*]
(4) [*Inserts new s.31(8)–(9) into the 1974 Act*]
(5) [*Inserts new s.32(9) into the 1974 Act*]

32 Winding-up of standard licensee's business

(1) [*Inserts new s.34A into the 1974 Act*]
(2) [*Inserts new s.29(3A) into the 1974 Act*]
(3) [*Repeals s.29(5) of the 1974 Act*]
(4) [*Substitutes new s.31(2)(b) into the 1974 Act*]
(5) [*Substitutes new s.32(2)(b) into the 1974 Act*]
(6) [*Repeals s.32(5) of the 1974 Act*]

33 Consequential amendments relating to ss. 27 to 32

(1) [*Amends s.21(1) of the 1974 Act*]
(2) [*Inserts new s.22(5A) into the 1974 Act*]
(3) [*Amends s.23(1) of the 1974 Act*]
(4) [*Amends s.23(4) of the 1974 Act*]
(5) [*Inserts new s.27A into the 1974 Act*]

(6) [*Amends s.41 of the 1974 Act*]

(7) In sections 194(3) and 203(4) of the 2000 Act (powers of intervention and prohibition) for '(a) to (d) of section 25(2)' substitute '(a) to (e) of section 25(2A)'.

(8) In section 203(10) of that Act (definitions relating to Consumer Credit Act businesses) in the definition of 'associate' for '25(2)' substitute '25(2A)'.

(9) In paragraph 15(3) of Schedule 3 to that Act (EEA passport rights) for '21, 39(1) and 147(1)' substitute '21 and 39(1)'.

(10) In paragraph 23 of that Schedule in sub-paragraph (1) for 'Sub-paragraph (2) applies' substitute 'Sub-paragraphs (2) and (2A) apply'.

(11) In sub-paragraph (2) of that paragraph for '(a) to (d) of section 25(2)' substitute '(a) to (e) of section 25(2A)'.

(12) After that sub-paragraph insert –

'(2A) The Authority may also exercise its power under section 45 in respect of the firm if the Office of Fair Trading has informed the Authority that it has concerns about any of the following –

(a) the firm's skills, knowledge and experience in relation to Consumer Credit Act businesses;

(b) such skills, knowledge and experience of other persons who are participating in any Consumer Credit Act business being carried on by the firm;

(c) practices and procedures that the firm is implementing in connection with any such business.'

Duration of licences and charges

34 Definite and indefinite licences

(1) [*Amends s.22(1)(a)–(b) of the 1974 Act*]
(2) [*Inserts new s.22(1A)–(1E) into the 1974 Act*]
(3) [*Amends s.29(1) and (4) of the 1974 Act*]
(4) [*Amends s.31(1) of the 1974 Act*]
(5) [*Inserts new s.31(1B) into the 1974 Act*]
(6) [*Amends s.32(1) of the 1974 Act*]
(7) [*Amends s.35(1)(b) of the 1974 Act*]
(8) [*Inserts new s.37(1A)–(1B) into the 1974 Act*]
(9) [*Amends s.37(3)(a) of the 1974 Act*]

35 Charges for indefinite licences

[*Inserts new s.28A into the 1974 Act*]

36 Extension of period to pay charge for indefinite licence

[*Inserts new s.28B into the 1974 Act*]

37 Failure to pay charge for indefinite licence

(1) [*Inserts new s.28C into the 1974 Act*]
(2) [*Amends s.35(1)(b) of the 1974 Act*]

38 Power of OFT to impose requirements on licensees

[*Inserts new s.33A into the 1974 Act*]

39 Power of OFT to impose requirements on supervisory bodies

[*Inserts new s.33B into the 1974 Act*]

40 Supplementary provision relating to requirements
[*Inserts new s.33C into the 1974 Act*]

41 Procedure in relation to requirements
[*Inserts new s.33D into the 1974 Act*]

42 Guidance on requirements
[*Inserts new s.33E into the 1974 Act*]

43 Consequential amendments relating to requirements
(1)   [*Inserts new s.35(1)(ba) into the 1974 Act*]
(2)   [*Amends s.41 of the 1974 Act*]

Powers and duties in relation to information

44 Provision of information etc. by applicants
(1)   [*Amends s.6(2) of the 1974 Act*]
(2)   [*Substitutes new s.6(3) into the 1974 Act*]
(3)   [*Inserts new s.6(5)–(9) into the 1974 Act*]

45 Duties to notify changes in information etc.
[*Inserts new s.36A into the 1974 Act*]

46 Power of OFT to require information generally
[*Inserts new s.36B into the 1974 Act*]

47 Power of OFT to require access to premises
[*Inserts new s.36C into the 1974 Act*]

48 Entry to premises under warrant
[*Inserts new s.36D into the 1974 Act*]

49 Failure to comply with information requirement
[*Inserts new s.36E into the 1974 Act*]

50 Officers of enforcement authorities other than OFT
[Inserts new s.36F into the 1974 Act]

51 Consequential amendments relating to information
(1)   [*Substitutes new s.7 into the 1974 Act*]
(2)   [*Amends s.162(1)(b)(ii) of the 1974 Act*]
(3)   [*Inserts new s.162(8) into the 1974 Act*]
(4)   [*Inserts new s.165(1A) into the 1974 Act*]
(5)   [*Inserts new s.174A into the 1974 Act*]
(6)   [*Amends s.189(1) of the 1974 Act*]
(7)   In Part 1 of Schedule 1 to the Criminal Justice and Police Act 2001 (c. 16) (powers of seizure to which section 50 applies) before paragraph 19 insert –

   '18A The power of seizure conferred by section 36D(3) of the Consumer Credit Act 1974.'

Civil penalties

52 Power of OFT to impose civil penalties

[*Inserts new s.39A into the 1974 Act*]

53 Further provision relating to civil penalties

(1) [*Inserts s.39B into the 1974 Act*]
(2) [*Amends s.41 of the 1974 Act*]
(3) [*Amends s.181(1)–(2) of the 1974 Act*]

54 Statement of policy in relation to civil penalties

[*Inserts new s.39C into the 1974 Act*]

Appeals

55 The Consumer Credit Appeals Tribunal

(1) [*Inserts new s.40A into the 1974 Act*]
(2) [*Inserts new Schedule A1 into the 1974 Act*]

56 Appeals to the Consumer Credit Appeals Tribunal

(1) [*Amends s.41(1) of the 1974 Act*]
(2) [*Inserts s.41(1A)–(1D) into the 1974 Act*]
(3) [*Repeals s.41(2)–(5) of the 1974 Act*]

57 Appeals from the Consumer Credit Appeals Tribunal

[*Inserts new s.41A into the 1974 Act*]

58 Consequential amendments relating to appeals

(1) [*Amends s.2(7) of the 1974 Act*]
(2) [*Inserts new s.182(1A) into the 1974 Act*]
(3) [*Amends s.182(2) of the 1974 Act*]
(4) [*Amends s.189(1) of the 1974 Act*]
(5) In Schedule 1 to the Tribunals and Inquiries Act 1992 (c. 53) (tribunals under supervision of Council on Tribunals) after paragraph 9A insert –

'Consumer Credit   9B.   The   Consumer   Credit   Appeals
                          Tribunal established by section 40A of the
                          Consumer Credit Act 1974.'

Ombudsman scheme

59 Financial services ombudsman scheme to apply to consumer credit licensees

(1) After section 226 of the 2000 Act insert –

'226A Consumer credit jurisdiction

(1) A complaint which relates to an act or omission of a person ("the respondent") is to be dealt with under the ombudsman scheme if the conditions mentioned in subsection (2) are satisfied.

(2) The conditions are that –

(a) the complainant is eligible and wishes to have the complaint dealt with under the scheme;

(b) the complaint falls within a description specified in consumer credit rules;

(c)   at the time of the act or omission the respondent was the licensee under a standard licence or was authorised to carry on an activity by virtue of section 34A of the Consumer Credit Act 1974;

(d)   the act or omission occurred in the course of a business being carried on by the respondent which was of a type mentioned in subsection (3);

(e)   at the time of the act or omission that type of business was specified in an order made by the Secretary of State; and

(f)   the complaint cannot be dealt with under the compulsory jurisdiction.

(3)   The types of business referred to in subsection (2)(d) are –

(a)   a consumer credit business;

(b)   a consumer hire business;

(c)   a business so far as it comprises or relates to credit brokerage;

(d)   a business so far as it comprises or relates to debt-adjusting;

(e)   a business so far as it comprises or relates to debt-counselling;

(f)   a business so far as it comprises or relates to debt-collecting;

(g)   a business so far as it comprises or relates to debt administration;

(h)   a business so far as it comprises or relates to the provision of credit information services;

(i)   a business so far as it comprises or relates to the operation of a credit reference agency.

(4)   A complainant is eligible if –

(a)   he is –

(i)   an individual; or

(ii)   a surety in relation to a security provided to the respondent in connection with the business mentioned in subsection (2)(d); and

(b)   he falls within a class of person specified in consumer credit rules.

(5)   The approval of the Treasury is required for an order under subsection (2)(e).

(6)   The jurisdiction of the scheme which results from this section is referred to in this Act as the "consumer credit jurisdiction".

(7)   In this Act "consumer credit rules" means rules made by the scheme operator with the approval of the Authority for the purposes of the consumer credit jurisdiction.

(8)   Consumer credit rules under this section may make different provision for different cases.

(9)   Expressions used in the Consumer Credit Act 1974 have the same meaning in this section as they have in that Act.'

(2)   In Schedule 17 to that Act (the ombudsman scheme) after Part 3 insert the Part 3A set out in Schedule 2 to this Act.

60 Funding of ombudsman scheme

In Part 16 of the 2000 Act after section 234 insert –

'234A Funding by consumer credit licensees etc.

(1)   For the purpose of funding –

(a)   the establishment of the ombudsman scheme so far as it relates to the consumer credit jurisdiction (whenever any relevant expense is incurred), and

(b)   its operation in relation to the consumer credit jurisdiction, the scheme operator may from time to time with the approval of the Authority determine a sum which is to be raised by way of contributions under this section.

(2)   A sum determined under subsection (1) may include a component to cover the costs of the collection of contributions to that sum ("collection costs") under this section.

(3) The scheme operator must notify the OFT of every determination under subsection (1).

(4) The OFT must give general notice of every determination so notified.

(5) The OFT may by general notice impose requirements on –

(a) licensees to whom this section applies, or

(b) persons who make applications to which this section applies, to pay contributions to the OFT for the purpose of raising sums determined under subsection (1).

(6) The amount of the contribution payable by a person under such a requirement –

(a) shall be the amount specified in or determined under the general notice; and

(b) shall be paid before the end of the period or at the time so specified or determined.

(7) A general notice under subsection (5) may –

(a) impose requirements only on descriptions of licensees or applicants specified in the notice;

(b) provide for exceptions from any requirement imposed on a description of licensees or applicants;

(c) impose different requirements on different descriptions of licensees or applicants;

(d) make provision for refunds in specified circumstances.

(8) Contributions received by the OFT must be paid to the scheme operator.

(9) As soon as practicable after the end of –

(a) each financial year of the scheme operator, or

(b) if the OFT and the scheme operator agree that this paragraph is to apply instead of paragraph (a) for the time being, each period agreed by them,

the scheme operator must pay to the OFT an amount representing the extent to which collection costs are covered in accordance with subsection (2) by the total amount of the contributions paid by the OFT to it during the year or (as the case may be) the agreed period.

(10) Amounts received by the OFT from the scheme operator are to be retained by it for the purpose of meeting its costs.

(11) The Secretary of State may by order provide that the functions of the OFT under this section are for the time being to be carried out by the scheme operator.

(12) An order under subsection (11) may provide that while the order is in force this section shall have effect subject to such modifications as may be set out in the order.

(13) The licensees to whom this section applies are licensees under standard licences which cover to any extent the carrying on of a type of business specified in an order under section 226A(2)(e).

(14) The applications to which this section applies are applications for –

(a) standard licences covering to any extent the carrying on of a business of such a type;

(b) the renewal of standard licences on terms covering to any extent the carrying on of a business of such a type.

(15) Expressions used in the Consumer Credit Act 1974 have the same meaning in this section as they have in that Act.'

61 Consequential amendments relating to ombudsman scheme

(1) [Amends s.4 of the 1974 Act]

(2) In section 227(2)(e) of the 2000 Act (conditions for exercise of voluntary jurisdiction) after 'jurisdiction' insert 'or the consumer credit jurisdiction'.

(3) In sections 228(1) and 229(1) of that Act (determinations and awards by ombudsman) after 'jurisdiction' insert 'and to the consumer credit jurisdiction'.

(4) In subsection (4) of section 229 of that Act (awards by ombudsman) after 'specify' insert 'for the purposes of the compulsory jurisdiction'.

(5) After that subsection insert –

'(4A) The scheme operator may specify for the purposes of the consumer credit jurisdiction the maximum amount which may be regarded as fair compensation for a particular kind of loss or damage specified under subsection (3)(b).'

(6) In subsection (8)(b) of that section after '17' insert 'or (as the case may be) Part 3A of that Schedule'.

(7) For subsection (11) of that section substitute –

'(11) "Specified" means –

(a)   for the purposes of the compulsory jurisdiction, specified in compulsory jurisdiction rules;
(b)   for the purposes of the consumer credit jurisdiction, specified in consumer credit rules.

(12) Consumer credit rules under this section may make different provision for different cases.'

(8) In section 230 of that Act (costs) –

(a)   in subsection (1) after 'jurisdiction' insert 'or the consumer credit jurisdiction';
(b)   in subsection (7) after '17' insert 'or (as the case may be) paragraph 16D of that Schedule'.

(9) In section 353(1) of that Act (power to permit disclosure of information) after paragraph (b) insert –

'(c)   by the scheme operator to the Office of Fair Trading for the purpose of assisting or enabling that Office to discharge prescribed functions under the Consumer Credit Act 1974.'

(10) In Schedule 17 to that Act (the ombudsman scheme) –

(a)   in paragraph 3(4) after '227' insert ', the function of making consumer credit rules, the function of making determinations under section 234A(1)';
(b)   in paragraph 7(2) after 'compulsory jurisdiction' insert ', functions in relation to its consumer credit jurisdiction';
(c)   in paragraph 9(3) after 'compulsory' insert ', consumer credit';
(d)   in paragraphs 10(1) and 11 after 'jurisdiction' insert 'or to the consumer credit jurisdiction'.

Miscellaneous

62 Monitoring of businesses by OFT

[Inserts new s.1(1)(ba) into the 1974 Act]

63 Disapplication of s.101 of the 1974 Act

(1)   [Inserts new s.101(8A) into the 1974 Act]
(2)   [Amends s.101(8) of the 1974 Act]

64 Determinations etc. by OFT

[Substitutes new s.183 into the 1974 Act]

65 Sums received by OFT

[*Amends s.190(2) of the 1974 Act*]

Final provisions

66 Financial provision

There shall be payable out of money provided by Parliament–

(a) any expenditure incurred by a Minister of the Crown or the Office of Fair Trading by virtue of this Act; and

(b) any increase attributable to this Act in the sums payable out of money so provided by virtue of any other Act.

67 Interpretation

In this Act –

'the 1974 Act' means the Consumer Credit Act 1974 (c. 39);
'the 2000 Act' means the Financial Services and Markets Act 2000 (c. 8).

68 Consequential amendments

(1) The Secretary of State may by order made by statutory instrument make such modifications of –

(a) any Act or subordinate legislation (within the meaning of the Interpretation Act 1978 (c. 30)), or

(b) any Northern Ireland legislation or instrument made under such legislation, as he thinks fit in consequence of any provision of this Act.

(2) An order under this section may include transitional or transitory provisions and savings.

(3) A statutory instrument containing an order under this section may not be made by the Secretary of State unless a draft has been laid before and approved by a resolution of each House of Parliament.

69 Transitional provision and savings

(1) Schedule 3 (which sets out transitional provision and savings) has effect.

(2) The Secretary of State may by order made by statutory instrument make such transitional or transitory provisions and savings as he thinks fit in connection with the coming into force of any provision of this Act.

(3) An order under this section may (amongst other things) –

(a) where a provision of this Act is brought into force for limited purposes only, make provision about how references in Schedule 3 to the commencement of that provision of this Act are to apply;

(b) make provision for or in connection with the application of any provision of this Act in relation to –

(i) things existing or done, or

(ii) persons who have done something or in relation to whom something has been done,

before the coming into force of that provision of this Act.

(4) An order under this section may –

(a) modify any Act or any subordinate legislation (within the meaning of the Interpretation Act 1978);

(b) modify any Northern Ireland legislation or any instrument made under such legislation;

(c) make different provision for different cases.

(5) Schedule 3 does not restrict the power under this section to make transitional or transitory provisions or savings.

70 Repeals

The enactments and instruments set out in Schedule 4 are repealed or revoked to the extent shown in that Schedule.

71 Short title, commencement and extent

(1) This Act may be cited as the Consumer Credit Act 2006.

(2) This Act (apart from this section) shall come into force on such day as the Secretary of State may by order made by statutory instrument appoint; and different days may be appointed for different purposes.

(3) This Act extends to Northern Ireland.

SCHEDULE 1 (SECTION 55)

[Reproduces Schedule A1 as inserted into the 1974 Act by s.55 of this Act]

SCHEDULE 2 (SECTION 59)

PART 3A OF SCHEDULE 17 TO THE 2000 ACT

PART 3A

THE CONSUMER CREDIT JURISDICTION

Introduction

16A This Part of this Schedule applies only in relation to the consumer credit jurisdiction.

Procedure for complaints etc.

16B (1) Consumer credit rules –

   (a) must provide that a complaint is not to be entertained unless the complainant has referred it under the ombudsman scheme before the applicable time limit (determined in accordance with the rules) has expired;

   (b) may provide that an ombudsman may extend that time limit in specified circumstances;

   (c) may provide that a complaint is not to be entertained (except in specified circumstances) if the complainant has not previously communicated its substance to the respondent and given him a reasonable opportunity to deal with it;

   (d) may make provision about the procedure for the reference of complaints and for their investigation, consideration and determination by an ombudsman.

   (2) Sub-paragraphs (2) and (3) of paragraph 14 apply in relation to consumer credit rules under sub-paragraph (1) of this paragraph as they apply in relation to scheme rules under that paragraph.

(3) Consumer credit rules may require persons falling within sub-paragraph (6) to establish such procedures as the scheme operator considers appropriate for the resolution of complaints which may be referred to the scheme.

(4) Consumer credit rules under sub-paragraph (3) may make different provision in relation to persons of different descriptions or to complaints of different descriptions.

(5) Consumer credit rules under sub-paragraph (3) may authorise the scheme operator to dispense with or modify the application of such rules in particular cases where the scheme operator –

(a) considers it appropriate to do so; and
(b) is satisfied that the specified conditions (if any) are met.

(6) A person falls within this sub-paragraph if he is licensed by a standard licence (within the meaning of the Consumer Credit Act 1974) to carry on to any extent a business of a type specified in an order under section 226A(2)(e) of this Act.

Fees

16C (1) Consumer credit rules may require a respondent to pay to the scheme operator such fees as may be specified in the rules.

(2) Sub-paragraph (2) of paragraph 15 applies in relation to consumer credit rules under this paragraph as it applies in relation to scheme rules under that paragraph.

Enforcement of money awards

16D A money award, including interest, which has been registered in accordance with consumer credit rules may –

(a) if a county court so orders in England and Wales, be recovered by execution issued from the county court (or otherwise) as if it were payable under an order of that court;
(b) be enforced in Northern Ireland as a money judgment under the Judgments Enforcement (Northern Ireland) Order 1981;
(c) be enforced in Scotland as if it were a decree of the sheriff and whether or not the sheriff could himself have granted such a decree.

Procedure for consumer credit rules

16E (1) If the scheme operator makes any consumer credit rules, it must give a copy of them to the Authority without delay.

(2) If the scheme operator revokes any such rules, it must give written notice to the Authority without delay.

(3) The power to make such rules is exercisable in writing.

(4) Immediately after the making of such rules, the scheme operator must arrange for them to be printed and made available to the public.

(5) The scheme operator may charge a reasonable fee for providing a person with a copy of any such rules.

Verification of consumer credit rules

16F (1) The production of a printed copy of consumer credit rules purporting to be made by the scheme operator –

(a)   on which there is endorsed a certificate signed by a member of the scheme operator's staff authorised by the scheme operator for that purpose, and

(b)   which contains the required statements,

is evidence (or in Scotland sufficient evidence) of the facts stated in the certificate.

(2)   The required statements are –

(a)   that the rules were made by the scheme operator;

(b)   that the copy is a true copy of the rules; and

(c)   that on a specified date the rules were made available to the public in accordance with paragraph 16E(4).

(3)   A certificate purporting to be signed as mentioned in sub-paragraph (1) is to be taken to have been duly signed unless the contrary is shown.

Consultation

16G (1)   If the scheme operator proposes to make consumer credit rules, it must publish a draft of the proposed rules in the way appearing to it to be best calculated to bring the draft to the attention of the public.

(2)   The draft must be accompanied by –

(a)   an explanation of the proposed rules; and

(b)   a statement that representations about the proposals may be made to the scheme operator within a specified time.

(3)   Before making any consumer credit rules, the scheme operator must have regard to any representations made to it in accordance with sub-paragraph (2)(b).

(4)   If consumer credit rules made by the scheme operator differ from the draft published under sub-paragraph (1) in a way which the scheme operator considers significant, the scheme operator must publish a statement of the difference.

SCHEDULE 3 (SECTION 69)

TRANSITIONAL PROVISION AND SAVINGS

Interpretation

1   (1)   Expressions used in the 1974 Act have the same meaning in this Schedule (apart from paragraphs 14 to 16 and 26) as they have in that Act.

(2)   For the purposes of this Schedule an agreement becomes a completed agreement once –

(a)   there is no sum payable under the agreement; and

(b)   there is no sum which will or may become so payable.

Statements to be provided in relation to regulated agreements

2   (1)   Section 77A of the 1974 Act applies in relation to agreements whenever made.

(2)   Section 77A shall have effect in relation to agreements made before the commencement of section 6 of this Act as if the period mentioned in subsection (1)(a) were the period of one year beginning with the day of the commencement of section 6.

3   Regulations made under section 78(4A) of the 1974 Act may apply in relation to agreements regardless of when they were made.

4   (1) Section 7(3) of this Act shall have effect in relation to agreements whenever made.

(2) A dispensing notice given under section 185(2) of the 1974 Act which is operative immediately before the commencement of section 7(3) –

(a) shall, on the commencement of section 7(3), be treated as having been given under section 185(2) as substituted by section 7(3); and

(b) shall continue to be operative accordingly.

Default under regulated agreements

5   The OFT shall prepare, and give general notice of, the arrears information sheet and the default information sheet required under section 86A of the 1974 Act as soon as practicable after the commencement of section 8 of this Act.

6   (1) Section 86B of the 1974 Act applies in relation to agreements whenever made.

(2) In the application of section 86B in relation to an agreement made before the commencement of section 9 of this Act, the conditions under subsection (1) can be satisfied only if the two payments mentioned in paragraph (c) were not required to have been made before the commencement of section 9.

(3) In the case of an agreement within subsection (9) of section 86B, subparagraph (2) has effect as if for 'two' there were substituted 'four'.

7   (1) Section 86C of the 1974 Act applies in relation to agreements whenever made.

(2) In the application of section 86C in relation to an agreement made before the commencement of section 10 of this Act, the conditions mentioned in subsection (1) can be satisfied only if the two payments mentioned in paragraph (b) were not required to have been made before the commencement of section 10.

8   Section 86E of the 1974 Act applies in relation to agreements whenever made but only as regards default sums which become payable after the commencement of section 12 of this Act.

9   (1) Section 86F of the 1974 Act applies in relation to agreements whenever made but only as regards default sums which become payable after the commencement of section 13 of this Act.

(2) Where section 86F applies in relation to an agreement made before the commencement of section 13, the agreement shall have effect as if any right of the creditor or owner to recover compound interest in connection with the default sum in question at a particular rate were a right to recover simple interest in that connection at that rate.

10   Section 14 of this Act shall have effect in relation to any default notice served after the commencement of that section, regardless of –

(a) when the breach of the agreement in question occurred; or

(b) when that agreement was made.

11   The repeal by this Act of –

(a) the words '(subject to subsections (3) and (4))' in subsection (1) of section 127 of the 1974 Act,

(b) subsections (3) to (5) of that section, and

(c) the words 'or 127(3)' in subsection (3) of section 185 of that Act,

has no effect in relation to improperly-executed agreements made before the commencement of section 15 of this Act.

12   A debtor or hirer under an agreement may make an application under section 129(1)(ba) of the 1974 Act regardless of when that agreement was made.

13   Section 130A of the 1974 Act applies in relation to agreements whenever made but only as regards sums that are required to be paid under judgments given after the commencement of section 17 of this Act.

Unfair relationships

14 (1) The court may make an order under section 140B of the 1974 Act in connection with a credit agreement made before the commencement of section 20 of this Act but only –

   (a) on an application of the kind mentioned in paragraph (a) of subsection (2) of section 140B made at a time after the end of the transitional period; or

   (b) at the instance of the debtor or a surety in any proceedings of the kind mentioned in paragraph (b) or (c) of that subsection which were commenced at such a time.

   (2) But the court shall not make such an order in connection with such an agreement so made if the agreement–

   (a) became a completed agreement before the commencement of section 20; or

   (b) becomes a completed agreement during the transitional period.

   (3) Expressions used in sections 140A to 140C of the 1974 Act have the same meaning in this paragraph as they have in those sections.

   (4) In this paragraph 'the transitional period' means the period of one year beginning with the day of the commencement of section 20.

   (5) An order under section 69 of this Act may extend, or further extend, the transitional period.

15 (1) The repeal by this Act of sections 137 to 140 of the 1974 Act shall not affect the court's power to reopen an existing agreement under those sections as set out in this paragraph.

   (2) The court's power to reopen an existing agreement which –

   (a) became a completed agreement before the commencement of section 22(3) of this Act, or

   (b) becomes a completed agreement during the transitional period,

   is not affected at all.

   (3) The court may also reopen an existing agreement –

   (a) on an application of the kind mentioned in paragraph (a) of subsection (1) of section 139 made at a time before the end of the transitional period; or

   (b) at the instance of the debtor or a surety in any proceedings of the kind mentioned in paragraph (b) or (c) of that subsection which were commenced at such a time.

   (4) Nothing in section 16A or 16B of the 1974 Act shall affect the application of sections 137 to 140 (whether by virtue of this paragraph or otherwise).

   (5) The repeal or revocation by this Act of the following provisions has no effect in relation to existing agreements so far as they may be reopened as set out in this paragraph –

   (a) section 16(7) of the 1974 Act;

   (b) in section 143(b) of that Act, the words ', 139(1)(a)';

   (c) section 171(7) of that Act;

   (d) in subsection (1) of section 181 of that Act, the words '139(5) and (7),';

   (e) in subsection (2) of that section, the words 'or 139(5) or (7)';

   (f) in section 61(6) of the Bankruptcy (Scotland) Act 1985 (c. 66), the words from the beginning to 'but';

   (g) in section 343(6) of the Insolvency Act 1986 (c. 45), the words from the beginning to 'But';

   (h) Article 316(6) of the Insolvency (Northern Ireland) Order 1989 (S.I. 1989/2405 (N.I. 19)).

   (6) Expressions used in sections 137 to 140 of the 1974 Act have the same meaning in this paragraph as they have in those sections.

(7) In this paragraph –

'existing agreement' means a credit agreement made before the commencement of section 22(3) of this Act;

'the transitional period' means the period of one year beginning with the day of the commencement of section 22(3).

(8) An order under section 69 of this Act may extend, or further extend, the transitional period.

16 (1) It is immaterial for the purposes of section 140C(4)(a) to (c) of the 1974 Act when (as the case may be) a credit agreement or a linked transaction was made or a security was provided.

(2) In relation to an order made under section 140B of the 1974 Act during the transitional period in connection with a credit agreement –

(a) references in subsection (1) of that section to any related agreement shall not include references to a related agreement to which this subparagraph applies;

(b) the reference to a security in paragraph (d) of that subsection shall not include a reference to a security to which this sub-paragraph applies;

and the order shall not under paragraph (g) of that subsection direct accounts to be taken, or (in Scotland) an accounting to be made, between any persons in relation to a related agreement to which this sub-paragraph applies.

(3) Sub-paragraph (2) applies to a related agreement or a security if –

(a) it was made or provided before the commencement of section 21 of this Act; and

(b) it ceased to have any operation before the order under section 140B is made.

(4) In relation to an order made under section 140B after the end of the transitional period in connection with a credit agreement –

(a) references in subsection (1) of that section to any related agreement shall not include references to a related agreement to which this subparagraph applies;

(b) the reference to a security in paragraph (d) of that subsection shall not include a reference to a security to which this sub-paragraph applies;

and the order shall not under paragraph (g) of that subsection direct accounts to be taken, or (in Scotland) an accounting to be made, between any persons in relation to a related agreement to which this sub-paragraph applies.

(5) Sub-paragraph (4) applies to a related agreement or a security if –

(a) it was made or provided before the commencement of section 21; and

(b) it ceased to have any operation before the end of the transitional period.

(6) Expressions used in sections 140A to 140C of the 1974 Act have the same meanings in this paragraph as they have in those sections.

(7) In this paragraph 'the transitional period' means the period of one year beginning with the day of the commencement of section 21.

(8) An order under section 69 of this Act may extend, or further extend, the transitional period.

17 Section 1 of this Act shall have no effect for the purposes of section 140C(1) of the 1974 Act in relation to agreements made before the commencement of section 1.

Applications for licences and fitness to hold a licence etc.

18 (1) Section 6A of the 1974 Act shall not apply in relation to applications made before the commencement of section 27 of this Act.

(2) Section 6(2A) of the 1974 Act shall not apply in relation to applications so made.

(3) The repeal by this Act of the words 'and must be accompanied by the specified fee' in section 6(2) of the 1974 Act has no effect in relation to applications so made.

19 (1) The OFT shall prepare and publish the guidance required by section 25A of the 1974 Act as soon as practicable after the commencement of section 30 of this Act.

(2) The requirements of subsection (4) of section 25A may be satisfied in relation to the preparation of that guidance by steps taken wholly or partly before the commencement of section 30.

Further powers of OFT to regulate conduct of licensees etc.

20 The cases in which the OFT may impose requirements under section 33A of the 1974 Act include cases where the matter with which the OFT is dissatisfied arose before the commencement of section 38 of this Act.

21 The cases in which the OFT may impose requirements under section 33B of the 1974 Act include cases where the matters giving rise to the OFT's dissatisfaction arose before the commencement of section 39 of this Act.

22 (1) The OFT shall prepare and publish the guidance required by section 33E of the 1974 Act as soon as practicable after the commencement of section 42 of this Act.

(2) The requirements of subsection (4) of section 33E may be satisfied in relation to the preparation of that guidance by steps taken wholly or partly before the commencement of section 42.

Powers and duties in relation to information

23 (1) Section 44 of this Act has no effect in relation to applications made before the commencement of that section.

(2) Paragraph 12(6) of Schedule A1 to the 1974 Act does not apply in relation to applications so made.

24 A person is not required by section 36A of the 1974 Act to do anything in relation to an application made by him before the commencement of section 45 of this Act.

Civil penalties

25 (1) The OFT shall prepare and publish the statement of policy required by section 39C of the 1974 Act as soon as practicable after the commencement of section 54 of this Act.

(2) The requirements of subsection (5) of section 39C may be satisfied in relation to the preparation of that statement of policy by steps taken wholly or partly before the commencement of section 54.

Appeals

26 (1) A person who –

(a) immediately before the commencement of section 55 of this Act is a member of a panel established under regulation 24 of the appeals regulations, and

(b) at the time of his appointment to that panel fell within paragraph (2)(a) of that regulation,

shall be treated as having been appointed to the panel of chairmen on the day of the commencement of section 55.

(2) A person who –

    (a) immediately before the commencement of section 55 is a member of a panel established under regulation 24 of the appeals regulations, and

    (b) is not to be treated as having been appointed to the panel of chairmen in accordance with sub-paragraph (1),

shall be treated as having been appointed to the lay panel on the day of the commencement of section 55.

(3) A person who is to be treated as having been appointed to the panel of chairmen or to the lay panel in accordance with this paragraph shall, subject to paragraph 4(2) and (3) of Schedule A1 to the 1974 Act, hold office as a member of the panel in question –

    (a) for the remainder of the period for which he was appointed under regulation 24 of the appeals regulations; and

    (b) on the terms on which he was so appointed (except as to the renewal of his appointment).

(4) In this paragraph –

'appeals regulations' means the Consumer Credit Licensing (Appeals) Regulations 1998 (S.I. 1998/1203);

'lay panel' and 'panel of chairmen' have the same meanings as in Schedule A1 to the 1974 Act.

27 (1) Neither –

    (a) subsections (1) and (2) of section 56 of this Act, nor

    (b) the repeal by this Act of subsections (2) to (5) of section 41 of the 1974 Act,

has effect in relation to determinations of the OFT made before the commencement of section 56.

(2) This Act, so far as it repeals section 11 of the Tribunals and Inquiries Act 1992 (c. 53), has no effect in relation to such determinations so made.

(3) The repeal by this Act of paragraph 27(2) of Schedule 25 to the Enterprise Act 2002 (c. 40) has no effect in relation to such determinations so made.

28 Neither subsection (1) nor (4)(a) of section 58 of this Act has effect in relation to determinations of the OFT made before the commencement of that section.

Ombudsman scheme

29 Section 1 of this Act shall have no effect for the purposes of section 226A(4)(a) of the 2000 Act in relation to a complaint which relates to an act or omission occurring before the commencement of section 1.

SCHEDULE 4 (SECTION 70)   REPEALS

Act or instrument	Extent of repeal
Consumer Credit Act 1974 (c. 39)	In section 2(7), the words 'or 150'. In section 6(2), the words 'and must be accompanied by the specified fee'. Section 8(2). In section 15, subsection (1)(c) and the 'and' immediately preceding it. Section 16(7).

Act or instrument	Extent of repeal
	Section 22(9) and (10).
	Section 23(2).
	Section 25(1A).
	Section 29(5).
	Section 32(5).
	Section 36(6).
	In section 40(6), the words ', other than a non-commercial agreement,'.
	In section 41 –
	(a) subsections (2) to (5); and
	(b) in the Table the entry relating to 'refusal to give directions in respect of a licensee under section 29(5) or 32(5)'.
	In section 43, subsection (3)(a) and the 'or' immediately after it.
	In section 127 –
	(a) in subsection (1) the words '(subject to subsections (3) and (4))'; and
	(b) subsections (3) to (5).
	Sections 137 to 140.
	In section 143(b), the words ', 139(1)(a)'.
	In section 147 –
	(a) subsection (1); and
	(b) in subsection (2) the words '(as applied by subsection (1))'.
	Section 150.
	In section 162 –
	(a) in subsection (1)(b)(i), the words 'books or';
	(b) in subsection (1)(b), the words 'and take copies of, or of any entry in, the books or documents';
	(c) in subsections (1)(d) and (e), (2) and (3) the word 'books'; and
	(d) subsection (7).
	Section 171(7).
	In section 181 –
	(a) in subsection (1) the words '43(3)(a),' and the words '139(5) and (7),'; and
	(b) in subsection (2) the words '43(3)(a),' and the words 'or 139(5) or (7)'.
	In section 185(3), the words 'or 127(3)'.
	In section 189(1) –
	(a) the definition of 'costs';
	(b) in the definition of 'licence' the words from '(including' onwards; and
	(c) the definition of 'personal credit agreement'.
	In Schedule 2, in Part 1, the entry relating to 'personal credit agreement'.
Bankruptcy (Scotland) Act 1985 (c. 66)	In section 61(6), the words from the beginning to 'but'.

Act or instrument	Extent of repeal
Insolvency Act 1986 (c. 45)	In section 343(6), the words from the beginning to 'But'.
Insolvency (Northern Ireland) Order 1989 (S.I. 1989/2405 (N.I. 19))	Article 316(6).
Tribunals and Inquiries Act 1992 (c. 53)	In section 11 – (a) subsection (6); (b) in subsection (7)(a), the words from 'or on an appeal' to 'Scotland' in the third place where it occurs; and (c) in subsection (8), the words from 'and in relation to' to 'Northern Ireland' in the third place where it occurs.
Enterprise Act 2002 (c. 40)	In Schedule 25, paragraphs 6(18)(b) and 27(2).

CONSUMER CREDIT ACT 1974 (AS AMENDED FOLLOWING CONSUMER CREDIT ACT 2006)

An Act to establish for the protection of consumers a new system, administered by the Director General of Fair Trading, of licensing and other control of traders concerned with the provision of credit, or the supply of goods on hire or hire-purchase, and their transactions, in place of the present enactments regulating moneylenders, pawnbrokers and hire-purchase traders and their transactions, and for related matters.

31st July 1974

BE IT ENACTED by the Queen's most Excellent Majesty, by and with the advice and consent of the Lords Spiritual and Temporal, and Commons, in this present Parliament assembled, and by the authority of the same, as follows: –

PART I   OFFICE OF FAIR TRADING

1 General functions of OFT
(1) It is the duty of the Office of Fair Trading ('the OFT') –
  (a) to administer the licensing system set up by this Act,
  (b) to exercise the adjudicating functions conferred on it by this Act in relation to the issue, renewal, variation, suspension and revocation of licences, and other matters,
  (ba) to monitor, as it sees fit, businesses being carried on under licences;
  (c) generally to superintend the working and enforcement of this Act, and regulations made under it, and
  (d) where necessary or expedient, itself to take steps to enforce this Act, and regulations so made.
(2) It is the duty of the OFT, so far as appears to it to be practicable and having regard both to the national interest and the interests of persons carrying on businesses to which this Act applies and their customers, to keep under review and from time to time advise the Secretary of State about –
  (a) social and commercial developments in the United Kingdom and elsewhere relating to the provision of credit or bailment or (in Scotland) hiring of goods to individuals, and related activities; and
  (b) the working and enforcement of this Act and orders and regulations made under it.

2 Powers of Secretary of State
(1) The Secretary of State may by order –
  (a) confer on the OFT additional functions concerning the provision of credit or bailment or (in Scotland) hiring of goods to individuals, and related activities, and

(b)   regulate the carrying out by the OFT of its functions under this Act.

(2)   The Secretary of State may give general directions indicating considerations to which the OFT should have particular regard in carrying out its functions under this Act, and may give specific directions on any matter connected with the carrying out by the OFT of those functions.

(3)   The Secretary of State, on giving any directions under subsection (2), shall arrange for them to be published in such manner as he thinks most suitable for drawing them to the attention of interested persons.

(4)   With the approval of the Secretary of State and the Treasury, the OFT may charge, for any service or facility provided by it under this Act, a fee of an amount specified by general notice (the 'specified fee').

(5)   Provision may be made under subsection (4) for reduced fees, or no fees at all, to be paid for certain services or facilities by persons of a specified description, and references in this Act to the specified fee shall, in such cases, be construed accordingly.

(6)   An order under subsection (1)(a) shall be made by statutory instrument and shall be of no effect unless a draft of the order has been laid before and approved by each House of Parliament.

(7)   References in subsection (2) to the functions of the OFT under this Act do not include the making of a determination to which section 41 (appeals from OFT to the Tribunal) applies.

3 . . .

4 Dissemination of information and advice

The OFT shall arrange for the dissemination, in such form and manner as it considers appropriate, of such information and advice as it may appear to it expedient to give to the public in the United Kingdom about the operation of this Act, the consumer credit jurisdiction under Part 16 of the Financial Services and Markets Act 2000, the credit facilities available to them, and other matters within the scope of its functions under this Act.

5 . . .

6 Form etc of application

(1)   An application to the OFT under this Act is of no effect unless the requirements of this section are satisfied.

(2)   The application must be in writing, and in such form, and accompanied by such information and documents, as the OFT may specify by or describe in a general notice.

(2A) The application must also be accompanied –

(a)   in the case of an application for a licence or for the renewal of a licence, by the charge payable by virtue of section 6A;

(b)   in any other case, by the specified fee.

(3)   Where the OFT receives an application, it may by notice to the applicant at any time before the determination of the application require him to provide such information or documents relevant to the application as may be specified or described in the notice.

(4)   The OFT may by notice require the applicant to publish details of his application at a time or times and in a manner specified in the notice.

(5)   Subsection (6) applies where a general notice under subsection (2) comes into effect –

(a)   after an application has been made; but

(b)   before its determination.

(6) The applicant shall, within such period as may be specified in the general notice, provide the OFT with any information or document –

    (a) which he has not previously provided in relation to the application by virtue of this section;

    (b) which he would have been required to provide with his application had it been made after the general notice came into effect; and

    (c) which the general notice requires to be provided for the purposes of this subsection.

(7) An applicant shall notify the OFT, giving details, if before his application is determined –

    (a) any information or document provided by him in relation to the application by virtue of this section is, to any extent, superseded or otherwise affected by a change in circumstances; or

    (b) he becomes aware of an error in or omission from any such information or document.

(8) A notification for the purposes of subsection (7) shall be given within the period of 28 days beginning with the day on which (as the case may be) –

    (a) the information or document is superseded;

    (b) the change in circumstances occurs; or

    (c) the applicant becomes aware of the error or omission.

(9) Subsection (7) does not require an applicant to notify the OFT about –

    (a) anything of which he is required to notify it under section 36; or

    (b) an error in or omission from any information or document which is a clerical error or omission not affecting the substance of the information or document.

6A Charge on applicants for licences etc.

(1) An applicant for a licence, or for the renewal of a licence, shall pay the OFT a charge towards the costs of carrying out its functions under this Act.

(2) The amount of the charge payable by an applicant shall be determined in accordance with provision made by the OFT by general notice.

(3) The provision that may be made by the OFT under subsection (2) includes –

    (a) different provision in relation to persons of different descriptions;

    (b) provision for no charge at all to be payable by persons of specified descriptions.

(4) The approval of the Secretary of State and the Treasury is required for a general notice under subsection (2).

7 Penalty for false information

A person commits an offence if, for the purposes of, or in connection with, any requirement imposed or other provision made by or under this Act, he knowingly or recklessly gives information to the OFT, or to an officer of the OFT, which, in a material particular, is false or misleading.

PART II   CREDIT AGREEMENTS, HIRE AGREEMENTS AND LINKED TRANSACTIONS

8 Consumer credit agreements

(1) A consumer credit agreement is an agreement between an individual ('the debtor') and any other person ('the creditor') by which the creditor provides the debtor with credit of any amount.

(2) . . .

(3)   A consumer credit agreement is a regulated agreement within the meaning of this Act
if it is not an agreement (an 'exempt agreement') specified in or under section 16, 16A
or 16B.

9 Meaning of credit

(1)   In this Act 'credit' includes a cash loan, and any other form of financial accommodation.
(2)   Where credit is provided otherwise than in sterling, it shall be treated for the purposes
of this Act as provided in sterling of an equivalent amount.
(3)   Without prejudice to the generality of subsection (1), the person by whom goods are
bailed or (in Scotland) hired to an individual under a hire-purchase agreement shall
be taken to provide him with fixed-sum credit to finance the transaction of an amount
equal to the total price of the goods less the aggregate of the deposit (if any) and the
total charge for credit.
(4)   For the purposes of this Act, an item entering into the total charge for credit shall not
be treated as credit even though time is allowed for its payment.

10 Running-account credit and fixed-sum credit

(1)   For the purposes of this Act –
   (a)   running-account credit is a facility under a consumer credit agreement whereby
the debtor is enabled to receive from time to time (whether in his own person,
or by another person) from the creditor or a third party cash, goods and services
(or any of them) to an amount or value such that, taking into account payments
made by or to the credit of the debtor, the credit limit (if any) is not at any time
exceeded; and
   (b)   fixed-sum credit is any other facility under a consumer credit agreement whereby
the debtor is enabled to receive credit (whether in one amount or by instalments).
(2)   In relation to running-account credit, 'credit limit' means, as respects any period, the
maximum debit balance which, under the credit agreement, is allowed to stand on the
account during that period, disregarding any term of the agreement allowing that
maximum to be exceeded merely temporarily.
(3)   For the purposes of paragraph (a) of section 16B(1), running-account credit shall be
taken not to exceed the amount specified in that paragraph ('the specified amount')
if –
   (a)   the credit limit does not exceed the specified amount; or
   (b)   whether or not there is a credit limit, and if there is, notwithstanding that it
exceeds the specified amount, –
      (i)   the debtor is not enabled to draw at any one time an amount which, so far
as (having regard to section 9(4)) it represents credit, exceeds the specified
amount, or
      (ii)   the agreement provides that, if the debit balance rises above a given amount
(not exceeding the specified amount), the rate of the total charge for credit
increases or any other condition favouring the creditor or his associate
comes into operation, or
      (iii)   at the time the agreement is made it is probable, having regard to the terms
of the agreement and any other relevant considerations, that the debit
balance will not at any time rise above the specified amount.

11 Restricted-use credit and unrestricted-use credit

(1)   A restricted-use credit agreement is a regulated consumer credit agreement –
   (a)   to finance a transaction between the debtor and the creditor, whether forming
part of that agreement or not, or
   (b)   to finance a transaction between the debtor and a person (the 'supplier') other
than the creditor, or

   (c) to refinance any existing indebtedness of the debtor's, whether to the creditor or another person,

and 'restricted-use credit' shall be construed accordingly.

(2) An unrestricted-use credit agreement is a regulated consumer credit agreement not falling within subsection (1), and 'unrestricted-use credit' shall be construed accordingly.

(3) An agreement does not fall within subsection (1) if the credit is in fact provided in such a way as to leave the debtor free to use it as he chooses, even though certain uses would contravene that or any other agreement.

(4) An agreement may fall within subsection (1)(b) although the identity of the supplier is unknown at the time the agreement is made.

12 Debtor-creditor-supplier agreements

A debtor-creditor-supplier agreement is a regulated consumer credit agreement being –

   (a) a restricted-use credit agreement which falls within section 11(1)(a), or

   (b) a restricted-use credit agreement which falls within section 11(1)(b) and is made by the creditor under pre-existing arrangements, or in contemplation of future arrangements, between himself and the supplier, or

   (c) an unrestricted-use credit agreement which is made by the creditor under pre-existing arrangements between himself and a person (the 'supplier') other than the debtor in the knowledge that the credit is to be used to finance a transaction between the debtor and the supplier.

13 Debtor-creditor agreements

A debtor-creditor agreement is a regulated consumer credit agreement being –

   (a) a restricted-use credit agreement which falls within section 11(1)(b) but is not made by the creditor under pre-existing arrangements, or in contemplation of future arrangements, between himself and the supplier, or

   (b) a restricted-use credit agreement which falls within section 11(1)(c), or

   (c) an unrestricted-use credit agreement which is not made by the creditor under pre-existing arrangements between himself and a person (the 'supplier') other than the debtor in the knowledge that the credit is to be used to finance a transaction between the debtor and the supplier.

14 Credit-token agreements

(1) A credit-token is a card, check, voucher, coupon, stamp, form, booklet or other document or thing given to an individual by a person carrying on a consumer credit business, who undertakes –

   (a) that on the production of it (whether or not some other action is also required) he will supply cash, goods and services (or any of them) on credit, or

   (b) that where, on the production of it to a third party (whether or not any other action is also required), the third party supplies cash, goods and services (or any of them), he will pay the third party for them (whether or not deducting any discount or commission), in return for payment to him by the individual.

(2) A credit-token agreement is a regulated agreement for the provision of credit in connection with the use of a credit-token.

(3) Without prejudice to the generality of section 9(1), the person who gives to an individual an undertaking falling within subsection (1)(b) shall be taken to provide him with credit drawn on whenever a third party supplies him with cash, goods or services.

(4) For the purposes of subsection (1), use of an object to operate a machine provided by the person giving the object or a third party shall be treated as the production of the object to him.

15 Consumer hire agreements

(1) A consumer hire agreement is an agreement made by a person with an individual (the 'hirer') for the bailment or (in Scotland) the hiring of goods to the hirer, being an agreement which –

    (a) is not a hire-purchase agreement, and

    (b) is capable of subsisting for more than three months, . . .

    (c) . . .

(2) A consumer hire agreement is a regulated agreement if it is not an exempt agreement.

16 Exempt agreements

(1) This Act does not regulate a consumer credit agreement where the creditor is a local authority . . ., or a body specified, or of a description specified, in an order made by the Secretary of State, being –

    (a) an insurer,

    (b) a friendly society,

    (c) an organisation of employers or organisation of workers,

    (d) a charity,

    (e) a land improvement company, . . .

    (f) a body corporate named or specifically referred to in any public general Act

    (ff) a body corporate named or specifically referred to in an order made under –

        section 156(4), 444(1) or 447(2)(a) of the Housing Act 1985,

        section 156(4) of that Act as it has effect by virtue of section 17 of the Housing Act 1996 (the right to acquire),

        section 2 of the Home Purchase Assistance and Housing Corporation Guarantee Act 1978 or section 31 of the Tenants' Rights, &c (Scotland) Act 1980, or

        Article 154(1)(a) or 156AA of the Housing (Northern Ireland) Order 1981 or Article 10(6A) of the Housing (Northern Ireland) Order 1983; or

    (g) a building society, or

    (h) a deposit-taker.

(2) Subsection (1) applies only where the agreement is –

    (a) a debtor-creditor-supplier agreement financing –

        (i)   the purchase of land, or

        (ii) the provision of dwellings on any land,

        and secured by a land mortgage on that land, or

    (b) a debtor-creditor agreement secured by any land mortgage; or

    (c) a debtor-creditor-supplier agreement financing a transaction which is a linked transaction in relation to –

        (i)   an agreement falling within paragraph (a), or

        (ii) an agreement falling within paragraph (b) financing –

            (aa) the purchase of any land, or

            (bb) the provision of dwellings on any land,

            and secured by a land mortgage on the land referred to in paragraph (a) or, as the case may be, the land referred to in sub-paragraph (ii).

(3) Before he makes, varies or revokes an order under subsection (1), the Secretary of State must undertake the necessary consultation.

(3A) The necessary consultation means consultation with the bodies mentioned in the following table in relation to the provision under which the order is to be made, varied or revoked:

Provision of subsection (1)	Consultee
Paragraph (a) or (b)	The Financial Services Authority
Paragraph (d)	The Charity Commissioners
Paragraph (e), (f) or (ff)	Any Minister of the Crown with responsibilities in relation to the body in question
Paragraph (g) or (h)	The Treasury and the Financial Services Authority

(4) An order under subsection (1) relating to a body may be limited so as to apply only to agreements by that body of a description specified in the order.

(5) The Secretary of State may by order provide that this Act shall not regulate other consumer credit agreements where –

    (a) the number of payments to be made by the debtor does not exceed the number specified for that purpose in the order, or

    (b) the rate of the total charge for credit does not exceed the rate so specified, or

    (c) an agreement has a connection with a country outside the United Kingdom.

(6) The Secretary of State may by order provide that this Act shall not regulate consumer hire agreements of a description specified in the order where –

    (a) the owner is a body corporate authorised by or under any enactment to supply electricity, gas or water, and

    (b) the subject of the agreement is a meter or metering equipment,

or where the owner is a provider of a public electronic communications service who is specified in the order.

(6A) This Act does not regulate a consumer credit agreement where the creditor is a housing authority and the agreement is secured by a land mortgage of a dwelling.

(6B) In subsection (6A) 'housing authority' means –

    (a) as regards England and Wales, the Housing Corporation. . . and an authority or body within section 80(1) of the Housing Act 1985 (the landlord condition for secure tenancies), other than a housing association or a housing trust which is a charity;

    (b) as regards Scotland, a development corporation established under an order made, or having effect as if made under the New Towns (Scotland) Act 1968, the Scottish Special Housing Association or the Housing Corporation;

    (c) as regards Northern Ireland, the Northern Ireland Housing Executive.

(6C) This Act does not regulate a consumer credit agreement if –

    (a) it is secured by a land mortgage; and

    (b) entering into that agreement as lender is a regulated activity for the purposes of the Financial Services and Markets Act 2000.

(6D) But section 126, and any other provision so far as it relates to section 126, applies to an agreement which would (but for subsection (6C)) be a regulated agreement.

(6E) Subsection (6C) must be read with –

    (a) section 22 of the Financial Services and Markets Act 2000 (regulated activities: power to specify classes of activity and categories of investment);

    (b) any order for the time being in force under that section; and

    (c) Schedule 2 to that Act.

(7) . . .

(7A) Nothing in this section affects the application of sections 140A to 140C.

(8) In the application of this section to Scotland, subsection (3A) shall have effect as if the reference to the Charity Commissioners were a reference to the Lord Advocate.

(9) In the application of this section to Northern Ireland subsection (3A) shall have effect as if any reference to a Minister of the Crown were a reference to a Northern Ireland department, . . . and any reference to the Charity Commissioners were a reference to the Department of Finance for Northern Ireland.

(10) In this section –

    (a) 'deposit-taker' means –

        (i) a person who has permission under Part 4 of the Financial Services and Markets Act 2000 to accept deposits,

        (ii) an EEA firm of the kind mentioned in paragraph 5(b) of Schedule 3 to that Act which has permission under paragraph 15 of that Schedule (as a result of qualifying for authorisation under paragraph 12 of that Schedule) to accept deposits,

        (iii) any wholly owned subsidiary (within the meaning of the Companies Act 1985) of a person mentioned in sub-paragraph (i), or

        (iv) any undertaking which, in relation to a person mentioned in sub-paragraph (ii), is a subsidiary undertaking within the meaning of any rule of law in force in the EEA State in question for purposes connected with the implementation of the European Council Seventh Company Law Directive of 13 June 1983 on consolidated accounts (No 83/349/EEC), and which has no members other than that person;

    (b) 'insurer' means –

        (i) a person who has permission under Part 4 of the Financial Services and Markets Act 2000 to effect or carry out contracts of insurance, or

        (ii) an EEA firm of the kind mentioned in paragraph 5(d) of Schedule 3 to that Act, which has permission under paragraph 15 of that Schedule (as a result of qualifying for authorisation under paragraph 12 of that Schedule) to effect or carry out contracts of insurance,

    but does not include a friendly society or an organisation of workers or of employers.

(11) Subsection (10) must be read with –

    (a) section 22 of the Financial Services and Markets Act 2000;

    (b) any relevant order under that section; and

    (c) Schedule 2 to that Act.

16A Exemption relating to high net worth debtors and hirers

(1) The Secretary of State may by order provide that this Act shall not regulate a consumer credit agreement or a consumer hire agreement where –

    (a) the debtor or hirer is a natural person;

    (b) the agreement includes a declaration made by him to the effect that he agrees to forgo the protection and remedies that would be available to him under this Act if the agreement were a regulated agreement;

    (c) a statement of high net worth has been made in relation to him; and

    (d) that statement is current in relation to the agreement and a copy of it was provided to the creditor or owner before the agreement was made.

(2) For the purposes of this section a statement of high net worth is a statement to the effect that, in the opinion of the person making it, the natural person in relation to whom it is made –

    (a) received during the previous financial year income of a specified description totalling an amount of not less than the specified amount; or

    (b) had throughout that year net assets of a specified description with a total value of not less than the specified value.

(3) Such a statement –

    (a) may not be made by the person in relation to whom it is made;

    (b) must be made by a person of a specified description; and

    (c) is current in relation to an agreement if it was made during the period of one year ending with the day on which the agreement is made.

(4) An order under this section may make provision about –

    (a) how amounts of income and values of net assets are to be determined for the purposes of subsection (2)(a) and (b);

    (b) the form, content and signing of –

        (i) statements of high net worth;

        (ii) declarations for the purposes of subsection (1)(b).

(5) Where an agreement has two or more debtors or hirers, for the purposes of paragraph (c) of subsection (1) a separate statement of high net worth must have been made in relation to each of them; and paragraph (d) of that subsection shall have effect accordingly.

(6) In this section –

'previous financial year' means, in relation to a statement of high net worth, the financial year immediately preceding the financial year during which the statement is made;

'specified' means specified in an order under this section.

(7) In subsection (6) 'financial year' means a period of one year ending with 31st March.

(8) Nothing in this section affects the application of sections 140A to 140C.

16B Exemption relating to businesses

(1) This Act does not regulate –

    (a) a consumer credit agreement by which the creditor provides the debtor with credit exceeding £25,000, or

    (b) a consumer hire agreement that requires the hirer to make payments exceeding £25,000,

if the agreement is entered into by the debtor or hirer wholly or predominantly for the purposes of a business carried on, or intended to be carried on, by him.

(2) If an agreement includes a declaration made by the debtor or hirer to the effect that the agreement is entered into by him wholly or predominantly for the purposes of a business carried on, or intended to be carried on, by him, the agreement shall be presumed to have been entered into by him wholly or predominantly for such purposes.

(3) But that presumption does not apply if, when the agreement is entered into –

    (a) the creditor or owner, or

    (b) any person who has acted on his behalf in connection with the entering into of the agreement,

knows, or has reasonable cause to suspect, that the agreement is not entered into by the debtor or hirer wholly or predominantly for the purposes of a business carried on, or intended to be carried on, by him.

(4) The Secretary of State may by order make provision about the form, content and signing of declarations for the purposes of subsection (2).

(5) Where an agreement has two or more creditors or owners, in subsection (3) references to the creditor or owner are references to any one or more of them.

(6) Nothing in this section affects the application of sections 140A to 140C.

17 Small agreements

(1) A small agreement is –

    (a) a regulated consumer credit agreement for credit not exceeding £50, other than a hire-purchase or conditional sale agreement; or

    (b) a regulated consumer hire agreement which does not require the hirer to make payments exceeding £50,

being an agreement which is either unsecured or secured by a guarantee or indemnity only (whether or not the guarantee or indemnity is itself secured).

(2) Section 10(3)(a) applies for the purposes of subsection (1) as it applies for the purposes of section 16B(1)(a).

(3) Where –

(a) two or more small agreements are made at or about the same time between the same parties, and

(b) it appears probable that they would instead have been made as a single agreement but for the desire to avoid the operation of provisions of this Act which would have applied to that single agreement but, apart from this subsection, are not applicable to the small agreements,

this Act applies to the small agreements as if they were regulated agreements other than small agreements.

(4) If, apart from this subsection, subsection (3) does not apply to any agreements but would apply if, for any party or parties to any of the agreements, there were substituted an associate of that party, or associates of each of those parties, as the case may be, then subsection (3) shall apply to the agreements.

18 Multiple agreements

(1) This section applies to an agreement (a 'multiple agreement') if its terms are such as –

(a) to place a part of it within one category of agreement mentioned in this Act, and another part of it within a different category of agreements so mentioned, or within a category of agreement not so mentioned, or

(b) to place it, or a part of it, within two or more categories of agreement so mentioned.

(2) Where a part of an agreement falls within subsection (1), that part shall be treated for the purposes of this Act as a separate agreement.

(3) Where an agreement falls within subsection (1)(b), it shall be treated as an agreement in each of the categories in question, and this Act shall apply to it accordingly.

(4) Where under subsection (2) a part of a multiple agreement is to be treated as a separate agreement, the multiple agreement shall (with any necessary modifications) be construed accordingly; and any sum payable under the multiple agreement, if not apportioned by the parties, shall for the purposes of proceedings in any court relating to the multiple agreement be apportioned by the court as may be requisite.

(5) In the case of an agreement for running-account credit, a term of the agreement allowing the credit limit to be exceeded merely temporarily shall not be treated as a separate agreement or as providing fixed-sum credit in respect of the excess.

(6) This Act does not apply to a multiple agreement so far as the agreement relates to goods if under the agreement payments are to be made in respect of the goods in the form of rent (other than a rent-charge) issuing out of land.

19 Linked transactions

(1) A transaction entered into by the debtor or hirer, or a relative of his, with any other person ('the other party'), except one for the provision of security, is a linked transaction in relation to an actual or prospective regulated agreement (the 'principal agreement') of which it does not form part if –

(a) the transaction is entered into in compliance with a term of the principal agreement; or

(b) the principal agreement is a debtor-creditor-supplier agreement and the transaction is financed, or to be financed, by the principal agreement; or

(c) the other party is a person mentioned in subsection (2), and a person so mentioned initiated the transaction by suggesting it to the debtor or hirer, or his relative, who enters into it –

(i)   to induce the creditor or owner to enter into the principal agreement, or

(ii)   for another purpose related to the principal agreement, or

(iii) where the principal agreement is a restricted-use credit agreement, for a purpose related to a transaction financed, or to be financed, by the principal agreement.

(2) The persons referred to in subsection (1)(c) are –

(a) the creditor or owner, or his associate;

(b) a person who, in the negotiation of the transaction, is represented by a credit-broker who is also a negotiator in antecedent negotiations for the principal agreement;

(c) a person who, at the time the transaction is initiated, knows that the principal agreement has been made or contemplates that it might be made.

(3) A linked transaction entered into before the making of the principal agreement has no effect until such time (if any) as that agreement is made.

(4) Regulations may exclude linked transactions of the prescribed description from the operation of subsection (3).

20 Total charge for credit

(1) The Secretary of State shall make regulations containing such provisions as appear to him appropriate for determining the true cost to the debtor of the credit provided or to be provided under an actual or prospective consumer credit agreement (the 'total charge for credit'), and regulations so made shall prescribe –

(a) what items are to be treated as entering into the total charge for credit, and how their amount is to be ascertained;

(b) the method of calculating the rate of the total charge for credit.

(2) Regulations under subsection (1) may provide for the whole or part of the amount payable by the debtor or his relative under any linked transaction to be included in the total charge for credit, whether or not the creditor is a party to the transaction or derives benefit from it.

PART III   LICENSING OF CREDIT AND HIRE BUSINESSES

Licensing principles

21 Businesses needing a licence

(1) Subject to this section, a licence is required to carry on a consumer credit business or a consumer hire business or an ancillary credit business.

(2) A local authority does not need a licence to carry on a business.

(3) A body corporate empowered by a public general Act naming it to carry on a business does not need a licence to do so.

22 Standard and group licences

(1) A licence may be –

(a) a standard licence, that is a licence, issued by the OFT to a person named in the licence on an application made by him, which, whilst the licence is in effect, covers such activities as are described in the licence, or

(b) a group licence, that is a licence, issued by the OFT (whether on the application of any person or of its own motion), which, whilst the licence is in effect, covers such persons and activities as are described in the licence.

(1A) The terms of a licence shall specify –

(a) whether it has effect indefinitely or only for a limited period; and

(b) if it has effect for a limited period, that period.

(1B) For the purposes of subsection (1A)(b) the period specified shall be such period not exceeding the prescribed period as the OFT thinks fit (subject to subsection (1E)).

(1C) A standard licence shall have effect indefinitely unless –

(a) the application for its issue requests that it have effect for a limited period only; or

(b) the OFT otherwise thinks there is good reason why it should have effect for such a period only.

(1D) A group licence shall have effect for a limited period only unless the OFT thinks there is good reason why it should have effect indefinitely.

(1E) Where a licence which has effect indefinitely is to be varied under section 30 or 31 for the purpose of limiting the licence's duration, the variation shall provide for the licence to expire –

(a) in the case of a variation under section 30, at the end of such period from the time of the variation as is set out in the application for the variation; or

(b) in the case of a variation under section 31, at the end of such period from the time of the variation as the OFT thinks fit;

but a period mentioned in paragraph (a) or (b) shall not exceed the prescribed period.

(2) A licence is not assignable or, subject to section 37, transmissible on death or in any other way.

(3) Except in the case of a partnership or an unincorporated body of persons, a standard licence shall not be issued to more than one person.

(4) A standard licence issued to a partnership or an unincorporated body of persons shall be issued in the name of the partnership or body.

(5) The OFT may issue a group licence only if it appears to it that the public interest is better served by doing so than by obliging the persons concerned to apply separately for standard licences.

(5A) A group licence to carry on a business may limit the activities it covers in any way the OFT thinks fit.

(6) The persons covered by a group licence may be described by general words, whether or not coupled with the exclusion of named persons, or in any other way the OFT thinks fit.

(7) The fact that a person is covered by a group licence in respect of certain activities does not prevent a standard licence being issued to him in respect of those activities or any of them.

(8) A group licence issued on the application of any person shall be issued to that person, and general notice shall be given of the issue of any group licence (whether on application or not).

(9)–(10) . . .

23 Authorisation of specific activities

(1) Subject to the terms of the licence, a licence to carry on a business covers all lawful activities done in the course of that business, whether by the licensee or other persons on his behalf.

(2) . . .

(3) A licence covers the canvassing off trade premises of debtor-creditor-supplier agreements or regulated consumer hire agreements only if, and to the extent that, the licence specifically so provides; and such provision shall not be included in a group licence.

(4) The OFT may by general notice specify other activities which, if engaged in by or on behalf of the person carrying on a business, require to be covered by an express term in his licence.

24 Control of name of business

A standard licence authorises the licensee to carry on a business under the name or names specified in the licence, but not under any other name.

24A Applications for standard licences

(1) An application for a standard licence shall, in relation to each type of business which is covered by the application, state whether the applicant is applying –

    (a) for the licence to cover the carrying on of that type of business with no limitation; or

    (b) for the licence to cover the carrying on of that type of business only so far as it falls within one or more descriptions of business.

(2) An application within subsection (1)(b) in relation to a type of business shall set out the description or descriptions of business in question.

(3) References in this Part to a type of business are references to a type of business within subsection (4).

(4) The types of business within this subsection are –

    (a) a consumer credit business;

    (b) a consumer hire business;

    (c) a business so far as it comprises or relates to credit brokerage;

    (d) a business so far as it comprises or relates to debt-adjusting;

    (e) a business so far as it comprises or relates to debt-counselling;

    (f) a business so far as it comprises or relates to debt-collecting;

    (g) a business so far as it comprises or relates to debt administration;

    (h) a business so far as it comprises or relates to the provision of credit information services;

    (i) a business so far as it comprises or relates to the operation of a credit reference agency.

(5) The OFT –

    (a) shall by general notice specify the descriptions of business which can be set out in an application for the purposes of subsection (2) in relation to a type of business;

    (b) may by general notice provide that applications within subsection (1)(b) cannot be made in relation to one or more of the types of business within subsection (4)(c) to (i).

(6) The power of the OFT under subsection (5) includes power to make different provision for different cases or classes of case.

25 Licensee to be a fit person

(1) If an applicant for a standard licence –

    (a) makes an application within section 24A(1)(a) in relation to a type of business, and

    (b) satisfies the OFT that he is a fit person to carry on that type of business with no limitation,

he shall be entitled to be issued with a standard licence covering the carrying on of that type of business with no limitation.

(1AA) If such an applicant –

    (a) makes an application within subsection (1)(b) of section 24A in relation to a type of business, and

    (b) satisfies the OFT that he is a fit person to carry on that type of business so far as it falls within the description or descriptions of business set out in his application in accordance with subsection (2) of that section, he shall be entitled to be issued with a standard licence covering the carrying on of that type of business so far as it falls within the description or descriptions in question.

(1AB) If such an applicant makes an application within section 24A(1)(a) or (b) in relation to a type of business but fails to satisfy the OFT as mentioned in subsection (1) or (1AA) (as the case may be), he shall nevertheless be entitled to be issued with a standard licence covering the carrying on of that type of business so far as it falls within one or more descriptions of business if –

(a) he satisfies the OFT that he is a fit person to carry on that type of business so far as it falls within the description or descriptions in question;
(b) he could have applied for the licence to be limited in that way; and
(c) the licence would not cover any activity which was not covered by his application.

(1AC) In this section 'description of business' means, in relation to a type of business, a description of business specified in a general notice under section 24A(5)(a).

(1AD) An applicant shall not, by virtue of this section, be issued with a licence unless he satisfies the OFT that the name or names under which he would be licensed is or are not misleading or otherwise undesirable.

(1A) . . .

(1B) If an application for the grant of a standard licence –

(a) is made by a person with permission under Part 4 of the Financial Services and Markets Act 2000 to accept deposits, and
(b) relates to a listed activity,

the Financial Services Authority may, if it considers that the OFT ought to refuse the application, notify him of that fact.

(1C) In subsection (1B) 'listed activity' means an activity listed in Annex 1 to the banking consolidation directive (2000/12/EC) or in the Annex to the investment services directive (93/22/EEC) and references to deposits and to their acceptance must be read with –

(a) section 22 of the Financial Services and Markets Act 2000;
(b) any relevant order under that section; and
(c) Schedule 2 to that Act.

(2) In determining whether an applicant for a licence is a fit person for the purposes of this section the OFT shall have regard to any matters appearing to it to be relevant including (amongst other things) –

(a) the applicant's skills, knowledge and experience in relation to consumer credit businesses, consumer hire businesses or ancillary credit businesses;
(b) such skills, knowledge and experience of other persons who the applicant proposes will participate in any business that would be carried on by him under the licence;
(c) practices and procedures that the applicant proposes to implement in connection with any such business;
(d) evidence of the kind mentioned in subsection (2A).

(2A) That evidence is evidence tending to show that the applicant, or any of the applicant's employees, agents or associates (whether past or present) or, where the applicant is a body corporate, any person appearing to the OFT to be a controller of the body corporate or an associate of any such person, has –

(a) committed any offence involving fraud or other dishonesty or violence;
(b) contravened any provision made by or under –

   (i)   this Act;
   (ii) Part 16 of the Financial Services and Markets Act 2000 so far as it relates to the consumer credit jurisdiction under that Part;

      (iii) any other enactment regulating the provision of credit to individuals or other transactions with individuals;

    (c) contravened any provision in force in an EEA State which corresponds to a provision of the kind mentioned in paragraph (b);

    (d) practised discrimination on grounds of sex, colour, race or ethnic or national origins in, or in connection with, the carrying on of any business; or

    (e) engaged in business practices appearing to the OFT to be deceitful or oppressive or otherwise unfair or improper (whether unlawful or not).

(2B) For the purposes of subsection (2A)(e), the business practices which the OFT may consider to be deceitful or oppressive or otherwise unfair or improper include practices in the carrying on of a consumer credit business that appear to the OFT to involve irresponsible lending.

(3) In subsection (2A), 'associate', in addition to the persons specified in section 184, includes a business associate.

25A Guidance on fitness test

(1) The OFT shall prepare and publish guidance in relation to how it determines, or how it proposes to determine, whether persons are fit persons as mentioned in section 25.

(2) If the OFT revises the guidance at any time after it has been published, the OFT shall publish it as revised.

(3) The guidance shall be published in such manner as the OFT thinks fit for the purpose of bringing it to the attention of those likely to be affected by it.

(4) In preparing or revising the guidance the OFT shall consult such persons as it thinks fit.

(5) In carrying out its functions under this Part the OFT shall have regard to the guidance as most recently published.

26 Conduct of business

(1) Regulations may be made as to –

    (a) the conduct by a licensee of his business; and

    (b) the conduct by a consumer credit EEA firm of its business in the United Kingdom.

(2) The regulations may in particular specify –

    (a) the books or other records to be kept by any person to whom the regulations apply;

    (b) the information to be furnished by such a person to those persons with whom –

        (i) that person does business, or

        (ii) that person seeks to do business,

and the way in which that information is to be furnished.

Issue of licences

27 Determination of applications

(1) Unless the OFT determines to issue a licence in accordance with an application it shall, before determining the application, by notice –

    (a) inform the applicant, giving its reasons, that, as the case may be, it is minded to refuse the application, or to grant it in terms different from those applied for, describing them, and

    (b) invite the applicant to submit to the OFT representations in support of his application in accordance with section 34.

(2) If the OFT grants the application in terms different from those applied for then, whether or not the applicant appeals, the OFT shall issue the licence in the terms approved by it unless the applicant by notice informs it that he does not desire a licence in those terms.

27A Consumer credit EEA firms

(1) Where –

    (a) a consumer credit EEA firm makes an application for a standard licence, and

    (b) the activities covered by the application are all permitted activities,

    the OFT shall refuse the application.

(2) Subsection (3) applies where –

    (a) a consumer credit EEA firm makes an application for a standard licence; and

    (b) some (but not all) of the activities covered by the application are permitted activities.

(3) In order to be entitled to be issued with a standard licence in accordance with section 25(1) to (1AB) in relation to a type of business, the firm need not satisfy the OFT that it is a fit person to carry on that type of business so far as it would involve any of the permitted activities covered by the application.

(4) A standard licence held by a consumer credit EEA firm does not at any time authorise the carrying on of an activity which is a permitted activity at that time.

(5) In this section 'permitted activity' means, in relation to a consumer credit EEA firm, an activity for which the firm has, or could obtain, permission under paragraph 15 of Schedule 3 to the Financial Services and Markets Act 2000.

28 Exclusion from group licence

Where the OFT is minded to issue a group licence (whether on the application of any person or not), and in doing so to exclude any person from the group by name, it shall, before determining the matter, –

    (a) give notice of that fact to the person proposed to be excluded, giving its reasons, and

    (b) invite that person to submit to the OFT representations against his exclusion in accordance with section 34.

Charges for indefinite licences

28A Charges to be paid by licensees etc. before end of payment periods

(1) The licensee under a standard licence which has effect indefinitely shall, before the end of each payment period of his, pay the OFT a charge towards the costs of carrying out its functions under this Act.

(2) The original applicant for a group licence which has effect indefinitely shall, before the end of each payment period of his, pay the OFT such a charge.

(3) The amount of the charge payable by a person under subsection (1) or (2) before the end of a payment period shall be determined in accordance with provision which –

    (a) is made by the OFT by general notice; and

    (b) is current on such day as may be determined in accordance with provision made by regulations.

(4) The provision that may be made by the OFT under subsection (3)(a) includes –

    (a) different provision in relation to persons of different descriptions (including persons whose payment periods end at different times);

    (b) provision for no charge at all to be payable by persons of specified descriptions.

(5) The approval of the Secretary of State and the Treasury is required for a general notice under subsection (3)(a).

(6) For the purposes of this section a person's payment periods are to be determined in accordance with provision made by regulations.

28B Extension of period to pay charge under s. 28A

(1) A person who is required under section 28A to pay a charge before the end of a period may apply once to the OFT for that period to be extended.

(2) The application shall be made before such day as may be determined in accordance with provision made by the OFT by general notice.

(3) If the OFT is satisfied that there is a good reason –

    (a) why the applicant has not paid that charge prior to his making of the application, and

    (b) why he cannot pay that charge before the end of that period,

it may, if it thinks fit, by notice to him extend that period by such time as it thinks fit having regard to that reason.

(4) The power of the OFT under this section to extend a period in relation to a charge –

    (a) includes the power to extend the period in relation to a part of the charge only;

    (b) may be exercised even though the period has ended.

28C Failure to pay charge under s. 28A

(1) This section applies if a person (the 'defaulter') fails to pay a charge –

    (a) before the end of a period (the 'payment period') as required under section 28A; or

    (b) where the payment period is extended under section 28B, before the end of the payment period as extended (subject to subsection (2)).

(2) Where the payment period is extended under section 28B in relation to a part of the charge only, this section applies if the defaulter fails –

    (a) to pay so much of the charge as is not covered by the extension before the end of the payment period disregarding the extension; or

    (b) to pay so much of the charge as is covered by the extension before the end of the payment period as extended.

(3) Subject to subsection (4), if the charge is a charge under section 28A(1), the defaulter's licence terminates.

(4) If the defaulter has applied to the OFT under section 28B for the payment period to be extended and that application has not been determined –

    (a) his licence shall not terminate before the application has been determined and the OFT has notified him of the determination; and

    (b) if the OFT extends the payment period on that application, this section shall have effect accordingly.

(5) If the charge is a charge under section 28A(2), the charge shall be recoverable by the OFT.

Renewal, variation, suspension and revocation of licences

29 Renewal

(1) If the licensee under a standard licence of limited duration, or the original applicant for, or any licensee under, a group licence of limited duration, wishes the OFT to renew the licence, whether on the same terms (except as to expiry) or on varied terms, he must, during the period specified by the OFT by general notice or such longer period as the OFT may allow, make an application to the OFT for its renewal.

(2) The OFT may of its own motion renew any group licence.

(3) The preceding provisions of this Part apply to the renewal of a licence as they apply to the issue of a licence, except that section 28 does not apply to a person who was already excluded in the licence up for renewal.

(3A) In its application to the renewal of standard licences by virtue of subsection (3) of this section, section 27(1) shall have effect as if for paragraph (b) there were substituted –

'(b) invite the applicant to submit to the OFT in accordance with section 34 representations –

(i)   in support of his application; and

(ii) about the provision (if any) that should be included under section 34A as part of the determination were the OFT to refuse the application or grant it in terms different from those applied for.'

(4) Until the determination of an application under subsection (1) and, where an appeal lies from the determination, until the end of the appeal period, the licence shall continue to have effect, notwithstanding that apart from this subsection it would expire earlier.

(5) . . .

(6) General notice shall be given of the renewal of a group licence.

30 Variation by request

(1) If it thinks fit, the OFT may by notice to the licensee under a standard licence –

(a) in the case of a licence which covers the carrying on of a type of business only so far as it falls within one or more descriptions of business, vary the licence by –

(i)   removing that limitation;

(ii) adding a description of business to that limitation; or

(iii) removing a description of business from that limitation;

(b) in the case of a licence which covers the carrying on of a type of business with no limitation, vary the licence so that it covers the carrying on of that type of business only so far as it falls within one or more descriptions of business;

(c) vary the licence so that it no longer covers the carrying on of a type of business at all;

(d) vary the licence so that a type of business the carrying on of which is not covered at all by the licence is covered either –

(i)   with no limitation; or

(ii) only so far as it falls within one or more descriptions of business; or

(e) vary the licence in any other way except for the purpose of varying the descriptions of activities covered by the licence.

(1A) The OFT may vary a licence under subsection (1) only in accordance with an application made by the licensee.

(1B) References in this section to a description of business in relation to a type of business –

(a) are references to a description of business specified in a general notice under section 24A(5)(a); and

(b) in subsection (1)(a) (apart from sub-paragraph (ii)) include references to a description of business that was, but is no longer, so specified.

(2) In the case of a group licence issued on the application of any person, the OFT, on an application made by that person, may if it thinks fit by notice to that person vary the terms of the licence in accordance with the application; but the OFT shall not vary a group licence under this subsection by excluding a named person, other than the

person making the request, unless that named person consents in writing to his exclusion.

(3) In the case of a group licence from which (whether by name or description) a person is excluded, the OFT, on an application made by that person, may if it thinks fit, by notice to that person, vary the terms of the licence so as to remove the exclusion.

(4) Unless the OFT determines to vary a licence in accordance with an application it shall, before determining the application, by notice –

(a) inform the applicant, giving its reasons, that it is minded to refuse the application, and

(b) invite the applicant to submit to the OFT representations in support of his application in accordance with section 34.

(5) General notice shall be given that a variation of a group licence has been made under this section.

31 Compulsory variation

(1) Where at a time during the currency of a licence the OFT is of the opinion that, if the licence had expired at that time (assuming, in the case of a licence which has effect indefinitely, that it were a licence of limited duration), it would, on an application for its renewal or further renewal on the same terms (except as to expiry), have been minded to grant the application but on different terms, and that therefore it should take steps mentioned in subsection (1A), it shall proceed as follows.

(1A) Those steps are –

(a)   in the case of a standard licence, steps mentioned in section 30(1)(a)(ii) and (iii), (b), (c) and (e);

(b)   in the case of a group licence, the varying of terms of the licence.

(1B) The OFT shall also proceed as follows if, having regard to section 22(1B) to (1E), it is of the opinion –

(a)   that a licence which has effect indefinitely should have its duration limited; or

(b)   in the case of a licence of limited duration, that the period during which it has effect should be shortened.

(2) In the case of a standard licence the OFT shall, by notice –

(a)   inform the licensee of the variations the OFT is minded to make in the terms of the licence, stating its reasons, and

(b)   invite him to submit to the OFT in accordance with section 34 representations –

(i)   as to the proposed variations; and

(ii)   about the provision (if any) that should be included under section 34A as part of the determination were the OFT to vary the licence.

(3) In the case of a group licence the OFT shall –

(a)   give general notice of the variations it is minded to make in the terms of the licence, stating its reasons, and

(b)   in the notice invite any licensee to submit to it representations as to the proposed variations in accordance with section 34.

(4) In the case of a group licence issued on application the OFT shall also –

(a)   inform the original applicant of the variations the OFT is minded to make in the terms of the licence, stating its reasons, and

(b)   invite him to submit to the OFT representations as to the proposed variations in accordance with section 34.

(5) If the OFT is minded to vary a group licence by excluding any person (other than the original applicant) from the group by name the OFT shall, in addition, take the like steps under section 28 as are required in the case mentioned in that section.

(6) General notice shall be given that a variation of any group licence has been made under this section.

(7) A variation under this section shall not take effect before the end of the appeal period.

(8) Subsection (1) shall have effect in relation to a standard licence as if an application could be made for the renewal or further renewal of the licence on the same terms (except as to expiry) even if such an application could not be made because of provision made in a general notice under section 24A(5).

(9) Accordingly, in applying subsection (1AA) of section 25 in relation to the licence for the purposes of this section, the OFT shall treat references in that subsection to the description or descriptions of business in relation to a type of business as references to the description or descriptions of business included in the licence in relation to that type of business, notwithstanding that provision under section 24A(5).

32 Suspension and revocation

(1) Where at a time during the currency of a licence the OFT is of the opinion that if the licence had expired at that time (assuming, in the case of a licence which has effect indefinitely, that it were a licence of limited duration) it would have been minded not to renew it, and that therefore it should be revoked or suspended, it shall proceed as follows.

(2) In the case of a standard licence the OFT shall, by notice –

    (a) inform the licensee that, as the case may be, the OFT is minded to revoke the licence, or suspend it until a specified date or indefinitely, stating its reasons, and

    (b) invite him to submit to the OFT in accordance with section 34 representations –

        (i) as to the proposed revocation or suspension; and

        (ii) about the provision (if any) that should be included under section 34A as part of the determination were the OFT to revoke or suspend the licence.

(3) In the case of a group licence the OFT shall –

    (a) give general notice that, as the case may be, it is minded to revoke the licence, or suspend it until a specified date or indefinitely, stating its reasons, and

    (b) in the notice invite any licensee to submit to it representations as to the proposed revocation or suspension in accordance with section 34.

(4) In the case of a group licence issued on application the OFT shall also –

    (a) inform the original applicant that, as the case may be, the OFT is minded to revoke the licence, or suspend it until a specified date or indefinitely, stating its reasons, and

    (b) invite him to submit representations as to the proposed revocation or suspension in accordance with section 34.

(5) . . .

(6) General notice shall be given of the revocation or suspension of a group licence.

(7) A revocation or suspension under this section shall not take effect before the end of the appeal period.

(8) Except for the purposes of section 29, a licensee under a suspended licence shall be treated, in respect of the period of suspension, as if the licence had not been issued; and where the suspension is not expressed to end on a specified date it may, if the OFT thinks fit, be ended by notice given by it to the licensee or, in the case of a group licence, by general notice.

(9) The OFT has no power to revoke or to suspend a standard licence simply because, by virtue of provision made in a general notice under section 24A(5), a person cannot apply for the renewal of such a licence on terms which are the same as the terms of the licence in question.

33 Application to end suspension

(1) On an application made by a licensee the OFT may, if it thinks fit, by notice to the licensee end the suspension of a licence, whether the suspension was for a fixed or indefinite period.

(2) Unless the OFT determines to end the suspension in accordance with the application it shall, before determining the application, by notice –

    (a) inform the applicant, giving its reasons, that it is minded to refuse the application, and

    (b) invite the applicant to submit to the OFT representations in support of his application in accordance with section 34.

(3) General notice shall be given that a suspension of a group licence has been ended under this section.

(4) In the case of a group licence issued on application –

    (a) the references in subsection (1) to a licensee include the original applicant;

    (b) the OFT shall inform the original applicant that a suspension of a group licence has been ended under this section.

Further powers of OFT to regulate conduct of licensees etc.

33A Power of OFT to impose requirements on licensees

(1) This section applies where the OFT is dissatisfied with any matter in connection with –

    (a) a business being carried on, or which has been carried on, by a licensee or by an associate or a former associate of a licensee;

    (b) a proposal to carry on a business which has been made by a licensee or by an associate or a former associate of a licensee; or

    (c) any conduct not covered by paragraph (a) or (b) of a licensee or of an associate or a former associate of a licensee.

(2) The OFT may by notice to the licensee require him to do or not to do (or to cease doing) anything specified in the notice for purposes connected with –

    (a) addressing the matter with which the OFT is dissatisfied; or

    (b) securing that matters of the same or a similar kind do not arise.

(3) A requirement imposed under this section on a licensee shall only relate to a business which the licensee is carrying on, or is proposing to carry on, under the licence under which he is a licensee.

(4) Such a requirement may be framed by reference to a named person other than the licensee.

(5) For the purposes of subsection (1) it is immaterial whether the matter with which the OFT is dissatisfied arose before or after the licensee became a licensee.

(6) If –

    (a) a person makes an application for a standard licence, and

    (b) while dealing with that application the OFT forms the opinion that, if such a licence were to be issued to that person, it would be minded to impose on him a requirement under this section, the OFT may, before issuing such a licence to that person, do (in whole or in part) anything that it must do under section 33D or 34(1) or (2) in relation to the imposing of the requirement.

(7) In this section 'associate', in addition to the persons specified in section 184, includes a business associate.

33B Power of OFT to impose requirements on supervisory bodies

(1) This section applies where the OFT is dissatisfied with the way in which a responsible person in relation to a group licence –

    (a) is regulating or otherwise supervising, or has regulated or otherwise supervised, persons who are licensees under that licence; or

    (b) is proposing to regulate or otherwise to supervise such persons.

(2) The OFT may by notice to the responsible person require him to do or not to do (or to cease doing) anything specified in the notice for purposes connected with –

    (a) addressing the matters giving rise to the OFT's dissatisfaction; or

    (b) securing that matters of the same or a similar kind do not arise.

(3) A requirement imposed under this section on a responsible person in relation to a group licence shall only relate to practices and procedures for regulating or otherwise supervising licensees under the licence in connection with their carrying on of businesses under the licence.

(4) For the purposes of subsection (1) it is immaterial whether the matters giving rise to the OFT's dissatisfaction arose before or after the issue of the group licence in question.

(5) If –

    (a) a person makes an application for a group licence, and

    (b) while dealing with that application the OFT forms the opinion that, if such a licence were to be issued to that person, it would be minded to impose on him a requirement under this section,

the OFT may, before issuing such a licence to that person, do (in whole or in part) anything that it must do under section 33D or 34(1) or (2) in relation to the imposing of the requirement.

(6) For the purposes of this Part a person is a responsible person in relation to a group licence if –

    (a) he is the original applicant for it; and

    (b) he has a responsibility (whether by virtue of an enactment, an agreement or otherwise) for regulating or otherwise supervising persons who are licensees under the licence.

33C Supplementary provision relating to requirements

(1) A notice imposing a requirement under section 33A or 33B may include provision about the time at or by which, or the period during which, the requirement is to be complied with.

(2) A requirement imposed under section 33A or 33B shall not have effect after the licence by reference to which it is imposed has itself ceased to have effect.

(3) A person shall not be required under section 33A or 33B to compensate, or otherwise to make amends to, another person.

(4) The OFT may by notice to the person on whom a requirement has been imposed under section 33A or 33B vary or revoke the requirement (including any provision made under subsection (1) of this section in relation to it) with effect from such date as may be specified in the notice.

(5) The OFT may exercise its power under subsection (4) in relation to a requirement either on its own motion or on the application of a person falling within subsection (6) or (7) in relation to the requirement.

(6) A person falls within this subsection in relation to a requirement if he is the person on whom the requirement is imposed.

(7) A person falls within this subsection in relation to a requirement if –

    (a) the requirement is imposed under section 33A;

    (b) he is not the person on whom the requirement is imposed;

(c) the requirement is framed by reference to him by name; and
(d) the effect of the requirement is –

    (i)   to prevent him being an employee of the person on whom the requirement is imposed;

    (ii) to restrict the activities that he may engage in as an employee of that person; or

    (iii) otherwise to prevent him from doing something, or to restrict his doing something, in connection with a business being carried on by that person.

33D Procedure in relation to requirements

(1) Before making a determination –

    (a) to impose a requirement on a person under section 33A or 33B,

    (b) to refuse an application under section 33C(5) in relation to a requirement imposed under either of those sections, or

    (c) to vary or to revoke a requirement so imposed,

the OFT shall proceed as follows.

(2) The OFT shall give a notice to every person to whom subsection (3) applies in relation to the determination –

    (a) informing him, with reasons, that it is minded to make the determination; and

    (b) inviting him to submit to it representations as to the determination under section 34.

(3) This subsection applies to a person in relation to the determination if he falls within, or as a consequence of the determination would fall within, section 33C(6) or (7) in relation to the requirement in question.

(4) This section does not require the OFT to give a notice to a person if the determination in question is in the same terms as a proposal made to the OFT by that person (whether as part of an application under this Part or otherwise).

33E Guidance on requirements

(1) The OFT shall prepare and publish guidance in relation to how it exercises, or how it proposes to exercise, its powers under sections 33A to 33C.

(2) If the OFT revises the guidance at any time after it has been published, the OFT shall publish it as revised.

(3) The guidance shall be published in such manner as the OFT thinks fit for the purpose of bringing it to the attention of those likely to be affected by it.

(4) In preparing or revising the guidance the OFT shall consult such persons as it thinks fit.

(5) In exercising its powers under sections 33A to 33C the OFT shall have regard to the guidance as most recently published.

Miscellaneous

34 Representations to OFT

(1) Where this section applies to an invitation by the OFT to any person to submit representations, the OFT shall invite that person, within 21 days after the notice containing the invitation is given to him or published, or such longer period as the OFT may allow, –

    (a) to submit his representations in writing to the OFT, and

    (b) to give notice to the OFT, if he thinks fit, that he wishes to make representations orally,

and where notice is given under paragraph (b) the OFT shall arrange for the oral representations to be heard.

(2) In reaching its determination the OFT shall take into account any representations submitted or made under this section.

(3) The OFT shall give notice of its determination to the persons who were required to be invited to submit representations about it or, where the invitation to submit representations was required to be given by general notice, shall give general notice of the determination.

34A Winding-up of standard licensee's business

(1) If it thinks fit, the OFT may, for the purpose of enabling the licensee's business, or any part of his business, to be transferred or wound up, include as part of a determination to which subsection (2) applies provision authorising the licensee to carry on for a specified period –

(a) specified activities, or

(b) activities of specified descriptions,

which, because of that determination, the licensee will no longer be licensed to carry on.

(2) This subsection applies to the following determinations –

(a) a determination to refuse to renew a standard licence in accordance with the terms of the application for its renewal;

(b) a determination to vary such a licence under section 31;

(c) a determination to suspend or revoke such a licence.

(3) Such provision –

(a) may specify different periods for different activities or activities of different descriptions;

(b) may provide for persons other than the licensee to carry on activities under the authorisation;

(c) may specify requirements which must be complied with by a person carrying on activities under the authorisation in relation to those activities;

and, if a requirement specified under paragraph (c) is not complied with, the OFT may by notice to a person carrying on activities under the authorisation terminate the authorisation (in whole or in part) from a specified date.

(4) Without prejudice to the generality of paragraph (c) of subsection (3), a requirement specified under that paragraph may have the effect of –

(a) preventing a named person from being an employee of a person carrying on activities under the authorisation, or restricting the activities he may engage in as an employee of such a person;

(b) preventing a named person from doing something, or restricting his doing something, in connection with activities being carried on by a person under the authorisation;

(c) securing that access to premises is given to officers of the OFT for the purpose of enabling them to inspect documents or to observe the carrying on of activities.

(5) Activities carried on under an authorisation shall be treated for the purposes of sections 39(1), 40, 148 and 149 as if carried on under a standard licence.

35 The register

(1) The OFT shall establish and maintain a register, in which it shall cause to be kept particulars of –

(a) applications not yet determined for the issue, variation or renewal of licences, or for ending the suspension of a licence;

(b) licences which are in effect, or have at any time been suspended or revoked or terminated by section 28C, with details of any variation of the terms of a licence;

(ba) requirements imposed under section 33A or 33B which are in effect or which have been in effect, with details of any variation of such a requirement;

(c) decisions given by it under this Act, and any appeal from those decisions; and

(d) such other matters (if any) as it thinks fit.

(1A) The OFT shall also cause to be kept in the register any copy of any notice or other document relating to a consumer credit EEA firm which is given to the OFT by the Financial Services Authority for inclusion in the register.

(2) The OFT shall give general notice of the various matters required to be entered in the register, and of any change in them made under subsection (1)(d).

(3) Any person shall be entitled, on payment of the specified fee –

(a) to inspect the register during ordinary office hours and take copies of any entry, or

(b) to obtain from the OFT a copy, certified by the OFT to be correct, of any entry in the register.

(4) The OFT may, if it thinks fit, determine that the right conferred by subsection (3)(a) shall be exercisable in relation to a copy of the register instead of, or in addition to, the original.

(5) The OFT shall give general notice of the place or places where, and times when, the register or a copy of it may be inspected.

36 Duty to notify changes

(1) Within 21 working days after a change takes place in any particulars entered in the register in respect of a standard licence or the licensee under section 35(1)(d) (not being a change resulting from action taken by the OFT), the licensee shall give the OFT notice of the change; and the OFT shall cause any necessary amendment to be made in the register.

(2) Within 21 working days after –

(a) any change takes place in the officers of –

(i) a body corporate, or an unincorporated body of persons, which is the licensee under a standard licence, or

(ii) a body corporate which is a controller of a body corporate which is such a licensee, or

(b) a body corporate which is such a licensee becomes aware that a person has become or ceased to be a controller of the body corporate, or

(c) any change takes place in the members of a partnership which is such a licensee (including a change on the amalgamation of the partnership with another firm, or a change whereby the number of partners is reduced to one),

the licensee shall give the OFT notice of the change.

(3) Within 14 working days after any change takes place in the officers of a body corporate which is a controller of another body corporate which is a licensee under a standard licence, the controller shall give the licensee notice of the change.

(4) Within 14 working days after a person becomes or ceases to be a controller of a body corporate which is a licensee under a standard licence, that person shall give the licensee notice of the fact.

(5) Where a change in a partnership has the result that the business ceases to be carried on under the name, or any of the names, specified in a standard licence the licence shall cease to have effect.

(6) . . .

36A Further duties to notify changes etc.

(1) Subsections (2) to (4) apply where a general notice under section 6(2) comes into effect.

(2) A person who is the licensee under a standard licence or who is the original applicant for a group licence shall, in relation to each relevant application which he has made and which was determined before the general notice came into effect, provide the OFT with any information or document –

(a) which he would have been required to provide with the application had the application been made after the general notice came into effect; and

(b) which the general notice requires to be provided for the purposes of this subsection.

(3) Any such information or document shall be provided within such period as may be specified in the general notice.

(4) Subsection (2) does not require a person to provide any information or document –

(a) which he provided in relation to the application by virtue of section 6;

(b) which he has previously provided in relation to the application by virtue of this section; or

(c) which he would have been required to provide in relation to the application by virtue of subsection (5) but for subsection (6).

(5) A person who is the licensee under a standard licence or who is the original applicant for a group licence shall, in relation to each relevant application which he has made, notify the OFT giving details if, after the application is determined, any information or document which he –

(a) provided in relation to the application by virtue of section 6, or

(b) has so provided by virtue of this section,

is, to any extent, superseded or otherwise affected by a change in circumstances.

(6) Subsection (5) does not require a person to notify the OFT about a matter unless it falls within a description of matters specified by the OFT in a general notice.

(7) A description may be specified for the purposes of subsection (6) only if the OFT is satisfied that the matters which would fall within that description are matters which would be relevant to the question of –

(a) whether, having regard to section 25(2), a person is a fit person to carry on a business under a standard licence; or

(b) whether the public interest is better served by a group licence remaining in effect than by obliging the licensees under it to apply separately for standard licences.

(8) A person who is the licensee under a standard licence or who is the original applicant for a group licence shall, in relation to each relevant application which he has made, notify the OFT about every error or omission –

(a) in or from any information or document which he provided by virtue of section 6, or which he has provided by virtue of this section, in relation to the application; and

(b) of which he becomes aware after the determination of the application.

(9) A notification for the purposes of subsection (5) or (8) shall be given within the period of 28 days beginning with the day on which (as the case may be) –

(a) the information or document is superseded;

(b) the change in circumstances occurs; or

(c) the licensee or the original applicant becomes aware of the error or omission.

(10) This section does not require a person to notify the OFT about –

(a) anything of which he is required to notify it under section 36; or

(b) an error in or omission from any information or document which is a clerical error or omission not affecting the substance of the information or document.

(11) In this section 'relevant application' means, in relation to a person who is the licensee under a standard licence or who is the original applicant for a group licence –

(a) the original application for the licence; or

(b) an application for its renewal or for its variation.

36B Power of OFT to require information generally

(1) The OFT may by notice to a person require him –

(a) to provide such information as may be specified or described in the notice; or

(b) to produce such documents as may be so specified or described.

(2) The notice shall set out the reasons why the OFT requires the information or documents to be provided or produced.

(3) The information or documents shall be provided or produced –

(a) before the end of such reasonable period as may be specified in the notice; and

(b) at such place as may be so specified.

(4) A requirement may be imposed under subsection (1) on a person who is –

(a) the licensee under a standard licence, or

(b) the original applicant for a group licence,

only if the provision or production of the information or documents in question is reasonably required for purposes connected with the OFT's functions under this Act.

(5) A requirement may be imposed under subsection (1) on any other person only if –

(a) an act or omission mentioned in subsection (6) has occurred or the OFT has reason to suspect that such an act or omission has occurred; and

(b) the provision or production of the information or documents in question is reasonably required for purposes connected with –

(i)   the taking by the OFT of steps under this Part as a consequence; or

(ii) its consideration of whether to take such steps as a consequence.

(6) Those acts or omissions are acts or omissions which –

(a) cast doubt on whether, having regard to section 25(2), a person is a fit person to carry on a business under a standard licence;

(b) cast doubt on whether the public interest is better served by a group licence remaining in effect, or being issued, than by obliging the persons who are licensees under it, or who would be licensees under it, to apply separately for standard licences;

(c) give rise, or are likely to give rise, to dissatisfaction for the purposes of section 33A(1) or 33B(1); or

(d) constitute or give rise to a failure of the kind mentioned in section 39A(1).

36C Power of OFT to require access to premises

(1) The OFT may by notice to a licensee under a licence require him to secure that access to the premises specified or described in the notice is given to an officer of an enforcement authority in order for the officer –

(a) to observe the carrying on of a business under the licence by the licensee; or

(b) to inspect such documents of the licensee relating to such a business as are –

(i)   specified or described in the notice; and

(ii) situated on the premises.

(2) The notice shall set out the reasons why the access is required.

(3) The premises which may be specified or described in the notice –

(a) include premises which are not premises of the licensee if they are premises from which he carries on activities in connection with the business in question; but

(b) do not include premises which are used only as a dwelling.

(4) The licensee shall secure that the required access is given at such times as the OFT reasonably requires.

(5) The OFT shall give reasonable notice of those times.

(6) Where an officer is given access to any premises by virtue of this section, the licensee shall also secure that persons on the premises give the officer such assistance or information as he may reasonably require in connection with his observation or inspection of documents (as the case may be).

(7) The assistance that may be required under subsection (6) includes (amongst other things) the giving to the officer of an explanation of a document which he is inspecting.

(8) A requirement may be imposed under subsection (1) on a person who is –

(a) the licensee under a standard licence, or

(b) the original applicant for a group licence, only if the observation or inspection in question is reasonably required for purposes connected with the OFT's functions under this Act.

(9) A requirement may be imposed under subsection (1) on any other person only if –

(a) an act or omission mentioned in section 36B(6) has occurred or the OFT has reason to suspect that such an act or omission has occurred; and

(b) the observation or inspection in question is reasonably required for purposes connected with –

(i) the taking by the OFT of steps under this Part as a consequence; or

(ii) its consideration of whether to take such steps as a consequence.

(10) In this section –

(a) references to a licensee under a licence include, in relation to a group licence issued on application, references to the original applicant; and

(b) references to a business being carried on under a licence by a licensee include, in relation to the original applicant for a group licence, activities being carried on by him for the purpose of regulating or otherwise supervising (whether by virtue of an enactment, an agreement or otherwise) licensees under that licence in connection with their carrying on of businesses under that licence.

36D Entry to premises under warrant

(1) A justice of the peace may issue a warrant under this section if satisfied on information on oath given on behalf of the OFT that there are reasonable grounds for believing that the following conditions are satisfied.

(2) Those conditions are –

(a) that there is on the premises specified in the warrant information or documents in relation to which a requirement could be imposed under section 36B; and

(b) that if such a requirement were to be imposed in relation to the information or documents –

(i) it would not be complied with; or

(ii) the information or documents would be tampered with.

(3) A warrant under this section shall authorise an officer of an enforcement authority –

(a) to enter the premises specified in the warrant;

(b) to search the premises and to seize and detain any information or documents appearing to be information or documents specified in the warrant or information or documents of a description so specified;

(c) to take any other steps which may appear to be reasonably necessary for preserving such information or documents or preventing interference with them; and

(d) to use such force as may be reasonably necessary.

(4) An officer entering premises by virtue of this section may take such persons and equipment with him as he thinks necessary.

(5) In the application of this section to Scotland –

    (a) the reference to a justice of the peace includes a reference to a sheriff;

    (b) for 'information on oath' there is substituted 'evidence on oath'.

(6) In the application of this section to Northern Ireland the reference to a justice of the peace shall be construed as a reference to a lay magistrate.

36E Failure to comply with information requirement

(1) If on an application made by the OFT it appears to the court that a person (the 'information defaulter') has failed to do something that he was required to do by virtue of section 36B or 36C, the court may make an order under this section.

(2) An order under this section may require the information defaulter –

    (a) to do the thing that it appears he failed to do within such period as may be specified in the order;

    (b) otherwise to take such steps to remedy the consequences of the failure as may be so specified.

(3) If the information defaulter is a body corporate, a partnership or an unincorporated body of persons which is not a partnership, the order may require any officer who is (wholly or partly) responsible for the failure to meet such costs of the application as are specified in the order.

(4) In this section –

'court' means –

    (a) in England and Wales and Northern Ireland, the High Court or the county court;

    (b) in Scotland, the Court of Session or the sheriff;

'officer' means –

    (a) in relation to a body corporate, a person holding a position of director, manager or secretary of the body or any similar position;

    (b) in relation to a partnership or to an unincorporated body of persons, a member of the partnership or body.

(5) In subsection (4) 'director' means, in relation to a body corporate whose affairs are managed by its members, a member of the body.

36F Officers of enforcement authorities other than OFT

(1) A relevant officer may only exercise powers by virtue of section 36C or 36D in pursuance of arrangements made with the OFT by or on behalf of the enforcement authority of which he is an officer.

(2) Anything done or omitted to be done by, or in relation to, a relevant officer in the exercise or purported exercise of a power by virtue of section 36C or 36D shall be treated for all purposes as having been done or omitted to be done by, or in relation to, an officer of the OFT.

(3) Subsection (2) does not apply for the purposes of any criminal proceedings brought against the officer, the enforcement authority of which he is an officer or the OFT in respect of anything done or omitted to be done by the officer.

(4) A relevant officer shall not disclose to a person other than the OFT information obtained by his exercise of a power by virtue of section 36C or 36D unless –

    (a) he has the approval of the OFT to do so; or

    (b) he is under a duty to make the disclosure.

(5) In this section 'relevant officer' means an officer of an enforcement authority other than the OFT.

37 Death, bankruptcy etc of licensee

(1) A licence held by one individual terminates if he –

  (a) dies, or
  (b) is adjudged bankrupt, or
  (c) *becomes a patient within the meaning of Part VIII of the Mental Health Act 1959*
  (c) becomes a person who lacks capacity (within the meaning of the Mental Capacity Act 2005) to carry on the activities covered by the licence.

(1A) A licence terminates if the licensee gives the OFT a notice under subsection (1B).

(1B) A notice under this subsection shall –

  (a) be in such form as the OFT may by general notice specify;
  (b) contain such information as may be so specified;
  (c) be accompanied by the licence or give reasons as to why it is not accompanied by the licence; and
  (d) be signed by or on behalf of the licensee.

(2) In relation to a licence held by one individual, or a partnership or other unincorporated body of persons, or a body corporate, regulations may specify other events relating to the licensee on the occurrence of which the licence is to terminate.

(3) Regulations may –

  (a) provide for the termination of a licence by subsection (1) or (1A), or under subsection (2), to be deferred for a period not exceeding 12 months, and
  (b) authorise the business of the licensee to be carried on under the licence by some other person during the period of deferment, subject to such conditions as may be prescribed.

(4) This section does not apply to group licences.

38 Application of s.37 to Scotland and Northern Ireland

(1) In the application of section 37 to Scotland the following shall be substituted for paragraphs (b) and (c) of subsection (1) –

  '(b) has his estate sequestrated, or
  (c) becomes incapable of managing his own affairs'.

(2) In the application of section 37 to Northern Ireland the following shall be substituted for subsection (1) –

  '(1) A licence held by one individual terminates if –

  (a) he dies, or
  (b) he is adjudged bankrupt or his estate and effects vest in the official assignee under section 349 of the Irish Bankrupt and Insolvent Act 1857, or
  (c) a declaration is made under section 15 of the Lunacy Regulation (Ireland) Act 1871 that he is of unsound mind and incapable of managing his person or property, or an order is made under section 68 of that Act in consequence of its being found that he is of unsound mind and incapable of managing his affairs.'.

39 Offences against Part III

(1) A person who engages in any activities for which a licence is required when he is not a licensee under a licence covering those activities commits an offence.

(2) A licensee under a standard licence who carries on business under a name not specified in the licence commits an offence.

(3) A person who fails to give the OFT or a licensee notice under section 36 within the period required commits an offence.

39A Power of OFT to impose civil penalties

(1) Where the OFT is satisfied that a person (the 'defaulter') has failed or is failing to comply with a requirement imposed on him by virtue of section 33A, 33B or 36A, it may by notice to him (a 'penalty notice') impose on him a penalty of such amount as it thinks fit.

(2) The penalty notice shall –

    (a) specify the amount of the penalty that is being imposed;
    (b) set out the OFT's reasons for imposing a penalty and for specifying that amount;
    (c) specify how the payment of the penalty may be made to the OFT; and
    (d) specify the period within which the penalty is required to be paid.

(3) The amount of the penalty shall not exceed £50,000.

(4) The period specified in the penalty notice for the purposes of subsection (2)(d) shall not end earlier than the end of the period during which an appeal may be brought against the imposition of the penalty under section 41.

(5) If the defaulter does not pay the penalty to the OFT within the period so specified –

    (a) the unpaid balance from time to time shall carry interest at the rate for the time being specified in section 17 of the Judgments Act 1838; and
    (b) the penalty and any interest payable on it shall be recoverable by the OFT.

39B Further provision relating to civil penalties

(1) Before determining to impose a penalty on a person under section 39A the OFT shall give a notice to that person –

    (a) informing him that it is minded to impose a penalty on him;
    (b) stating the proposed amount of the penalty;
    (c) setting out its reasons for being minded to impose a penalty on him and for proposing that amount;
    (d) setting out the proposed period for the payment of the penalty; and
    (e) inviting him to submit representations to it about the matters mentioned in the preceding paragraphs in accordance with section 34.

(2) In determining whether and how to exercise its powers under section 39A in relation to a person's failure, the OFT shall have regard to (amongst other things) –

    (a) any penalty or fine that has been imposed on that person by another body in relation to the conduct giving rise to the failure;
    (b) other steps that the OFT has taken or might take under this Part in relation to that conduct.

(3) General notice shall be given of the imposition of a penalty under section 39A on a person who is a responsible person in relation to a group licence.

(4) That notice shall include the matters set out in the notice imposing the penalty in accordance with section 39A(2)(a) and (b).

39C Statement of policy in relation to civil penalties

(1) The OFT shall prepare and publish a statement of policy in relation to how it exercises, or how it proposes to exercise, its powers under section 39A.

(2) If the OFT revises the statement of policy at any time after it has been published, the OFT shall publish it as revised.

(3) No statement of policy shall be published without the approval of the Secretary of State.

(4) The statement of policy shall be published in such manner as the OFT thinks fit for the purpose of bringing it to the attention of those likely to be affected by it.

(5) In preparing or revising the statement of policy the OFT shall consult such persons as it thinks fit.

(6) In determining whether and how to exercise its powers under section 39A in relation to a person's failure, the OFT shall have regard to the statement of policy as most recently published at the time the failure occurred.

(7) The OFT shall not impose a penalty on a person under section 39A in relation to a failure occurring before it has published a statement of policy.

40 Enforcement of agreements made by unlicensed trader

(1) A regulated agreement is not enforceable against the debtor or hirer by a person acting in the course of a consumer credit business or a consumer hire business (as the case may be) if that person is not licensed to carry on a consumer credit business or a consumer hire business (as the case may be) of a description which covers the enforcement of the agreement.

(1A) Unless the OFT has made an order under subsection (2) which applies to the agreement, a regulated agreement is not enforceable against the debtor or hirer if –

(a) it was made by the creditor or owner in the course of a consumer credit business or a consumer hire business (as the case may be); and

(b) at the time the agreement was made he was not licensed to carry on a consumer credit business or a consumer hire business (as the case may be) of a description which covered the making of the agreement.

(2) Where –

(a) during any period a person (the 'trader') has made regulated agreements in the course of a consumer credit business or a consumer hire business (as the case may be), and

(b) during that period he was not licensed to carry on a consumer credit business or a consumer hire business (as the case may be) of a description which covered the making of those agreements, he or his successor in title may apply to the OFT for an order that the agreements are to be treated for the purposes of subsection (1A) as if he had been licensed as required.

(3) Unless the OFT determines to make an order under subsection (2) in accordance with the application, it shall, before determining the application, by notice –

(a) inform the applicant, giving its reasons, that, as the case may be, it is minded to refuse the application, or to grant it in terms different from those applied for, describing them, and

(b) invite the applicant to submit to the OFT representations in support of his application in accordance with section 34.

(4) In determining whether or not to make an order under subsection (2) in respect of any period the OFT shall consider, in addition to any other relevant factors –

(a) how far, if at all, debtors or hirers under the regulated agreements in question were prejudiced by the trader's conduct,

(b) whether or not the OFT would have been likely to grant a licence covering the making of those agreements during that period on an application by the trader, and

(c) the degree of culpability for the failure to be licensed as required.

(5) If the OFT thinks fit, it may in an order under subsection (2) –

(a) limit the order to specified agreements, or agreements of a specified description or made at a specified time;

(b) make the order conditional on the doing of specified acts by the applicant.

(6) This section (apart from subsection (1)) does not apply to a regulated agreement made by a consumer credit EEA firm unless at the time it was made that firm was precluded from entering into it as a result of

(a) a consumer credit prohibition imposed under section 203 of the Financial Services and Markets Act 2000; or

(b) a restriction imposed on the firm under section 204 of that Act.

(7) Subsection (1) does not apply to the enforcement of a regulated agreement by a consumer credit EEA firm unless that firm is precluded from enforcing it as a result of a prohibition or restriction mentioned in subsection (6)(a) or (b).

(8) This section (apart from subsection (1)) does not apply to a regulated agreement made by a person if by virtue of section 21(2) or (3) he was not required to be licensed to make the agreement.

(9) Subsection (1) does not apply to the enforcement of a regulated agreement by a person if by virtue of section 21(2) or (3) he is not required to be licensed to enforce the agreement.

Appeals

40A The Consumer Credit Appeals Tribunal

(1) There shall be a tribunal known as the Consumer Credit Appeals Tribunal ('the Tribunal').

(2) The Tribunal shall have the functions conferred on it by or under this Part.

(3) The Lord Chancellor may by rules make such provision as he thinks fit for regulating the conduct and disposal of appeals before the Tribunal.

(4) Schedule A1 (which makes provision about the Tribunal and proceedings before it) shall have effect.

(5) But that Schedule does not limit the Lord Chancellor's powers under subsection (3).

41 Appeals to Secretary of State under Part III

(1) If, in the case of a determination by the OFT such as is mentioned in column 1 of the table set out at the end of this section, a person mentioned in relation to that determination in column 2 of the table is aggrieved by the determination he may, within the specified period, appeal to the Tribunal.

(1A) The means for making an appeal is by sending the Tribunal a notice of appeal.

(1B) The notice of appeal shall –

(a) be in the specified form;

(b) set out the grounds of appeal in the specified manner; and

(c) include the specified information and documents.

(1C) An appeal to the Tribunal is to be by way of a rehearing of the determination appealed against.

(1D) In this section 'specified' means specified by rules under section 40A(3).

(2)–(5) . . .

Determination	Appellant
Refusal to issue, renew or vary licence in accordance with terms of application.	The applicant.
Exclusion of person from group licence.	The person excluded.
. . .	. . .
Compulsory variation, or suspension or revocation, of standard licence.	The licensee.
Compulsory variation, or suspension or revocation, of group licence.	The original applicant or any licensee.
Refusal to end suspension of licence in accordance with terms of application.	The applicant.

Determination	Appellant
Determination – (a) to impose a requirement under section 33A or 33B; (b) to refuse an application under section 33C(5) in relation to a requirement imposed under either of those sections; or (c) to vary or revoke a requirement so imposed.	A person who falls within section 33C(6) or (7) in relation to the requirement unless the OFT was not required to give a notice to him in relation to the determination by virtue of section 33D(4)
Imposition of penalty under section 39A.	The person on whom the penalty is imposed.
Refusal to make order under section 40(2), 148(2) or 149(2) in accordance with terms of application.	The applicant.
Imposition of, or refusal to withdraw, consumer credit prohibition under section 203 of the Financial Services and Markets Act 2000.	The consumer credit EEA firm concerned.
Imposition of, or refusal to withdraw, a restriction under section 204 of the Financial Services and Markets Act 2000.	The consumer credit EEA firm concerned.

41A Appeals from the Consumer Credit Appeals Tribunal

(1) A party to an appeal to the Tribunal may with leave appeal –

    (a) in England and Wales and Northern Ireland, to the Court of Appeal, or

    (b) in Scotland, to the Court of Session,

    on a point of law arising from a decision of the Tribunal.

(2) For the purposes of subsection (1) leave to appeal may be given by –

    (a) the Tribunal; or

    (b) the Court of Appeal or the Court of Session.

(3) An application for leave to appeal may be made to the Court of Appeal or the Court of Session only if the Tribunal has refused such leave.

(4) If on an appeal under this section the court considers that the decision of the Tribunal was wrong in law, it may do one or more of the following –

    (a) quash or vary that decision;

    (b) substitute for that decision a decision of its own;

    (c) remit the matter to the Tribunal for rehearing and determination in accordance with the directions (if any) given to it by the court.

(5) An appeal may be brought from a decision of the Court of Appeal under this section only if leave to do so is given by the Court of Appeal or the House of Lords.

(6) Rules under section 40A(3) may make provision for regulating or prescribing any matters incidental to or consequential on an appeal under this section.

(7) In this section 'party' means, in relation to an appeal to the Tribunal, the appellant or the OFT.

42   . . .

PART IV   SEEKING BUSINESS

Advertising

43 Advertisements to which Part IV applies

(1) This Part applies to any advertisement, published for the purposes of a business carried on by the advertiser, indicating that he is willing –

    (a) to provide credit, or

    (b) to enter into an agreement for the bailment or (in Scotland) the hiring of goods by him.

(2) An advertisement does not fall within subsection (1) if the advertiser does not carry on –

    (a) a consumer credit business or consumer hire business, or

    (b) a business in the course of which he provides credit to individuals secured on land, or

    (c) a business which comprises or relates to unregulated agreements where –

        (i) the law applicable to the agreement is the law of a country outside the United Kingdom, and

        (ii) if the law applicable to the agreement were the law of a part of the United Kingdom it would be a regulated agreement.

(3) An advertisement does not fall within subsection (1)(a) if it indicates –

    (a) . . .

    (b) that the credit is available only to a body corporate.

(3A) An advertisement does not fall within subsection (1)(a) in so far as it is a communication of an invitation or inducement to engage in investment activity within the meaning of section 21 of the Financial Services and Markets Act 2000, other than an exempt generic communication.

(3B) An 'exempt generic communication' is a communication to which subsection (1) of section 21 of the Financial Services and Markets Act 2000 does not apply, as a result of an order under subsection (5) of that section, because it does not identify a person as providing an investment or as carrying on an activity to which the communication relates.

(4) An advertisement does not fall within subsection (1)(b) if it indicates that the advertiser is not willing to enter into a consumer hire agreement.

(5) The Secretary of State may by order provide that this Part shall not apply to other advertisements of a description specified in the order.

44 Form and content of advertisements

(1) The Secretary of State shall make regulations as to the form and content of advertisements to which this Part applies, and the regulations shall contain such provisions as appear to him appropriate with a view to ensuring that, having regard to its subject-matter and the amount of detail included in it, an advertisement conveys a fair and reasonably comprehensive indication of the nature of the credit or hire facilities offered by the advertiser and of their true cost to persons using them.

(2) Regulations under subsection (1) may in particular –

    (a) require specified information to be included in the prescribed manner in advertisements, and other specified material to be excluded;

    (b) contain requirements to ensure that specified information is clearly brought to the attention of persons to whom advertisements are directed, and that one part of an advertisement is not given insufficient or excessive prominence compared with another.

45 Prohibition of advertisement where goods etc not sold for cash

If an advertisement to which this Part applies indicates that the advertiser is willing to provide credit under a restricted-use credit agreement relating to goods or services to be supplied by any person, but at the time when the advertisement is published that person is not holding himself out as prepared to sell the goods or provide the services (as the case may be) for cash, the advertiser commits an offence.

46 False or misleading advertisements

(1) If an advertisement to which this Part applies conveys information which in a material respect is false or misleading the advertiser commits an offence.

(2) Information stating or implying an intention on the advertiser's part which he has not got is false.

47 Advertising infringements

(1) Where an advertiser commits an offence against regulations made under section 44 or against section 45 or 46, or would be taken to commit such an offence but for the defence provided by section 168, a like offence is committed by –

(a) the publisher of the advertisement, and

(b) any person who, in the course of a business carried on by him, devised the advertisement, or a part of it relevant to the first-mentioned offence, and

(c) where the advertiser did not procure the publication of the advertisement, the person who did procure it.

(2) In proceedings for an offence under subsection (1)(a) it is a defence for the person charged to prove that –

(a) the advertisement was published in the course of a business carried on by him, and

(b) he received the advertisement in the course of that business, and did not know and had no reason to suspect that its publication would be an offence under this Part.

Canvassing etc

48 Definition of canvassing off trade premises (regulated agreements)

(1) An individual (the 'canvasser') canvasses a regulated agreement off trade premises if he solicits the entry (as debtor or hirer) of another individual (the 'consumer') into the agreement by making oral representations to the consumer, or any other individual, during a visit by the canvasser to any place (not excluded by subsection (2)) where the consumer, or that other individual, as the case may be, is, being a visit –

(a) carried out for the purpose of making such oral representations to individuals who are at that place, but

(b) not carried out in response to a request made on a previous occasion.

(2) A place is excluded from subsection (1) if it is a place where a business is carried on (whether on a permanent or temporary basis) by –

(a) the creditor or owner, or

(b) a supplier, or

(c) the canvasser, or the person whose employee or agent the canvasser is, or

(d) the consumer.

49 Prohibition of canvassing debtor-creditor agreements off trade premises

(1)   It is an offence to canvass debtor-creditor agreements off trade premises.

(2)   It is also an offence to solicit the entry of an individual (as debtor) into a debtor-creditor agreement during a visit carried out in response to a request made on a previous occasion, where –

  (a)   the request was not in writing signed by or on behalf of the person making it, and

  (b)   if no request for the visit had been made, the soliciting would have constituted the canvassing of a debtor-creditor agreement off trade premises.

(3)   Subsections (1) and (2) do not apply to any soliciting for an agreement enabling the debtor to overdraw on a current account of any description kept with the creditor, where –

  (a)   the OFT has determined that current accounts of that description kept with the creditor are excluded from subsections (1) and (2), and

  (b)   the debtor already keeps an account with the creditor (whether a current account or not).

(4)   A determination under subsection (3)(a) –

  (a)   may be made subject to such conditions as the OFT thinks fit, and

  (b)   shall be made only where the OFT is of opinion that it is not against the interests of debtors.

(5)   If soliciting is done in breach of a condition imposed under subsection (4)(a), the determination under subsection (3)(a) does not apply to it.

50 Circulars to minors

(1)   A person commits an offence who, with a view to financial gain, sends to a minor any document inviting him to –

  (a)   borrow money, or

  (b)   obtain goods on credit or hire, or

  (c)   obtain services on credit, or

  (d)   apply for information or advice on borrowing money or otherwise obtaining credit, or hiring goods.

(2)   In proceedings under subsection (1) in respect of the sending of a document to a minor, it is a defence for the person charged to prove that he did not know, and had no reasonable cause to suspect, that he was a minor.

(3)   Where a document is received by a minor at any school or educational establishment for minors, a person sending it to him at that establishment knowing or suspecting it to be such an establishment shall be taken to have reasonable cause to suspect that he is a minor.

51 Prohibition of unsolicited credit-tokens

(1)   It is an offence to give a person a credit-token if he has not asked for it.

(2)   To comply with subsection (1) a request must be contained in a document signed by the person making the request, unless the credit-token agreement is a small debtor-creditor-supplier agreement.

(3)   Subsection (1) does not apply to the giving of a credit-token to a person –

  (a)   for use under a credit-token agreement already made, or

  (b)   in renewal or replacement of a credit-token previously accepted by him under a credit-token agreement which continues in force, whether or not varied.

Miscellaneous

52 Quotations

(1) Regulations may be made –

    (a) as to the form and content of any document (a 'quotation') by which a person who carries on a consumer credit business or consumer hire business, or a business in the course of which he provides credit to individuals secured on land, gives prospective customers information about the terms on which he is prepared to do business;

    (b) requiring a person carrying on such a business to provide quotations to such persons and in such circumstances as are prescribed.

(2) Regulations under subsection (1)(a) may in particular contain provisions relating to quotations such as are set out in relation to advertisements in section 44.

(3) In this section, 'quotation' does not include –

    (a) any document which is a communication of an invitation or inducement to engage in investment activity within the meaning of section 21 of the Financial Services and Markets Act 2000; or

    (b) any document (other than one falling within paragraph (a)) provided by an authorised person (within the meaning of that Act) in connection with an agreement which would or might be an exempt agreement as a result of section 16(6C).

53 Duty to display information

Regulations may require a person who carries on a consumer credit business or consumer hire business, or a business in the course of which he provides credit to individuals secured on land (other than credit provided under an agreement which is an exempt agreement as a result of section 16(6C)), to display in the prescribed manner, at any premises where the business is carried on to which the public have access, prescribed information about the business.

54 Conduct of business regulations

Without prejudice to the generality of section 26, regulations under that section may include provisions further regulating the seeking of business by a person to whom the regulations apply who carries on a consumer credit business or a consumer hire business.

PART V   ENTRY INTO CREDIT OR HIRE AGREEMENTS

Preliminary matters

55 Disclosure of information

(1) Regulations may require specified information to be disclosed in the prescribed manner to the debtor or hirer before a regulated agreement is made.

(2) A regulated agreement is not properly executed unless regulations under subsection (1) were complied with before the making of the agreement.

56 Antecedent negotiations

(1) In this Act 'antecedent negotiations' means any negotiations with the debtor or hirer –

    (a) conducted by the creditor or owner in relation to the making of any regulated agreement, or

    (b) conducted by a credit-broker in relation to goods sold or proposed to be sold by the credit-broker to the creditor before forming the subject-matter of a debtor-creditor-supplier agreement within section 12(a), or

(c) conducted by the supplier in relation to a transaction financed or proposed to be financed by a debtor-creditor-supplier agreement within section 12(b) or (c),

and 'negotiator' means the person by whom negotiations are so conducted with the debtor or hirer.

(2) Negotiations with the debtor in a case falling within subsection (1)(b) or (c) shall be deemed to be conducted by the negotiator in the capacity of agent of the creditor as well as in his actual capacity.

(3) An agreement is void if, and to the extent that, it purports in relation to an actual or prospective regulated agreement –

(a) to provide that a person acting as, or on behalf of, a negotiator is to be treated as the agent of the debtor or hirer, or

(b) to relieve a person from liability for acts or omissions of any person acting as, or on behalf of, a negotiator.

(4) For the purposes of this Act, antecedent negotiations shall be taken to begin when the negotiator and the debtor or hirer first enter into communication (including communication by advertisement), and to include any representations made by the negotiator to the debtor or hirer and any other dealings between them.

57 Withdrawal from prospective agreement

(1) The withdrawal of a party from a prospective regulated agreement shall operate to apply this Part to the agreement, any linked transaction and any other thing done in anticipation of the making of the agreement as it would apply if the agreement were made and then cancelled under section 69.

(2) The giving to a party of a written or oral notice which, however expressed, indicates the intention of the other party to withdraw from a prospective regulated agreement operates as a withdrawal from it.

(3) Each of the following shall be deemed to be the agent of the creditor or owner for the purpose of receiving a notice under subsection (2) –

(a) a credit-broker or supplier who is the negotiator in antecedent negotiations, and

(b) any person who, in the course of a business carried on by him, acts on behalf of the debtor or hirer in any negotiations for the agreement.

(4) Where the agreement, if made, would not be a cancellable agreement, subsection (1) shall nevertheless apply as if the contrary were the case.

58 Opportunity for withdrawal from prospective land mortgage

(1) Before sending to the debtor or hirer, for his signature, an unexecuted agreement in a case where the prospective regulated agreement is to be secured on land (the 'mortgaged land'), the creditor or owner shall give the debtor or hirer a copy of the unexecuted agreement which contains a notice in the prescribed form indicating the right of the debtor or hirer to withdraw from the prospective agreement, and how and when the right is exercisable, together with a copy of any other document referred to in the unexecuted agreement.

(2) Subsection (1) does not apply to –

(a) a restricted-use credit agreement to finance the purchase of the mortgaged land, or

(b) an agreement for a bridging loan in connection with the purchase of the mortgaged land or other land.

59 Agreement to enter future agreement void

(1) An agreement is void if, and to the extent that, it purports to bind a person to enter as debtor or hirer into a prospective regulated agreement.

(2) Regulations may exclude from the operation of subsection (1) agreements such as are described in the regulations.

Making the agreement

60 Form and content of agreements

(1) The Secretary of State shall make regulations as to the form and content of documents embodying regulated agreements, and the regulations shall contain such provisions as appear to him appropriate with a view to ensuring that the debtor or hirer is made aware of –

   (a) the rights and duties conferred or imposed on him by the agreement,
   (b) the amount and rate of the total charge for credit (in the case of a consumer credit agreement),
   (c) the protection and remedies available to him under this Act, and
   (d) any other matters which, in the opinion of the Secretary of State, it is desirable for him to know about in connection with the agreement.

(2) Regulations under subsection (1) may in particular –

   (a) require specified information to be included in the prescribed manner in documents, and other specified material to be excluded;
   (b) contain requirements to ensure that specified information is clearly brought to the attention of the debtor or hirer, and that one part of a document is not given insufficient or excessive prominence compared with another.

(3) If, on an application made to the OFT by a person carrying on a consumer credit business or a consumer hire business, it appears to the OFT impracticable for the applicant to comply with any requirement of regulations under subsection (1) in a particular case, it may, by notice to the applicant, direct that the requirement be waived or varied in relation to such agreements, and subject to such conditions (if any), as it may specify, and this Act and the regulations shall have effect accordingly.

(4) The OFT shall give a notice under subsection (3) only if it is satisfied that to do so would not prejudice the interests of debtors or hirers.

61 Signing of agreement

(1) A regulated agreement is not properly executed unless –

   (a) a document in the prescribed form itself containing all the prescribed terms and conforming to regulations under section 60(1) is signed in the prescribed manner both by the debtor or hirer and by or on behalf of the creditor or owner, and
   (b) the document embodies all the terms of the agreement, other than implied terms, and
   (c) the document is, when presented or sent to the debtor or hirer for signature, in such a state that all its terms are readily legible.

(2) In addition, where the agreement is one to which section 58(1) applies, it is not properly executed unless –

   (a) the requirements of section 58(1) were complied with, and
   (b) the unexecuted agreement was sent, for his signature, to the debtor or hirer by an appropriate method not less than seven days after a copy of it was given to him under section 58(1), and
   (c) during the consideration period, the creditor or owner refrained from approaching the debtor or hirer (whether in person, by telephone or letter, or in any other way) except in response to a specific request made by the debtor or hirer after the beginning of the consideration period, and
   (d) no notice of withdrawal by the debtor or hirer was received by the creditor or owner before the sending of the unexecuted agreement.

(3) In subsection (2)(c), 'the consideration period' means the period beginning with the giving of the copy under section 58(1) and ending –

(a) at the expiry of seven days after the day on which the unexecuted agreement is sent, for his signature, to the debtor or hirer, or

(b) on its return by the debtor or hirer after signature by him,

whichever first occurs.

(4) Where the debtor or hirer is a partnership or an unincorporated body of persons, subsection (1)(a) shall apply with the substitution for 'by the debtor or hirer' of 'by or on behalf of the debtor or hirer'.

62 Duty to supply copy of unexecuted agreement

(1) If the unexecuted agreement is presented personally to the debtor or hirer for his signature, but on the occasion when he signs it the document does not become an executed agreement, a copy of it, and of any other document referred to in it, must be there and then delivered to him.

(2) If the unexecuted agreement is sent to the debtor or hirer for his signature, a copy of it, and of any other document referred to in it, must be sent to him at the same time.

(3) A regulated agreement is not properly executed if the requirements of this section are not observed.

63 Duty to supply copy of executed agreement

(1) If the unexecuted agreement is presented personally to the debtor or hirer for his signature, and on the occasion when he signs it the document becomes an executed agreement, a copy of the executed agreement, and of any other document referred to in it, must be there and then delivered to him.

(2) A copy of the executed agreement, and of any other document referred to in it, must be given to the debtor or hirer within the seven days following the making of the agreement unless –

(a) subsection (1) applies, or

(b) the unexecuted agreement was sent to the debtor or hirer for his signature and, on the occasion of his signing it, the document became an executed agreement.

(3) In the case of a cancellable agreement, a copy under subsection (2) must be sent by an appropriate method.

(4) In the case of a credit-token agreement, a copy under subsection (2) need not be given within the seven days following the making of the agreement if it is given before or at the time when the credit-token is given to the debtor.

(5) A regulated agreement is not properly executed if the requirements of this section are not observed.

64 Duty to give notice of cancellation rights

(1) In the case of a cancellable agreement, a notice in the prescribed form indicating the right of the debtor or hirer to cancel the agreement, how and when that right is exercisable, and the name and address of a person to whom notice of cancellation may be given, –

(a) must be included in every copy given to the debtor or hirer under section 62 or 63, and

(b) except where section 63(2) applied, must also be sent by an appropriate method to the debtor or hirer within the seven days following the making of the agreement.

(2) In the case of a credit-token agreement, a notice under subsection (1)(b) need not be sent by an appropriate method within the seven days following the making of the agreement if either –

(a) it is sent by an appropriate method to the debtor or hirer before the credit-token is given to him, or

(b) it is sent by an appropriate method to him together with the credit-token.

(3) Regulations may provide that except where section 63(2) applied a notice sent under subsection (1)(b) shall be accompanied by a further copy of the executed agreement, and of any other document referred to in it.

(4) Regulations may provide that subsection (1)(b) is not to apply in the case of agreements such as are described in the regulations, being agreements made by a particular person, if –

(a) on an application by that person to the OFT, the OFT has determined that, having regard to –

(i) the manner in which antecedent negotiations for agreements with the applicant of that description are conducted, and

(ii) the information provided to debtors or hirers before such agreements are made,

the requirement imposed by subsection (1)(b) can be dispensed with without prejudicing the interests of debtors or hirers; and

(b) any conditions imposed by the OFT in making the determination are complied with.

(5) A cancellable agreement is not properly executed if the requirements of this section are not observed.

65 Consequences of improper execution

(1) An improperly-executed regulated agreement is enforceable against the debtor or hirer on an order of the court only.

(2) A retaking of goods or land to which a regulated agreement relates is an enforcement of the agreement.

66 Acceptance of credit-tokens

(1) The debtor shall not be liable under a credit-token agreement for use made of the credit-token by any person unless the debtor had previously accepted the credit-token, or the use constituted an acceptance of it by him.

(2) The debtor accepts a credit-token when –

(a) it is signed, or

(b) a receipt for it is signed, or

(c) it is first used,

either by the debtor himself or by a person who, pursuant to the agreement, is authorised by him to use it.

Cancellation of certain agreements within cooling-off period

67 Cancellable agreements

A regulated agreement may be cancelled by the debtor or hirer in accordance with this Part if the antecedent negotiations included oral representations made when in the presence of the debtor or hirer by an individual acting as, or on behalf of, the negotiator, unless –

(a) the agreement is secured on land, or is a restricted-use credit agreement to finance the purchase of land or is an agreement for a bridging loan in connection with the purchase of land, or

(b) the unexecuted agreement is signed by the debtor or hirer at premises at which any of the following is carrying on any business (whether on a permanent or temporary basis) –

(i) the creditor or owner;

     (ii)   any party to a linked transaction (other than the debtor or hirer or a relative of his);

     (iii)   the negotiator in any antecedent negotiations.

68 Cooling-off period

The debtor or hirer may serve notice of cancellation of a cancellable agreement between his signing of the unexecuted agreement and –

    (a)   the end of the fifth day following the day on which he received a copy under section 63(2) or a notice under section 64(1)(b), or

    (b)   if (by virtue of regulations made under section 64(4)) section 64(1)(b) does not apply, the end of the fourteenth day following the day on which he signed the unexecuted agreement.

69 Notice of cancellation

(1)   If within the period specified in section 68 the debtor or hirer under a cancellable agreement serves on –

    (a)   the creditor or owner, or

    (b)   the person specified in the notice under section 64(1), or

    (c)   a person who (whether by virtue of subsection (6) or otherwise) is the agent of the creditor or owner,

    a notice (a 'notice of cancellation') which, however expressed and whether or not conforming to the notice given under section 64(1), indicates the intention of the debtor or hirer to withdraw from the agreement, the notice shall operate –

     (i)   to cancel the agreement, and any linked transaction, and

     (ii)   to withdraw any offer by the debtor or hirer, or his relative, to enter into a linked transaction.

(2)   In the case of a debtor-creditor-supplier agreement for restricted-use credit financing –

    (a)   the doing of work or supply of goods to meet an emergency, or

    (b)   the supply of goods which, before service of the notice of cancellation, had by the act of the debtor or his relative become incorporated in any land or thing not comprised in the agreement or any linked transaction,

    subsection (1) shall apply with the substitution of the following for paragraph (i) –

     '(i)   to cancel only such provisions of the agreement and any linked transaction as –

       (aa)   relate to the provision of credit, or

       (bb)   require the debtor to pay an item in the total charge for credit, or

       (cc)   subject the debtor to any obligation other than to pay for the doing of the said work, or the supply of the said goods'.

(3)   Except so far as is otherwise provided, references in this Act to the cancellation of an agreement or transaction do not include a case within subsection (2).

(4)   Except as otherwise provided by or under this Act, an agreement or transaction cancelled under subsection (1) shall be treated as if it had never been entered into.

(5)   Regulations may exclude linked transactions of the prescribed description from subsection (1)(i) or (ii).

(6)   Each of the following shall be deemed to be the agent of the creditor or owner for the purpose of receiving a notice of cancellation –

    (a)   a credit-broker or supplier who is the negotiator in antecedent negotiations, and

    (b)   any person who, in the course of a business carried on by him, acts on behalf of the debtor or hirer in any negotiations for the agreement.

(7) Whether or not it is actually received by him, a notice of cancellation sent to a person shall be deemed to be served on him –

    (a) in the case of a notice sent by post, at the time of posting, and

    (b) in the case of a notice transmitted in the form of an electronic communication in accordance with section 176A(1), at the time of the transmission.

70 Cancellation: recovery of money paid by debtor or hirer

(1) On the cancellation of a regulated agreement, and of any linked transaction, –

    (a) any sum paid by the debtor or hirer, or his relative, under or in contemplation of the agreement or transaction, including any item in the total charge for credit, shall become repayable, and

    (b) any sum, including any item in the total charge for credit, which but for the cancellation is, or would or might become, payable by the debtor or hirer, or his relative, under the agreement or transaction shall cease to be, or shall not become, so payable, and

    (c) in the case of a debtor-creditor-supplier agreement falling within section 12(b) any sum paid on the debtor's behalf by the creditor to the supplier shall become repayable to the creditor.

(2) If, under the terms of a cancelled agreement or transaction, the debtor or hirer, or his relative, is in possession of any goods, he shall have a lien on them for any sum repayable to him under subsection (1) in respect of that agreement or transaction, or any other linked transaction.

(3) A sum repayable under subsection (1) is repayable by the person to whom it was originally paid, but in the case of a debtor-creditor-supplier agreement falling within section 12(b) the creditor and the supplier shall be under a joint and several liability to repay sums paid by the debtor, or his relative, under the agreement or under a linked transaction falling within section 19(1)(b) and accordingly, in such a case, the creditor shall be entitled, in accordance with rules of court, to have the supplier made a party to any proceedings brought against the creditor to recover any such sums.

(4) Subject to any agreement between them, the creditor shall be entitled to be indemnified by the supplier for loss suffered by the creditor in satisfying his liability under subsection (3), including costs reasonably incurred by him in defending proceedings instituted by the debtor.

(5) Subsection (1) does not apply to any sum which, if not paid by a debtor, would be payable by virtue of section 71, and applies to a sum paid or payable by a debtor for the issue of a credit-token only where the credit-token has been returned to the creditor or surrendered to a supplier.

(6) If the total charge for credit includes an item in respect of a fee or commission charged by a credit-broker, the amount repayable under subsection (1) in respect of that item shall be the excess over £5 of the fee or commission.

(7) If the total charge for credit includes any sum payable or paid by the debtor to a credit-broker otherwise than in respect of a fee or commission charged by him, that sum shall for the purposes of subsection (6) be treated as if it were such a fee or commission.

(8) So far only as is necessary to give effect to section 69(2), this section applies to an agreement or transaction within that subsection as it applies to a cancelled agreement or transaction.

71 Cancellation: repayment of credit

(1) Notwithstanding the cancellation of a regulated consumer credit agreement, other than a debtor-creditor-supplier agreement for restricted-use credit, the agreement shall continue in force so far as it relates to repayment of credit and payment of interest.

(2) If, following the cancellation of a regulated consumer credit agreement, the debtor repays the whole or a portion of a credit –

(a) before the expiry of one month following service of the notice of cancellation, or

(b) in the case of a credit repayable by instalments, before the date on which the first instalment is due,

no interest shall be payable on the amount repaid.

(3) If the whole of a credit repayable by instalments is not repaid on or before the date specified in subsection (2) (b), the debtor shall not be liable to repay any of the credit except on receipt of a request in writing in the prescribed form, signed by or on behalf of the creditor, stating the amounts of the remaining instalments (recalculated by the creditor as nearly as may be in accordance with the agreement and without extending the repayment period), but excluding any sum other than principal and interest.

(4) Repayment of a credit, or payment of interest, under a cancelled agreement shall be treated as duly made if it is made to any person on whom, under section 69, a notice of cancellation could have been served, other than a person referred to in section 69(6)(b).

72 Cancellation: return of goods

(1) This section applies where any agreement or transaction relating to goods, being –

(a) a restricted-use debtor-creditor-supplier agreement, a consumer hire agreement, or a linked transaction to which the debtor or hirer under any regulated agreement is a party, or

(b) a linked transaction to which a relative of the debtor or hirer under any regulated agreement is a party,

is cancelled after the debtor or hirer (in a case within paragraph (a)) or the relative (in a case within paragraph (b)) has acquired possession of the goods by virtue of the agreement or transaction.

(2) In this section –

(a) 'the possessor' means the person who has acquired possession of the goods as mentioned in subsection (1),

(b) 'the other party' means the person from whom the possessor acquired possession, and

(c) 'the pre-cancellation period' means the period beginning when the possessor acquired possession and ending with the cancellation.

(3) The possessor shall be treated as having been under a duty throughout the pre-cancellation period –

(a) to retain possession of the goods, and

(b) to take reasonable care of them.

(4) On the cancellation, the possessor shall be under a duty, subject to any lien, to restore the goods to the other party in accordance with this section, and meanwhile to retain possession of the goods and take reasonable care of them.

(5) The possessor shall not be under any duty to deliver the goods except at his own premises and in pursuance of a request in writing signed by or on behalf of the other party and served on the possessor either before, or at the time when, the goods are collected from those premises.

(6) If the possessor –

(a) delivers the goods (whether at his own premises or elsewhere) to any person on whom, under section 69, a notice of cancellation could have been served (other than a person referred to in section 69(6)(b)), or

(b) sends the goods at his own expense to such a person,

he shall be discharged from any duty to retain the goods or deliver them to any person.

(7)   Where the possessor delivers the goods as mentioned in subsection (6)(a) his obligation to take care of the goods shall cease; and if he sends the goods as mentioned in subsection (6)(b), he shall be under a duty to take reasonable care to see that they are received by the other party and not damaged in transit, but in other respects his duty to take care of the goods shall cease.

(8)   Where, at any time during the period of 21 days following the cancellation, the possessor receives such a request as is mentioned in subsection (5), and unreasonably refuses or unreasonably fails to comply with it, his duty to take reasonable care of the goods shall continue until he delivers or sends the goods as mentioned in subsection (6), but if within that period he does not receive such a request his duty to take reasonable care of the goods shall cease at the end of that period.

(9)   The preceding provisions of this section do not apply to –

(a)   perishable goods, or

(b)   goods which by their nature are consumed by use and which, before the cancellation, were so consumed, or

(c)   goods supplied to meet an emergency, or

(d)   goods which, before the cancellation, had become incorporated in any land or thing not comprised in the cancelled agreement or a linked transaction.

(10) Where the address of the possessor is specified in the executed agreement, references in this section to his own premises are to that address and no other.

(11) Breach of a duty imposed by this section is actionable as a breach of statutory duty.

73 Cancellation: goods given in part-exchange

(1)   This section applies on the cancellation of a regulated agreement where, in antecedent negotiations, the negotiator agreed to take goods in part-exchange (the 'part-exchange goods') and those goods have been delivered to him.

(2)   Unless, before the end of the period of ten days beginning with the date of cancellation, the part-exchange goods are returned to the debtor or hirer in a condition substantially as good as when they were delivered to the negotiator, the debtor or hirer shall be entitled to recover from the negotiator a sum equal to the part-exchange allowance (as defined in subsection (7)(b)).

(3)   In the case of a debtor-creditor-supplier agreement within section 12(b), the negotiator and the creditor shall be under a joint and several liability to pay to the debtor a sum recoverable under subsection (2).

(4)   Subject to any agreement between them, the creditor shall be entitled to be indemnified by the negotiator for loss suffered by the creditor in satisfying his liability under subsection (3), including costs reasonably incurred by him in defending proceedings instituted by the debtor.

(5)   During the period of ten days beginning with the date of cancellation, the debtor or hirer, if he is in possession of goods to which the cancelled agreement relates, shall have a lien on them for –

(a)   delivery of the part-exchange goods, in a condition substantially as good as when they were delivered to the negotiator, or

(b)   a sum equal to the part-exchange allowance;

and if the lien continues to the end of that period it shall thereafter subsist only as a lien for a sum equal to the part-exchange allowance.

(6)   Where the debtor or hirer recovers from the negotiator or creditor, or both of them jointly, a sum equal to the part-exchange allowance, then, if the title of the debtor or hirer to the part-exchange goods has not vested in the negotiator, it shall so vest on the recovery of that sum.

(7)   For the purposes of this section –

(a)   the negotiator shall be treated as having agreed to take goods in part-exchange if, in pursuance of the antecedent negotiations, he either purchased or agreed to purchase those goods or accepted or agreed to accept them as part of the consideration for the cancelled agreement, and

(b) the part-exchange allowance shall be the sum agreed as such in the antecedent negotiations or, if no such agreement was arrived at, such sum as it would have been reasonable to allow in respect of the part-exchange goods if no notice of cancellation had been served.

(8) In an action brought against the creditor for a sum recoverable under subsection (2), he shall be entitled, in accordance with rules of court, to have the negotiator made a party to the proceedings.

Exclusion of certain agreements from Part V

74 Exclusion of certain agreements from Part V

(1) This Part (except section 56) does not apply to –

(a) a non-commercial agreement, or

(b) a debtor-creditor agreement enabling the debtor to overdraw on a current account, or

(c) a debtor-creditor agreement to finance the making of such payments arising on, or connected with, the death of a person as may be prescribed.

(2) This Part (except sections 55 and 56) does not apply to a small debtor-creditor-supplier agreement for restricted-use credit.

(2A) In the case of an agreement to which the Consumer Protection (Cancellation of Contracts Concluded away from Business Premises) Regulations 1987 apply the reference in subsection (2) to a small agreement shall be construed as if in section 17(1)(a) and (b) '£35' were substituted for '£50'.

(3) Subsection (1)(b) or (c) applies only where the OFT so determines, and such a determination –

(a) may be made subject to such conditions as the OFT thinks fit, and

(b) shall be made only if the OFT is of opinion that it is not against the interests of debtors.

(3A) Notwithstanding anything in subsection (3)(b) above, in relation to a debtor-creditor agreement under which the creditor is the Bank of England or a bank within the meaning of the Bankers' Books Evidence Act 1879, the OFT shall make a determination that subsection (1)(b) above applies unless it considers that it would be against the public interest to do so.

(4) If any term of an agreement falling within subsection (1)(c) or (2) is expressed in writing, regulations under section 60(1) shall apply to that term (subject to section 60(3)) as if the agreement was a regulated agreement not falling within subsection (1)(c) or (2).

PART VI   MATTERS ARISING DURING CURRENCY OF CREDIT OR HIRE AGREEMENTS

75 Liability of creditor for breaches by supplier

(1) If the debtor under a debtor-creditor-supplier agreement falling within section 12(b) or (c) has, in relation to a transaction financed by the agreement, any claim against the supplier in respect of a misrepresentation or breach of contract, he shall have a like claim against the creditor, who, with the supplier, shall accordingly be jointly and severally liable to the debtor.

(2) Subject to any agreement between them, the creditor shall be entitled to be indemnified by the supplier for loss suffered by the creditor in satisfying his liability under subsection (1), including costs reasonably incurred by him in defending proceedings instituted by the debtor.

(3) Subsection (1) does not apply to a claim –

    (a) under a non-commercial agreement, or

    (b) so far as the claim relates to any single item to which the supplier has attached a cash price not exceeding £100 or more than £30,000.

(4) This section applies notwithstanding that the debtor, in entering into the transaction, exceeded the credit limit or otherwise contravened any term of the agreement.

(5) In an action brought against the creditor under subsection (1) he shall be entitled, in accordance with rules of court, to have the supplier made a party to the proceedings.

76 Duty to give notice before taking certain action

(1) The creditor or owner is not entitled to enforce a term of a regulated agreement by –

    (a) demanding earlier payment of any sum, or

    (b) recovering possession of any goods or land, or

    (c) treating any right conferred on the debtor or hirer by the agreement as terminated, restricted or deferred,

except by or after giving the debtor or hirer not less than seven days' notice of intention to do so.

(2) Subsection (1) applies only where –

    (a) a period for the duration of the agreement is specified in the agreement, and

    (b) that period has not ended when the creditor or owner does an act mentioned in subsection (1),

but so applies notwithstanding that, under the agreement, any party is entitled to terminate it before the end of the period so specified.

(3) A notice under subsection (1) is ineffective if not in the prescribed form.

(4) Subsection (1) does not prevent a creditor from treating the right to draw on any credit as restricted or deferred and taking such steps as may be necessary to make the restriction or deferment effective.

(5) Regulations may provide that subsection (1) is not to apply to agreements described by the regulations.

(6) Subsection (1) does not apply to a right of enforcement arising by reason of any breach by the debtor or hirer of the regulated agreement.

77 Duty to give information to debtor under fixed-sum credit agreement

(1) The creditor under a regulated agreement for fixed-sum credit, within the prescribed period after receiving a request in writing to that effect from the debtor and payment of a fee of £1, shall give the debtor a copy of the executed agreement (if any) and of any other document referred to in it, together with a statement signed by or on behalf of the creditor showing, according to the information to which it is practicable for him to refer, –

    (a) the total sum paid under the agreement by the debtor;

    (b) the total sum which has become payable under the agreement by the debtor but remains unpaid, and the various amounts comprised in that total sum, with the date when each became due; and

    (c) the total sum which is to become payable under the agreement by the debtor, and the various amounts comprised in that total sum, with the date, or mode of determining the date, when each becomes due.

(2) If the creditor possesses insufficient information to enable him to ascertain the amounts and dates mentioned in subsection (1)(c), he shall be taken to comply with

that paragraph if his statement under subsection (1) gives the basis on which, under the regulated agreement, they would fall to be ascertained.

(3) Subsection (1) does not apply to –

(a) an agreement under which no sum is, or will or may become, payable by the debtor, or

(b) a request made less than one month after a previous request under that subsection relating to the same agreement was complied with.

(4) If the creditor under an agreement fails to comply with subsection (1) –

(a) he is not entitled, while the default continues, to enforce the agreement; and

(b) if the default continues for one month he commits an offence.

(5) This section does not apply to a non-commercial agreement.

77A Statements to be provided in relation to fixed-sum credit agreements

(1) The creditor under a regulated agreement for fixed-sum credit –

(a) shall, within the period of one year beginning with the day after the day on which the agreement is made, give the debtor a statement under this section; and

(b) after the giving of that statement, shall give the debtor further statements under this section at intervals of not more than one year.

(2) Regulations may make provision about the form and content of statements under this section.

(3) The debtor shall have no liability to pay any sum in connection with the preparation or the giving to him of a statement under this section.

(4) The creditor is not required to give the debtor any statement under this section once the following conditions are satisfied –

(a) that there is no sum payable under the agreement by the debtor; and

(b) that there is no sum which will or may become so payable.

(5) Subsection (6) applies if at a time before the conditions mentioned in subsection (4) are satisfied the creditor fails to give the debtor –

(a) a statement under this section within the period mentioned in subsection (1)(a); or

(b) such a statement within the period of one year beginning with the day after the day on which such a statement was last given to him.

(6) Where this subsection applies in relation to a failure to give a statement under this section to the debtor –

(a) the creditor shall not be entitled to enforce the agreement during the period of non-compliance;

(b) the debtor shall have no liability to pay any sum of interest to the extent calculated by reference to the period of non-compliance or to any part of it; and

(c) the debtor shall have no liability to pay any default sum which (apart from this paragraph) –

(i) would have become payable during the period of non-compliance; or

(ii) would have become payable after the end of that period in connection with a breach of the agreement which occurs during that period (whether or not the breach continues after the end of that period).

(7) In this section 'the period of non-compliance' means, in relation to a failure to give a statement under this section to the debtor, the period which –

(a) begins immediately after the end of the period mentioned in paragraph (a) or (as the case may be) paragraph (b) of subsection (5); and

(b) ends at the end of the day on which the statement is given to the debtor or on which the conditions mentioned in subsection (4) are satisfied, whichever is earlier.

(8) This section does not apply in relation to a non-commercial agreement or to a small agreement.

78 Duty to give information to debtor under running-account credit agreement

(1) The creditor under a regulated agreement for running-account credit, within the prescribed period after receiving a request in writing to that effect from the debtor and payment of a fee of £1, shall give the debtor a copy of the executed agreement (if any) and of any other document referred to in it, together with a statement signed by or on behalf of the creditor showing, according to the information to which it is practicable for him to refer, –

    (a) the state of the account, and

    (b) the amount, if any, currently payable under the agreement by the debtor to the creditor, and

    (c) the amounts and due dates of any payments which, if the debtor does not draw further on the account, will later become payable under the agreement by the debtor to the creditor.

(2) If the creditor possesses insufficient information to enable him to ascertain the amounts and dates mentioned in subsection (1)(c), he shall be taken to comply with that paragraph if his statement under subsection (1) gives the basis on which, under the regulated agreement, they would fall to be ascertained.

(3) Subsection (1) does not apply to –

    (a) an agreement under which no sum is, or will or may become, payable by the debtor, or

    (b) a request made less than one month after a previous request under that subsection relating to the same agreement was complied with.

(4) Where running-account credit is provided under a regulated agreement, the creditor shall give the debtor statements in the prescribed form, and with the prescribed contents –

    (a) showing according to the information to which it is practicable for him to refer, the state of the account at regular intervals of not more than twelve months, and

    (b) where the agreement provides, in relation to specified periods, for the making of payments by the debtor, or the charging against him of interest or any other sum, showing according to the information to which it is practicable for him to refer the state of the account at the end of each of those periods during which there is any movement in the account.

(4A) Regulations may require a statement under subsection (4) to contain also information in the prescribed terms about the consequences of the debtor –

    (a) failing to make payments as required by the agreement; or

    (b) only making payments of a prescribed description in prescribed circumstances.

(5) A statement under subsection (4) shall be given within the prescribed period after the end of the period to which the statement relates.

(6) If the creditor under an agreement fails to comply with subsection (1) –

    (a) he is not entitled, while the default continues, to enforce the agreement; and

    (b) if the default continues for one month he commits an offence.

(7) This section does not apply to a non-commercial agreement, and subsections (4) to (5) do not apply to a small agreement.

79 Duty to give hirer information

(1) The owner under a regulated consumer hire agreement, within the prescribed period after receiving a request in writing to that effect from the hirer and payment of a fee of £1, shall give to the hirer a copy of the executed agreement and of any other document referred to in it, together with a statement signed by or on behalf of the owner

showing, according to the information to which it is practicable for him to refer, the total sum which has become payable under the agreement by the hirer but remains unpaid and the various amounts comprised in that total sum, with the date when each became due.

(2) Subsection (1) does not apply to –

   (a) an agreement under which no sum is, or will or may become, payable by the hirer, or

   (b) a request made less than one month after a previous request under that subsection relating to the same agreement was complied with.

(3) If the owner under an agreement fails to comply with subsection (1) –

   (a) he is not entitled, while the default continues, to enforce the agreement; and

   (b) if the default continues for one month he commits an offence.

(4) This section does not apply to a non-commercial agreement.

80 Debtor or hirer to give information about goods

(1) Where a regulated agreement, other than a non-commercial agreement, requires the debtor or hirer to keep goods to which the agreement relates in his possession or control, he shall, within seven working days after he has received a request in writing to that effect from the creditor or owner, tell the creditor or owner where the goods are.

(2) If the debtor or hirer fails to comply with subsection (1), and the default continues for 14 days, he commits an offence.

81 Appropriation of payments

(1) Where a debtor or hirer is liable to make to the same person payments in respect of two or more regulated agreements, he shall be entitled, on making any payment in respect of the agreements which is not sufficient to discharge the total amount then due under all the agreements, to appropriate the sum so paid by him –

   (a) in or towards the satisfaction of the sum due under any one of the agreements, or

   (b) in or towards the satisfaction of the sums due under any two or more of the agreements in such proportions as he thinks fit.

(2) If the debtor or hirer fails to make any such appropriation where one or more of the agreements is –

   (a) a hire-purchase agreement or conditional sale agreement, or

   (b) a consumer hire agreement, or

   (c) an agreement in relation to which any security is provided,

the payment shall be appropriated towards the satisfaction of the sums due under the several agreements respectively in the proportions which those sums bear to one another.

82 Variation of agreements

(1) Where, under a power contained in a regulated agreement, the creditor or owner varies the agreement, the variation shall not take effect before notice of it is given to the debtor or hirer in the prescribed manner.

(2) Where an agreement (a 'modifying agreement') varies or supplements an earlier agreement, the modifying agreement shall for the purposes of this Act be treated as –

   (a) revoking the earlier agreement, and

   (b) containing provisions reproducing the combined effect of the two agreements,

and obligations outstanding in relation to the earlier agreement shall accordingly be treated as outstanding instead in relation to the modifying agreement.

(2A) Subsection (2) does not apply if the modifying agreement is an exempt agreement as a result of section 16(6C).

(3) If the earlier agreement is a regulated agreement but (apart from this subsection) the modifying agreement is not then, unless the modifying agreement is –

(a) for running account credit; or

(b) an exempt agreement as a result of section 16(6C),

it shall be treated as a regulated agreement.

(4) If the earlier agreement is a regulated agreement for running-account credit, and by the modifying agreement the creditor allows the credit limit to be exceeded but intends the excess to be merely temporary, Part V (except section 56) shall not apply to the modifying agreement.

(5) If –

(a) the earlier agreement is a cancellable agreement, and

(b) the modifying agreement is made within the period applicable under section 68 to the earlier agreement,

then, whether or not the modifying agreement would, apart from this subsection, be a cancellable agreement, it shall be treated as a cancellable agreement in respect of which a notice may be served under section 68 not later than the end of the period applicable under that section to the earlier agreement.

(5A) Subsection (5) does not apply where the modifying agreement is an exempt agreement as a result of section 16(6C).

(6) Except under subsection (5), a modifying agreement shall not be treated as a cancellable agreement.

(7) This section does not apply to a non-commercial agreement.

83 Liability for misuse of credit facilities

(1) The debtor under a regulated consumer credit agreement shall not be liable to the creditor for any loss arising from use of the credit facility by another person not acting, or to be treated as acting, as the debtor's agent.

(2) This section does not apply to a non-commercial agreement, or to any loss in so far as it arises from misuse of an instrument to which section 4 of the Cheques Act 1957 applies.

84 Misuse of credit-tokens

(1) Section 83 does not prevent the debtor under a credit-token agreement from being made liable to the extent of £50 (or the credit limit if lower) for loss to the creditor arising from use of the credit-token by other persons during a period beginning when the credit-token ceases to be in the possession of any authorised person and ending when the credit-token is once more in the possession of an authorised person.

(2) Section 83 does not prevent the debtor under a credit-token agreement from being made liable to any extent for loss to the creditor from use of the credit-token by a person who acquired possession of it with the debtor's consent.

(3) Subsections (1) and (2) shall not apply to any use of the credit-token after the creditor has been given oral or written notice that it is lost or stolen, or is for any other reason liable to misuse.

(3A) Subsections (1) and (2) shall not apply to any use, in connection with a distance contract (other than an excepted contract), of a card which is a credit-token.

(3B) In subsection (3A), 'distance contract' and 'excepted contract' have the meanings given in the Consumer Protection (Distance Selling) Regulations 2000.

(3C) Subsections (1) and (2) shall not apply to any use, in connection with a distance contract within the meaning of the Financial Services (Distance Marketing) Regulations 2004, of a card which is a credit-token.

(4) Subsections (1) and (2) shall not apply unless there are contained in the credit-token agreement in the prescribed manner particulars of the name, address and telephone

number of a person stated to be the person to whom notice is to be given under subsection (3).

(5) Notice under subsection (3) takes effect when received, but where it is given orally, and the agreement so requires, it shall be treated as not taking effect if not confirmed in writing within seven days.

(6) Any sum paid by the debtor for the issue of the credit-token, to the extent (if any) that it has not been previously offset by use made of the credit token, shall be treated as paid towards satisfaction of any liability under subsection (1) or (2).

(7) The debtor, the creditor, and any person authorised by the debtor to use the credit-token, shall be authorised persons for the purposes of subsection (1).

(8) Where two or more credit-tokens are given under one credit-token agreement, the preceding provisions of this section apply to each credit-token separately.

85 Duty on issue of new credit-tokens

(1) Whenever, in connection with a credit-token agreement, a credit-token (other than the first) is given by the creditor to the debtor, the creditor shall give the debtor a copy of the executed agreement (if any) and of any other document referred to in it.

(2) If the creditor fails to comply with this section –

(a) he is not entitled, while the default continues, to enforce the agreement; and

(b) if the default continues for one month he commits an offence.

(3) This section does not apply to a small agreement.

86 Death of debtor or hirer

(1) The creditor or owner under a regulated agreement is not entitled, by reason of the death of the debtor or hirer, to do an act specified in paragraphs (a) to (e) of section 87(1) if at the death the agreement is fully secured.

(2) If at the death of the debtor or hirer a regulated agreement is only partly secured or is unsecured, the creditor or owner is entitled, by reason of the death of the debtor or hirer, to do an act specified in paragraphs (a) to (e) of section 87(1) on an order of the court only.

(3) This section applies in relation to the termination of an agreement only where –

(a) a period for its duration is specified in the agreement, and

(b) that period has not ended when the creditor or owner purports to terminate the agreement,

but so applies notwithstanding that, under the agreement, any party is entitled to terminate it before the end of the period so specified.

(4) This section does not prevent the creditor from treating the right to draw on any credit as restricted or deferred, and taking such steps as may be necessary to make the restriction or deferment effective.

(5) This section does not affect the operation of any agreement providing for payment of sums –

(a) due under the regulated agreement, or

(b) becoming due under it on the death of the debtor or hirer,

out of the proceeds of a policy of assurance on his life.

(6) For the purposes of this section an act is done by reason of the death of the debtor or hirer if it is done under a power conferred by the agreement which is –

(a) exercisable on his death, or

(b) exercisable at will and exercised at any time after his death.

PART VII   DEFAULT AND TERMINATION

Information sheets

86A OFT to prepare information sheets on arrears and default

(1) The OFT shall prepare, and give general notice of, an arrears information sheet and a default information sheet.

(2) The arrears information sheet shall include information to help debtors and hirers who receive notices under section 86B or 86C.

(3) The default information sheet shall include information to help debtors and hirers who receive default notices.

(4) Regulations may make provision about the information to be included in an information sheet.

(5) An information sheet takes effect for the purposes of this Part at the end of the period of three months beginning with the day on which general notice of it is given.

(6) If the OFT revises an information sheet after general notice of it has been given, it shall give general notice of the information sheet as revised.

(7) A revised information sheet takes effect for the purposes of this Part at the end of the period of three months beginning with the day on which general notice of it is given.

Sums in arrears and default sums

86B Notice of sums in arrears under fixed-sum credit agreements etc.

(1) This section applies where at any time the following conditions are satisfied –

(a) that the debtor or hirer under an applicable agreement is required to have made at least two payments under the agreement before that time;

(b) that the total sum paid under the agreement by him is less than the total sum which he is required to have paid before that time;

(c) that the amount of the shortfall is no less than the sum of the last two payments which he is required to have made before that time;

(d) that the creditor or owner is not already under a duty to give him notices under this section in relation to the agreement; and

(e) if a judgment has been given in relation to the agreement before that time, that there is no sum still to be paid under the judgment by the debtor or hirer.

(2) The creditor or owner –

(a) shall, within the period of 14 days beginning with the day on which the conditions mentioned in subsection (1) are satisfied, give the debtor or hirer a notice under this section; and

(b) after the giving of that notice, shall give him further notices under this section at intervals of not more than six months.

(3) The duty of the creditor or owner to give the debtor or hirer notices under this section shall cease when either of the conditions mentioned in subsection (4) is satisfied; but if either of those conditions is satisfied before the notice required by subsection (2)(a) is given, the duty shall not cease until that notice is given.

(4) The conditions referred to in subsection (3) are –

(a) that the debtor or hirer ceases to be in arrears;

(b) that a judgment is given in relation to the agreement under which a sum is required to be paid by the debtor or hirer.

(5) For the purposes of subsection (4)(a) the debtor or hirer ceases to be in arrears when –

(a) no sum, which he has ever failed to pay under the agreement when required, is still owing;

    (b)   no default sum, which has ever become payable under the agreement in connection with his failure to pay any sum under the agreement when required, is still owing;

    (c)   no sum of interest, which has ever become payable under the agreement in connection with such a default sum, is still owing; and

    (d)   no other sum of interest, which has ever become payable under the agreement in connection with his failure to pay any sum under the agreement when required, is still owing.

(6)   A notice under this section shall include a copy of the current arrears information sheet under section 86A.

(7)   The debtor or hirer shall have no liability to pay any sum in connection with the preparation or the giving to him of a notice under this section.

(8)   Regulations may make provision about the form and content of notices under this section.

(9)   In the case of an applicable agreement under which the debtor or hirer must make all payments he is required to make at intervals of one week or less, this section shall have effect as if in subsection (1)(a) and (c) for 'two' there were substituted 'four'.

(10) If an agreement mentioned in subsection (9) was made before the beginning of the relevant period, only amounts resulting from failures by the debtor or hirer to make payments he is required to have made during that period shall be taken into account in determining any shortfall for the purposes of subsection (1)(c).

(11) In subsection (10) 'relevant period' means the period of 20 weeks ending with the day on which the debtor or hirer is required to have made the most recent payment under the agreement.

(12) In this section 'applicable agreement' means an agreement which –

    (a)   is a regulated agreement for fixed-sum credit or a regulated consumer hire agreement; and

    (b)   is neither a non-commercial agreement nor a small agreement.

86C Notice of sums in arrears under running-account credit agreements

(1)   This section applies where at any time the following conditions are satisfied –

    (a)   that the debtor under an applicable agreement is required to have made at least two payments under the agreement before that time;

    (b)   that the last two payments which he is required to have made before that time have not been made;

    (c)   that the creditor has not already been required to give a notice under this section in relation to either of those payments; and

    (d)   if a judgment has been given in relation to the agreement before that time, that there is no sum still to be paid under the judgment by the debtor.

(2)   The creditor shall, no later than the end of the period within which he is next required to give a statement under section 78(4) in relation to the agreement, give the debtor a notice under this section.

(3)   The notice shall include a copy of the current arrears information sheet under section 86A.

(4)   The notice may be incorporated in a statement or other notice which the creditor gives the debtor in relation to the agreement by virtue of another provision of this Act.

(5)   The debtor shall have no liability to pay any sum in connection with the preparation or the giving to him of the notice.

(6)   Regulations may make provision about the form and content of notices under this section.

(7)   In this section 'applicable agreement' means an agreement which –

    (a)   is a regulated agreement for running-account credit; and

    (b)   is neither a non-commercial agreement nor a small agreement.

86D Failure to give notice of sums in arrears

(1) This section applies where the creditor or owner under an agreement is under a duty to give the debtor or hirer notices under section 86B but fails to give him such a notice –

(a) within the period mentioned in subsection (2)(a) of that section; or
(b) within the period of six months beginning with the day after the day on which such a notice was last given to him.

(2) This section also applies where the creditor under an agreement is under a duty to give the debtor a notice under section 86C but fails to do so before the end of the period mentioned in subsection (2) of that section.

(3) The creditor or owner shall not be entitled to enforce the agreement during the period of non-compliance.

(4) The debtor or hirer shall have no liability to pay –

(a) any sum of interest to the extent calculated by reference to the period of non-compliance or to any part of it; or
(b) any default sum which (apart from this paragraph) –
    (i) would have become payable during the period of non-compliance; or
    (ii) would have become payable after the end of that period in connection with a breach of the agreement which occurs during that period (whether or not the breach continues after the end of that period).

(5) In this section 'the period of non-compliance' means, in relation to a failure to give a notice under section 86B or 86C to the debtor or hirer, the period which –

(a) begins immediately after the end of the period mentioned in (as the case may be) subsection (1)(a) or (b) or (2); and
(b) ends at the end of the day mentioned in subsection (6).

(6) That day is –

(a) in the case of a failure to give a notice under section 86B as mentioned in subsection (1)(a) of this section, the day on which the notice is given to the debtor or hirer;
(b) in the case of a failure to give a notice under that section as mentioned in subsection (1)(b) of this section, the earlier of the following –
    (i) the day on which the notice is given to the debtor or hirer;
    (ii) the day on which the condition mentioned in subsection (4)(a) of that section is satisfied;
(c) in the case of a failure to give a notice under section 86C, the day on which the notice is given to the debtor.

86E Notice of default sums

(1) This section applies where a default sum becomes payable under a regulated agreement by the debtor or hirer.

(2) The creditor or owner shall, within the prescribed period after the default sum becomes payable, give the debtor or hirer a notice under this section.

(3) The notice under this section may be incorporated in a statement or other notice which the creditor or owner gives the debtor or hirer in relation to the agreement by virtue of another provision of this Act.

(4) The debtor or hirer shall have no liability to pay interest in connection with the default sum to the extent that the interest is calculated by reference to a period occurring before the 29th day after the day on which the debtor or hirer is given the notice under this section.

(5) If the creditor or owner fails to give the debtor or hirer the notice under this section within the period mentioned in subsection (2), he shall not be entitled to enforce the agreement until the notice is given to the debtor or hirer.

(6) The debtor or hirer shall have no liability to pay any sum in connection with the preparation or the giving to him of the notice under this section.

(7) Regulations may –

    (a) provide that this section does not apply in relation to a default sum which is less than a prescribed amount;

    (b) make provision about the form and content of notices under this section.

(8) This section does not apply in relation to a non-commercial agreement or to a small agreement.

86F Interest on default sums

(1) This section applies where a default sum becomes payable under a regulated agreement by the debtor or hirer.

(2) The debtor or hirer shall only be liable to pay interest in connection with the default sum if the interest is simple interest.

Default notices

87 Need for default notice

(1) Service of a notice on the debtor or hirer in accordance with section 88 (a 'default notice') is necessary before the creditor or owner can become entitled, by reason of any breach by the debtor or hirer of a regulated agreement, –

    (a) to terminate the agreement, or

    (b) to demand earlier payment of any sum, or

    (c) to recover possession of any goods or land, or

    (d) to treat any right conferred on the debtor or hirer by the agreement as terminated, restricted or deferred, or

    (e) to enforce any security.

(2) Subsection (1) does not prevent the creditor from treating the right to draw upon any credit as restricted or deferred, and taking such steps as may be necessary to make the restriction or deferment effective.

(3) The doing of an act by which a floating charge becomes fixed is not enforcement of a security.

(4) Regulations may provide that subsection (1) is not to apply to agreements described by the regulations.

88 Contents and effect of default notice

(1) The default notice must be in the prescribed form and specify –

    (a) the nature of the alleged breach;

    (b) if the breach is capable of remedy, what action is required to remedy it and the date before which that action is to be taken;

    (c) if the breach is not capable of remedy, the sum (if any) required to be paid as compensation for the breach, and the date before which it is to be paid.

(2) A date specified under subsection (1) must not be less than 14 days after the date of service of the default notice, and the creditor or owner shall not take action such as is mentioned in section 87(1) before the date so specified or (if no requirement is made under subsection (1)) before those 14 days have elapsed.

(3) The default notice must not treat as a breach failure to comply with a provision of the agreement which becomes operative only on breach of some other provision, but if the breach of that other provision is not duly remedied or compensation demanded under subsection (1) is not duly paid, or (where no requirement is made under subsection (1)) if the 14 days mentioned in subsection (2) have elapsed, the creditor or owner may treat the failure as a breach and section 87(1) shall not apply to it.

(4) The default notice must contain information in the prescribed terms about the consequences of failure to comply with it and any other prescribed matters relating to the agreement.

(4A) The default notice must also include a copy of the current default information sheet under section 86A.

(5) A default notice making a requirement under subsection (1) may include a provision for the taking of action such as is mentioned in section 87(1) at any time after the restriction imposed by subsection (2) will cease, together with a statement that the provision will be ineffective if the breach is duly remedied or the compensation duly paid.

89 Compliance with default notice

If before the date specified for that purpose in the default notice the debtor or hirer takes the action specified under section 88(1)(b) or (c) the breach shall be treated as not having occurred.

Further restriction of remedies for default

90 Retaking of protected hire-purchase etc goods

(1) At any time when –

(a) the debtor is in breach of a regulated hire-purchase or a regulated conditional sale agreement relating to goods, and

(b) the debtor has paid to the creditor one-third or more of the total price of the goods, and

(c) the property in the goods remains in the creditor,

the creditor is not entitled to recover possession of the goods from the debtor except on an order of the court.

(2) Where under a hire-purchase or conditional sale agreement the creditor is required to carry out any installation and the agreement specifies, as part of the total price, the amount to be paid in respect of the installation (the 'installation charge') the reference in subsection (1)(b) to one third of the total price shall be construed as a reference to the aggregate of the installation charge and one third of the remainder of the total price.

(3) In a case where –

(a) subsection (1)(a) is satisfied, but not subsection (1)(b), and

(b) subsection (1)(b) was satisfied on a previous occasion in relation to an earlier agreement, being a regulated hire-purchase or regulated conditional sale agreement, between the same parties, and relating to any of the goods comprised in the later agreement (whether or not other goods were also included),

subsection (1) shall apply to the later agreement with the omission of paragraph (b).

(4) If the later agreement is a modifying agreement, subsection (3) shall apply with the substitution, for the second reference to the later agreement, of a reference to the modifying agreement.

(5) Subsection (1) shall not apply, or shall cease to apply, to an agreement if the debtor has terminated, or terminates, the agreement.

(6) Where subsection (1) applies to an agreement at the death of the debtor, it shall continue to apply (in relation to the possessor of the goods) until the grant of probate or administration, or (in Scotland) confirmation (on which the personal representative would fall to be treated as the debtor).

(7) Goods falling within this section are in this Act referred to as 'protected goods'.

91 Consequences of breach of s 90

If goods are recovered by the creditor in contravention of section 90 –

(a) the regulated agreement, if not previously terminated, shall terminate, and

(b) the debtor shall be released from all liability under the agreement, and shall be entitled to recover from the creditor all sums paid by the debtor under the agreement.

92 Recovery of possession of goods or land

(1) Except under an order of the court, the creditor or owner shall not be entitled to enter any premises to take possession of goods subject to a regulated hire-purchase agreement, regulated conditional sale agreement or regulated consumer hire agreement.

(2) At any time when the debtor is in breach of a regulated conditional sale agreement relating to land, the creditor is entitled to recover possession of the land from the debtor, or any person claiming under him, on an order of the court only.

(3) An entry in contravention of subsection (1) or (2) is actionable as a breach of statutory duty.

93 Interest not to be increased on default

The debtor under a regulated consumer credit agreement shall not be obliged to pay interest on sums which, in breach of the agreement, are unpaid by him at a rate –

(a) where the total charge for credit includes an item in respect of interest, exceeding the rate of that interest, or

(b) in any other case, exceeding what would be the rate of the total charge for credit if any items included in the total charge for credit by virtue of section 20(2) were disregarded.

Early payment by debtor

94 Right to complete payments ahead of time

(1) The debtor under a regulated consumer credit agreement is entitled at any time, by notice to the creditor and the payment to the creditor of all amounts payable by the debtor to him under the agreement (less any rebate allowable under section 95), to discharge the debtor's indebtedness under the agreement.

(2) A notice under subsection (1) may embody the exercise by the debtor of any option to purchase goods conferred on him by the agreement, and deal with any other matter arising on, or in relation to, the termination of the agreement.

95 Rebate on early settlement

(1) Regulations may provide for the allowance of a rebate of charges for credit to the debtor under a regulated consumer credit agreement where, under section 94, on refinancing, on breach of the agreement, or for any other reason, his indebtedness is discharged or becomes payable before the time fixed by the agreement, or any sum becomes payable by him before the time so fixed.

(2) Regulations under subsection (1) may provide for calculation of the rebate by reference to any sums paid or payable by the debtor or his relative under or in connection with the agreement (whether to the creditor or some other person), including sums under linked transactions and other items in the total charge for credit.

96 Effect on linked transactions

(1) Where for any reason the indebtedness of the debtor under a regulated consumer credit agreement is discharged before the time fixed by the agreement, he, and any

relative of his, shall at the same time be discharged from any liability under a linked transaction, other than a debt which has already become payable.

(2) Subsection (1) does not apply to a linked transaction which is itself an agreement providing the debtor or his relative with credit.

(3) Regulations may exclude linked transactions of the prescribed description from the operation of subsection (1).

97 Duty to give information

(1) The creditor under a regulated consumer credit agreement, within the prescribed period after he has received a request in writing to that effect from the debtor, shall give the debtor a statement in the prescribed form indicating, according to the information to which it is practicable for him to refer, the amount of the payment required to discharge the debtor's indebtedness under the agreement, together with the prescribed particulars showing how the amount is arrived at.

(2) Subsection (1) does not apply to a request made less than one month after a previous request under that subsection relating to the same agreement was complied with.

(3) If the creditor fails to comply with subsection (1) –

(a) he is not entitled, while the default continues, to enforce the agreement; and

(b) if the default continues for one month he commits an offence.

Termination of agreements

98 Duty to give notice of termination (non-default cases)

(1) The creditor or owner is not entitled to terminate a regulated agreement except by or after giving the debtor or hirer not less than seven days' notice of the termination.

(2) Subsection (1) applies only where –

(a) a period for the duration of the agreement is specified in the agreement, and

(b) that period has not ended when the creditor or owner does an act mentioned in subsection (1),

but so applies notwithstanding that, under the agreement, any party is entitled to terminate it before the end of the period so specified.

(3) A notice under subsection (1) is ineffective if not in the prescribed form.

(4) Subsection (1) does not prevent a creditor from treating the right to draw on any credit as restricted or deferred and taking such steps as may be necessary to make the restriction or deferment effective.

(5) Regulations may provide that subsection (1) is not to apply to agreements described by the regulations.

(6) Subsection (1) does not apply to the termination of a regulated agreement by reason of any breach by the debtor or hirer of the agreement.

99 Right to terminate hire-purchase etc agreements

(1) At any time before the final payment by the debtor under a regulated hire-purchase or regulated conditional sale agreement falls due, the debtor shall be entitled to terminate the agreement by giving notice to any person entitled or authorised to receive the sums payable under the agreement.

(2) Termination of an agreement under subsection (1) does not affect any liability under the agreement which has accrued before the termination.

(3) Subsection (1) does not apply to a conditional sale agreement relating to land after the title to the land has passed to the debtor.

(4) In the case of a conditional sale agreement relating to goods, where the property in the goods, having become vested in the debtor, is transferred to a person who does not become the debtor under the agreement, the debtor shall not thereafter be entitled to terminate the agreement under subsection (1).

(5) Subject to subsection (4), where a debtor under a conditional sale agreement relating to goods, terminates the agreement under this section after the property in the goods has become vested in him, the property in the goods shall thereupon vest in the person (the 'previous owner') in whom it was vested immediately before it became vested in the debtor:

> Provided that if the previous owner has died, or any other event has occurred whereby that property, if vested in him immediately before that event, would thereupon have vested in some other person, the property shall be treated as having devolved as if it had been vested in the previous owner immediately before his death or immediately before that event, as the case may be.

100 Liability of debtor on termination of hire-purchase etc agreement

(1) Where a regulated hire-purchase or regulated conditional sale agreement is terminated under section 99 the debtor shall be liable, unless the agreement provides for a smaller payment, or does not provide for any payment, to pay to the creditor the amount (if any) by which one-half of the total price exceeds the aggregate of the sums paid and the sums due in respect of the total price immediately before the termination.

(2) Where under a hire-purchase or conditional sale agreement the creditor is required to carry out any installation and the agreement specifies, as part of the total price, the amount to be paid in respect of the installation (the 'installation charge') the reference in subsection (1) to one-half of the total price shall be construed as a reference to the aggregate of the installation charge and one-half of the remainder of the total price.

(3) If in any action the court is satisfied that a sum less than the amount specified in subsection (1) would be equal to the loss sustained by the creditor in consequence of the termination of the agreement by the debtor, the court may make an order for the payment of that sum in lieu of the amount specified in subsection (1).

(4) If the debtor has contravened an obligation to take reasonable care of the goods or land, the amount arrived at under subsection (1) shall be increased by the sum required to recompense the creditor for that contravention, and subsection (2) shall have effect accordingly.

(5) Where the debtor, on the termination of the agreement, wrongfully retains possession of goods to which the agreement relates, then, in any action brought by the creditor to recover possession of the goods from the debtor, the court, unless it is satisfied that having regard to the circumstances it would not be just to do so, shall order the goods to be delivered to the creditor without giving the debtor an option to pay the value of the goods.

101 Right to terminate hire agreement

(1) The hirer under a regulated consumer hire agreement is entitled to terminate the agreement by giving notice to any person entitled or authorised to receive the sums payable under the agreement.

(2) Termination of an agreement under subsection (1) does not affect any liability under the agreement which has accrued before the termination.

(3) A notice under subsection (1) shall not expire earlier than eighteen months after the making of the agreement, but apart from that the minimum period of notice to be given under subsection (1), unless the agreement provides for a shorter period, is as follows.

(4) If the agreement provides for the making of payments by the hirer to the owner at equal intervals, the minimum period of notice is the length of one interval or three months, whichever is less.

(5) If the agreement provides for the making of such payments at differing intervals, the minimum period of notice is the length of the shortest interval or three months, whichever is less.

(6) In any other case, the minimum period of notice is three months.

(7) This section does not apply to –

    (a) any agreement which provides for the making by the hirer of payments which in total (and without breach of the agreement) exceed £1,500 in any year, or

    (b) any agreement where –

        (i) goods are bailed or (in Scotland) hired to the hirer for the purposes of a business carried on by him, or the hirer holds himself out as requiring the goods for those purposes, and

        (ii) the goods are selected by the hirer, and acquired by the owner for the purposes of the agreement at the request of the hirer from any person other than the owner's associate, or

    (c) any agreement where the hirer requires, or holds himself out as requiring, the goods for the purpose of bailing or hiring them to other persons in the course of a business carried on by him.

(8) If, on an application made to the OFT by a person carrying on a consumer hire business, it appears to the OFT that it would be in the interest of hirers to do so, it may by notice to the applicant direct that, subject to such conditions (if any) as it may specify, this section shall not apply to consumer hire agreements made by the applicant; and this Act shall have effect accordingly

(8A) If it appears to the OFT that it would be in the interests of hirers to do so, it may by general notice direct that, subject to such conditions (if any) as it may specify, this section shall not apply to a consumer hire agreement if the agreement falls within a specified description; and this Act shall have effect accordingly.

(9) In the case of a modifying agreement subsection (3) shall apply with the substitution, for 'the making of the agreement' of 'the making of the original agreement'.

102 Agency for receiving notice of rescission

(1) Where the debtor or hirer under a regulated agreement claims to have a right to rescind the agreement, each of the following shall be deemed to be the agent of the creditor or owner for the purpose of receiving any notice rescinding the agreement which is served by the debtor or hirer –

    (a) a credit-broker or supplier who was the negotiator in antecedent negotiations, and

    (b) any person who, in the course of a business carried on by him, acted on behalf of the debtor or hirer in any negotiations for the agreement.

(2) In subsection (1) 'rescind' does not include –

    (a) service of a notice of cancellation, or

    (b) termination of an agreement under section 99 or 101, or by the exercise of a right or power in that behalf expressly conferred by the agreement.

103 Termination statements

(1) If an individual (the 'customer') serves on any person (the 'trader') a notice –

    (a) stating that –

        (i) the customer was the debtor or hirer under a regulated agreement described in the notice, and the trader was the creditor or owner under the agreement, and

        (ii) the customer has discharged his indebtedness to the trader under the agreement, and

        (iii) the agreement has ceased to have any operation; and

    (b) requiring the trader to give the customer a notice, signed by or on behalf of the trader, confirming that those statements are correct,

the trader shall, within the prescribed period after receiving the notice, either comply with it or serve on the customer a counter-notice stating that, as the case may be, he disputes the correctness of the notice or asserts that the customer is not indebted to him under the agreement.

(2) Where the trader disputes the correctness of the notice he shall give particulars of the way in which he alleges it to be wrong.

(3) Subsection (1) does not apply in relation to any agreement if the trader has previously complied with that subsection on the service of a notice under it with respect to that agreement.

(4) Subsection (1) does not apply to a non-commercial agreement.

(5) If the trader fails to comply with subsection (1), and the default continues for one month, he commits an offence.

104 Goods not to be treated as subject to landlord's hypothec in Scotland

Goods comprised in a hire-purchase agreement or goods comprised in a conditional sale agreement which have not become vested in the debtor shall not be treated in Scotland as subject to the landlord's hypothec –

(a) during the period between the service of the default notice in respect of the goods and the date on which the notice expires or is earlier complied with; or

(b) if the agreement is enforceable on an order of the court only, during the period between the commencement and the termination of an action by the creditor to enforce the agreement.

PART VIII   SECURITY

General

105 Form and content of securities

(1) Any security provided in relation to a regulated agreement shall be expressed in writing.

(2) Regulations may prescribe the form and content of documents ('security instruments') to be made in compliance with subsection (1).

(3) Regulations under subsection (2) may in particular –

(a) require specified information to be included in the prescribed manner in documents, and other specified material to be excluded;

(b) contain requirements to ensure that specified information is clearly brought to the attention of the surety, and that one part of a document is not given insufficient or excessive prominence compared with another.

(4) A security instrument is not properly executed unless –

(a) a document in the prescribed form, itself containing all the prescribed terms and conforming to regulations under subsection (2), is signed in the prescribed manner by or on behalf of the surety, and

(b) the document embodies all the terms of the security, other than implied terms, and

(c) the document, when presented or sent for the purpose of being signed by or on behalf of the surety, is in such a state that its terms are readily legible, and

(d) when the document is presented or sent for the purpose of being signed by or on behalf of the surety there is also presented or sent a copy of the document.

(5) A security instrument is not properly executed unless –

(a) where the security is provided after, or at the time when, the regulated agreement is made, a copy of the executed agreement, together with a copy of any other document referred to in it, is given to the surety at the time the security is provided, or

(b)   where the security is provided before the regulated agreement is made, a copy of the executed agreement, together with a copy of any other document referred to in it, is given to the surety within seven days after the regulated agreement is made.

(6)   Subsection (1) does not apply to a security provided by the debtor or hirer.

(7)   If –

(a)   in contravention of subsection (1) a security is not expressed in writing, or

(b)   a security instrument is improperly executed,

the security (so far as provided in relation to a regulated agreement) is enforceable against the surety on an order of the court only.

(8)   If an application for an order under subsection (7) is dismissed (except on technical grounds only) section 106 (ineffective securities) shall apply to the security.

(9)   Regulations under section 60(1) shall include provision requiring documents embodying regulated agreements also to embody any security provided in relation to a regulated agreement by the debtor or hirer.

106 Ineffective securities

Where, under any provision of this Act, this section is applied to any security provided in relation to a regulated agreement, then, subject to section 177 (saving for registered charges), –

(a)   the security, so far as it is so provided, shall be treated as never having effect;

(b)   any property lodged with the creditor or owner solely for the purposes of the security as so provided shall be returned by him forthwith;

(c)   the creditor or owner shall take any necessary action to remove or cancel an entry in any register, so far as the entry relates to the security as so provided; and

(d)   any amount received by the creditor or owner on realisation of the security shall, so far as it is referable to the agreement, be repaid to the surety.

107 Duty to give information to surety under fixed-sum credit agreement

(1)   The creditor under a regulated agreement for fixed-sum credit in relation to which security is provided, within the prescribed period after receiving a request in writing to that effect from the surety and payment of a fee of £1, shall give to the surety (if a different person from the debtor) –

(a)   a copy of the executed agreement (if any) and of any other document referred to in it;

(b)   a copy of the security instrument (if any); and

(c)   a statement signed by or on behalf of the creditor showing, according to the information to which it is practicable for him to refer, –

(i)   the total sum paid under the agreement by the debtor,

(ii)   the total sum which has become payable under the agreement by the debtor but remains unpaid, and the various amounts comprised in that total sum, with the date when each became due, and

(iii)   the total sum which is to become payable under the agreement by the debtor, and the various amounts comprised in that total sum, with the date, or mode of determining the date, when each becomes due.

(2)   If the creditor possesses insufficient information to enable him to ascertain the amount and dates mentioned in subsection (1)(c) (iii), he shall be taken to comply with that sub-paragraph if his statement under subsection (1)(c) gives the basis on which, under the regulated agreement, they would fall to be ascertained.

(3)   Subsection (1) does not apply to –

(a)   an agreement under which no sum is, or will or may become, payable by the debtor, or

(b) a request made less than one month after a previous request under that subsection relating to the same agreement was complied with.

(4) If the creditor under an agreement fails to comply with subsection (1) –

(a) he is not entitled, while the default continues, to enforce the security, so far as provided in relation to the agreement; and

(b) if the default continues for one month he commits an offence.

(5) This section does not apply to a non-commercial agreement.

108 Duty to give information to surety under running-account credit agreement

(1) The creditor under a regulated agreement for running-account credit in relation to which security is provided, within the prescribed period after receiving a request in writing to that effect from the surety and payment of a fee of £1, shall give to the surety (if a different person from the debtor) –

(a) a copy of the executed agreement (if any) and of any other document referred to in it;

(b) a copy of the security instrument (if any); and

(c) a statement signed by or on behalf of the creditor showing, according to the information to which it is practicable for him to refer, –

(i) the state of the account, and

(ii) the amount, if any, currently payable under the agreement by the debtor to the creditor, and

(iii) the amounts and due dates of any payments which, if the debtor does not draw further on the account, will later become payable under the agreement by the debtor to the creditor.

(2) If the creditor possesses insufficient information to enable him to ascertain the amounts and dates mentioned in subsection (1)(c)(iii), he shall be taken to comply with that sub-paragraph if his statement under subsection (1)(c) gives basis on which, under the regulated agreement, they would fall to be ascertained.

(3) Subsection (1) does not apply to –

(a) an agreement under which no sum is, or will or may become, payable by the debtor, or

(b) a request made less than one month after a previous request under that subsection relating to the same agreement was complied with.

(4) If the creditor under an agreement fails to comply with subsection (1) –

(a) he is not entitled, while the default continues, to enforce the security, so far as provided in relation to the agreement; and

(b) if the default continues for one month he commits an offence.

(5) This section does not apply to a non-commercial agreement.

109 Duty to give information to surety under consumer hire agreement

(1) The owner under a regulated consumer hire agreement in relation to which security is provided, within the prescribed period after receiving a request in writing to that effect from the surety and payment of a fee of £1, shall give to the surety (if a different person from the hirer) –

(a) a copy of the executed agreement and of any other document referred to in it;

(b) a copy of the security instrument (if any); and

(c) a statement signed by or on behalf of the owner showing, according to the information to which it is practicable for him to refer, the total sum which has become payable under the agreement by the hirer but remains unpaid and the various amounts comprised in that total sum, with the date when each became due.

(2) Subsection (1) does not apply to –

(a) an agreement under which no sum is, or will or may become, payable by the hirer, or

(b) a request made less than one month after a previous request under that subsection relating to the same agreement was complied with.

(3) If the owner under an agreement fails to comply with subsection (1) –

(a) he is not entitled, while the default continues, to enforce the security, so far as provided in relation to the agreement; and

(b) if the default continues for one month he commits an offence.

(4) This section does not apply to a non-commercial agreement.

110 Duty to give information to debtor or hirer

(1) The creditor or owner under a regulated agreement, within the prescribed period after receiving a request in writing to that effect from the debtor or hirer and payment of a fee of £1, shall give the debtor or hirer a copy of any security instrument executed in relation to the agreement after the making of the agreement.

(2) Subsection (1) does not apply to –

(a) a non-commercial agreement, or

(b) an agreement under which no sum is, or will or may become, payable by the debtor or hirer, or

(c) a request made less than one month after a previous request under subsection (1) relating to the same agreement was complied with.

(3) If the creditor or owner under an agreement fails to comply with subsection (1) –

(a) he is not entitled, while the default continues, to enforce the security (so far as provided in relation to the agreement); and

(b) if the default continues for one month he commits an offence.

111 Duty to give surety copy of default etc notice

(1) When a default notice or a notice under section 76(1) or 98(1) is served on a debtor or hirer, a copy of the notice shall be served by the creditor or owner on any surety (if a different person from the debtor or hirer).

(2) If the creditor or owner fails to comply with subsection (1) in the case of any surety, the security is enforceable against the surety (in respect of the breach or other matter to which the notice relates) on an order of the court only.

112 Realisation of securities

Subject to section 121, regulations may provide for any matters relating to the sale or other realisation, by the creditor or owner, of property over which any right has been provided by way of security in relation to an actual or prospective regulated agreement, other than a non-commercial agreement.

113 Act not to be evaded by use of security

(1) Where a security is provided in relation to an actual or prospective regulated agreement, the security shall not be enforced so as to benefit the creditor or owner, directly or indirectly, to an extent greater (whether as respects the amount of any payment or the time or manner of its being made) than would be the case if the security were not provided and any obligations of the debtor or hirer, or his relative, under or in relation to the agreement were carried out to the extent (if any) to which they would be enforced under this Act.

(2) In accordance with subsection (1), where a regulated agreement is enforceable on an order of the court or the OFT only, any security provided in relation to the agreement is enforceable (so far as provided in relation to the agreement) where such an order has been made in relation to the agreement, but not otherwise.

(3) Where –

    (a) a regulated agreement is cancelled under section 69(1) or becomes subject to section 69(2), or

    (b) a regulated agreement is terminated under section 91, or

    (c) in relation to any agreement an application for an order under section 40(2), 65(1), 124(1) or 149(2) is dismissed (except on technical grounds only), or

    (d) a declaration is made by the court under section 142(1) (refusal of enforcement order) as respects any regulated agreement,

    section 106 shall apply to any security provided in relation to the agreement.

(4) Where subsection (3)(d) applies and the declaration relates to a part only of the regulated agreement, section 106 shall apply to the security only so far as it concerns that part.

(5) In the case of a cancelled agreement, the duty imposed on the debtor or hirer by section 71 or 72 shall not be enforceable before the creditor or owner has discharged any duty imposed on him by section 106 (as applied by subsection (3)(a)).

(6) If the security is provided in relation to a prospective agreement or transaction, the security shall be enforceable in relation to the agreement or transaction only after the time (if any) when the agreement is made; and until that time the person providing the security shall be entitled, by notice to the creditor or owner, to require that section 106 shall thereupon apply to the security.

(7) Where an indemnity or guarantee is given in a case where the debtor or hirer is a minor, or an indemnity is given in a case where he is otherwise not of full capacity, the reference in subsection (1) to the extent to which his obligations would be enforced shall be read in relation to the indemnity or guarantee as a reference to the extent to which those obligations would be enforced if he were of full capacity.

(8) Subsections (1) to (3) also apply where a security is provided in relation to an actual or prospective linked transaction, and in that case –

    (a) references to the agreement shall be read as references to the linked transaction, and

    (b) references to the creditor or owner shall be read as references to any person (other than the debtor or hirer, or his relative) who is a party, or prospective party, to the linked transaction.

Pledges

114 Pawn-receipts

(1) At the time he receives the article, a person who takes any article in pawn under a regulated agreement shall give to the person from whom he receives it a receipt in the prescribed form (a 'pawn-receipt').

(2) A person who takes any article in pawn from an individual whom he knows to be, or who appears to be and is, a minor commits an offence.

(3) This section and sections 115 to 122 do not apply to –

    (a) a pledge of documents of title or of bearer bonds, or

    (b) a non-commercial agreement.

115 Penalty for failure to supply copies of pledge agreement, etc

If the creditor under a regulated agreement to take any article in pawn fails to observe the requirements of sections 62 to 64 or 114(1) in relation to the agreement he commits an offence.

116 Redemption period

(1) A pawn is redeemable at any time within six months after it was taken.

(2) Subject to subsection (1), the period within which a pawn is redeemable shall be the same as the period fixed by the parties for the duration of the credit secured by the pledge, or such longer period as they may agree.

(3) If the pawn is not redeemed by the end of the period laid down by subsections (1) and (2) (the 'redemption period'), it nevertheless remains redeemable until it is realised by the pawnee under section 121, except where under section 120(1)(a) the property in it passes to the pawnee.

(4) No special charge shall be made for redemption of a pawn after the end of the redemption period, and charges in respect of the safe keeping of the pawn shall not be at a higher rate after the end of the redemption period than before.

117 Redemption procedure

(1) On surrender of the pawn-receipt, and payment of the amount owing, at any time when the pawn is redeemable, the pawnee shall deliver the pawn to the bearer of the pawn-receipt.

(2) Subsection (1) does not apply if the pawnee knows or has reasonable cause to suspect that the bearer of the pawn-receipt is neither the owner of the pawn nor authorised by the owner to redeem it.

(3) The pawnee is not liable to any person in tort or delict for delivering the pawn where subsection (1) applies, or refusing to deliver it where the person demanding delivery does not comply with subsection (1) or, by reason of subsection (2), subsection (1) does not apply.

118 Loss etc of pawn-receipt

(1) A person (the 'claimant') who is not in possession of the pawn-receipt but claims to be the owner of the pawn, or to be otherwise entitled or authorised to redeem it, may do so at any time when it is redeemable by tendering to the pawnee in place of the pawn-receipt –

(a) a statutory declaration made by the claimant in the prescribed form, and with the prescribed contents, or

(b) where the pawn is security for fixed-sum credit not exceeding £75 or running-account credit on which the credit limit does not exceed £75, and the pawnee agrees, a statement in writing in the prescribed form, and with the prescribed contents, signed by the claimant.

(2) On compliance by the claimant with subsection (1), section 117 shall apply as if the declaration or statement were the pawn-receipt, and the pawn-receipt itself shall become inoperative for the purposes of section 117.

119 Unreasonable refusal to deliver pawn

(1) If a person who has taken a pawn under a regulated agreement refuses without reasonable cause to allow the pawn to be redeemed, he commits an offence.

(2) On the conviction in England or Wales of a pawnee under subsection (1) where the offence does not amount to theft, section 148 of the Powers of Criminal Courts (Sentencing) Act 2000 (restitution orders) shall apply as if the pawnee had been convicted of stealing the pawn.

(3) On the conviction in Northern Ireland of a pawnee under subsection (1) where the offence does not amount to theft, section 27 (orders for restitution) of the Theft Act (Northern Ireland) 1969, and any provision of the Theft Act (Northern Ireland) 1969 relating to that section, shall apply as if the pawnee had been convicted of stealing the pawn.

120 Consequence of failure to redeem

(1) If at the end of the redemption period the pawn has not been redeemed –

    (a) notwithstanding anything in section 113, the property in the pawn passes to the pawnee where the redemption period is six months and the pawn is security for fixed-sum credit not exceeding £75 or running- account credit on which the credit limit does not exceed £75; or

    (b) in any other case the pawn becomes realisable by the pawnee.

(2) Where the debtor or hirer is entitled to apply to the court for a time order under section 129, subsection (1) shall apply with the substitution, for 'at the end of the redemption period' of 'after the expiry of five days following the end of the redemption period'.

121 Realisation of pawn

(1) When a pawn has become realisable by him, the pawnee may sell it, after giving to the pawnor (except in such cases as may be prescribed) not less than the prescribed period of notice of the intention to sell, indicating in the notice the asking price and such other particulars as may be prescribed.

(2) Within the prescribed period after the sale takes place, the pawnee shall give the pawnor the prescribed information in writing as to the sale, its proceeds and expenses.

(3) Where the net proceeds of sale are not less than the sum which, if the pawn had been redeemed on the date of the sale, would have been payable for its redemption, the debt secured by the pawn is discharged and any surplus shall be paid by the pawnee to the pawnor.

(4) Where subsection (3) does not apply, the debt shall be treated as from the date of sale as equal to the amount by which the net proceeds of sale fall short of the sum which would have been payable for the redemption of the pawn on that date.

(5) In this section the 'net proceeds of sale' is the amount realised (the 'gross amount') less the expenses (if any) of the sale.

(6) If the pawnor alleges that the gross amount is less than the true market value of the pawn on the date of sale, it is for the pawnee to prove that he and any agents employed by him in the sale used reasonable care to ensure that the true market value was obtained, and if he fails to do so subsections (3) and (4) shall have effect as if the reference in subsection (5) to the gross amount were a reference to the true market value.

(7) If the pawnor alleges that the expenses of the sale were unreasonably high, it is for the pawnee to prove that they were reasonable, and if he fails to do so subsections (3) and (4) shall have effect as if the reference in subsection (5) to expenses were a reference to reasonable expenses.

122 Order in Scotland to deliver pawn

(1) As respects Scotland where –

    (a) a pawn is either –

        (i) an article which has been stolen, or

        (ii) an article which has been obtained by fraud, and a person is convicted of any offence in relation to the theft or, as the case may be, the fraud; or

    (b) a person is convicted of an offence under section 119(1),

the court by which that person is so convicted may order delivery of the pawn to the owner or the person otherwise entitled thereto.

(2) A court making an order under subsection (1)(a) for delivery of a pawn may make the order subject to such conditions as to payment of the debt secured by the pawn as it thinks fit.

Negotiable instruments

123 Restrictions on taking and negotiating instruments

(1) A creditor or owner shall not take a negotiable instrument, other than a bank note or cheque, in discharge of any sum payable –

    (a) by the debtor or hirer under a regulated agreement, or

    (b) by any person as surety in relation to the agreement.

(2) The creditor or owner shall not negotiate a cheque taken by him in discharge of a sum payable as mentioned in subsection (1), except to a banker (within the meaning of the Bills of Exchange Act 1882).

(3) The creditor or owner shall not take a negotiable instrument as security for the discharge of any sum payable as mentioned in subsection (1).

(4) A person takes a negotiable instrument as security for the discharge of a sum if the sum is intended to be paid in some other way, and the negotiable instrument is to be presented for payment only if the sum is not paid in that way.

(5) This section does not apply where the regulated agreement is a non-commercial agreement.

(6) The Secretary of State may by order provide that this section shall not apply where the regulated agreement has a connection with a country outside the United Kingdom.

124 Consequences of breach of s 123

(1) After any contravention of section 123 has occurred in relation to a sum payable as mentioned in section 123(1)(a), the agreement under which the sum is payable is enforceable against the debtor or hirer on an order of the court only.

(2) After any contravention of section 123 has occurred in relation to a sum payable by any surety, the security is enforceable on an order of the court only.

(3) Where an application for an order under subsection (2) is dismissed (except on technical grounds only) section 106 shall apply to the security.

125 Holders in due course

(1) A person who takes a negotiable instrument in contravention of section 123(1) or (3) is not a holder in due course, and is not entitled to enforce the instrument.

(2) Where a person negotiates a cheque in contravention of section 123(2), his doing so constitutes a defect in his title within the meaning of the Bills of Exchange Act 1882.

(3) If a person mentioned in section 123(1)(a) or (b) ('the protected person') becomes liable to a holder in due course of an instrument taken from the protected person in contravention of section 123(1) or (3), or taken from the protected person and negotiated in contravention of section 123(2), the creditor or owner shall indemnify the protected person in respect of that liability.

(4) Nothing in this Act affects the rights of the holder in due course of any negotiable instrument.

Land mortgages

126 Enforcement of land mortgages

A land mortgage securing a regulated agreement is enforceable (so far as provided in relation to the agreement) on an order of the court only.

PART IX   JUDICIAL CONTROL

Enforcement of certain regulated agreements and securities

127 Enforcement orders in cases of infringement

(1)   In the case of an application for an enforcement order under –

    (a)   section 65(1) (improperly executed agreements), or

    (b)   section 105(7)(a) or (b) (improperly executed security instruments), or

    (c)   section 111(2) (failure to serve copy of notice on surety), or

    (d)   section 124(1) or (2) (taking of negotiable instrument in contravention of section 123),

the court shall dismiss the application if, but only if, it considers it just to do so having regard to –

    (i)   prejudice caused to any person by the contravention in question, and the degree of culpability for it; and

    (ii)   the powers conferred on the court by subsection (2) and sections 135 and 136.

(2)   If it appears to the court just to do so, it may in an enforcement order reduce or discharge any sum payable by the debtor or hirer, or any surety, so as to compensate him for prejudice suffered as a result of the contravention in question.

(3)–(5)   . . .

128 Enforcement orders on death of debtor or hirer

The court shall make an order under section 86(2) if, but only if, the creditor or owner proves that he has been unable to satisfy himself that the present and future obligations of the debtor or hirer under the agreement are likely to be discharged.

Extension of time

129 Time orders

(1)   Subject to subsection (3) below, if it appears to the court just to do so –

    (a)   on an application for an enforcement order; or

    (b)   on an application made by a debtor or hirer under this paragraph after service on him of –

        (i)   a default notice, or

        (ii)   a notice under section 76(1) or 98(1); or

    (ba) on an application made by a debtor or hirer under this paragraph after he has been given a notice under section 86B or 86C; or

    (c)   in an action brought by a creditor or owner to enforce a regulated agreement or any security, or recover possession of any goods or land to which a regulated agreement relates,

the court may make an order under this section (a 'time order').

(2)   A time order shall provide for one or both of the following, as the court considers just –

    (a)   the payment by the debtor or hirer or any surety of any sum owed under a regulated agreement or a security by such instalments, payable at such times, as the court, having regard to the means of the debtor or hirer and any surety, considers reasonable;

    (b)   the remedying by the debtor or hirer of any breach of a regulated agreement (other than the non-payment of money) within such period as the court may specify.

(3) Where in Scotland a time to pay direction or a time to pay order has been made in relation to a debt, it shall not thereafter be competent to make a time order in relation to the same debt.

129A Debtor or hirer to give notice of intent etc. to creditor or owner

(1) A debtor or hirer may make an application under section 129(1)(ba) in relation to a regulated agreement only if –

    (a) following his being given the notice under section 86B or 86C, he gave a notice within subsection (2) to the creditor or owner; and

    (b) a period of at least 14 days has elapsed after the day on which he gave that notice to the creditor or owner.

(2) A notice is within this subsection if it –

    (a) indicates that the debtor or hirer intends to make the application;

    (b) indicates that he wants to make a proposal to the creditor or owner in relation to his making of payments under the agreement; and

    (c) gives details of that proposal.

130 Supplemental provisions about time orders

(1) Where in accordance with rules of court an offer to pay any sum by instalments is made by the debtor or hirer and accepted by the creditor or owner, the court may in accordance with rules of court make a time order under section 129(2)(a) giving effect to the offer without hearing evidence of means.

(2) In the case of a hire-purchase or conditional sale agreement only, a time order under section 129(2)(a) may deal with sums which, although not payable by the debtor at the time the order is made, would if the agreement continued in force become payable under it subsequently.

(3) A time order under section 129(2)(a) shall not be made where the regulated agreement is secured by a pledge if, by virtue of regulations made under section 76(5), 87(4) or 98(5), service of a notice is not necessary for enforcement of the pledge.

(4) Where, following the making of a time order in relation to a regulated hire-purchase or conditional sale agreement or a regulated consumer hire agreement, the debtor or hirer is in possession of the goods, he shall be treated (except in the case of a debtor to whom the creditor's title has passed) as a bailee or (in Scotland) a custodier of the goods under the terms of the agreement, notwithstanding that the agreement has been terminated.

(5) Without prejudice to anything done by the creditor or owner before the commencement of the period specified in a time order made under section 129(2)(b) ('the relevant period'), –

    (a) he shall not while the relevant period subsists take in relation to the agreement any action such as is mentioned in section 87(1);

    (b) where –

       (i) a provision of the agreement ('the secondary provision') becomes operative only on breach of another provision of the agreement ('the primary provision'), and

       (ii) the time order provides for the remedying of such a breach of the primary provision within the relevant period,

    he shall not treat the secondary provision as operative before the end of that period;

    (c) if while the relevant period subsists the breach to which the order relates is remedied it shall be treated as not having occurred.

(6) On the application of any person affected by a time order, the court may vary or revoke the order.

Interest

130A Interest payable on judgment debts etc.

(1)   If the creditor or owner under a regulated agreement wants to be able to recover from the debtor or hirer post-judgment interest in connection with a sum that is required to be paid under a judgment given in relation to the agreement (the 'judgment sum'), he –

(a)   after the giving of that judgment, shall give the debtor or hirer a notice under this section (the 'first required notice'); and

(b)   after the giving of the first required notice, shall give the debtor or hirer further notices under this section at intervals of not more than six months.

(2)   The debtor or hirer shall have no liability to pay post-judgment interest in connection with the judgment sum to the extent that the interest is calculated by reference to a period occurring before the day on which he is given the first required notice.

(3)   If the creditor or owner fails to give the debtor or hirer a notice under this section within the period of six months beginning with the day after the day on which such a notice was last given to the debtor or hirer, the debtor or hirer shall have no liability to pay post-judgment interest in connection with the judgment sum to the extent that the interest is calculated by reference to the whole or to a part of the period which –

(a)   begins immediately after the end of that period of six months; and

(b)   ends at the end of the day on which the notice is given to the debtor or hirer.

(4)   The debtor or hirer shall have no liability to pay any sum in connection with the preparation or the giving to him of a notice under this section.

(5)   A notice under this section may be incorporated in a statement or other notice which the creditor or owner gives the debtor or hirer in relation to the agreement by virtue of another provision of this Act.

(6)   Regulations may make provision about the form and content of notices under this section.

(7)   This section does not apply in relation to post-judgment interest which is required to be paid by virtue of any of the following –

(a)   section 4 of the Administration of Justice (Scotland) Act 1972;

(b)   Article 127 of the Judgments Enforcement (Northern Ireland) Order 1981;

(c)   section 74 of the County Courts Act 1984.

(8)   This section does not apply in relation to a non-commercial agreement or to a small agreement.

(9)   In this section 'post-judgment interest' means interest to the extent calculated by reference to a period occurring after the giving of the judgment under which the judgment sum is required to be paid.

Protection of property pending proceedings

131 Protection orders

The court, on the application of the creditor or owner under a regulated agreement, may make such orders as it thinks just for protecting any property of the creditor or owner, or property subject to any security, from damage or depreciation pending the determination of any proceedings under this Act, including orders restricting or prohibiting use of the property or giving directions as to its custody.

Hire and hire-purchase etc agreements

132 Financial relief for hirer

(1) Where the owner under a regulated consumer hire agreement recovers possession of goods to which the agreement relates otherwise than by action, the hirer may apply to the court for an order that –

   (a) the whole or part of any sum paid by the hirer to the owner in respect of the goods shall be repaid, and

   (b) the obligation to pay the whole or part of any sum owed by the hirer to the owner in respect of the goods shall cease,

and if it appears to the court just to do so, having regard to the extent of the enjoyment of the goods by the hirer, the court shall grant the application in full or in part.

(2) Where in proceedings relating to a regulated consumer hire agreement the court makes an order for the delivery to the owner of goods to which the agreement relates the court may include in the order the like provision as may be made in an order under subsection (1).

133 Hire-purchase etc agreements: special powers of court

(1) If, in relation to a regulated hire-purchase or conditional sale agreement, it appears to the court just to do so –

   (a) on an application for an enforcement order or time order; or

   (b) in an action brought by the creditor to recover possession of goods to which the agreement relates,

the court may –

    (i) make an order (a 'return order') for the return to the creditor of goods to which the agreement relates,

    (ii) make an order (a 'transfer order') for the transfer to the debtor of the creditor's title to certain goods to which the agreement relates ('the transferred goods'), and the return to the creditor of the remainder of the goods.

(2) In determining for the purposes of this section how much of the total price has been paid ('the paid-up sum'), the court may –

   (a) treat any sum paid by the debtor, or owed by the creditor, in relation to the goods as part of the paid-up sum;

   (b) deduct any sum owed by the debtor in relation to the goods (otherwise than as part of the total price) from the paid-up sum,

and make corresponding reductions in amounts so owed.

(3) Where a transfer order is made, the transferred goods shall be such of the goods to which the agreement relates as the court thinks just; but a transfer order shall be made only where the paid-up sum exceeds the part of the total price referable to the transferred goods by an amount equal to at least one-third of the unpaid balance of the total price.

(4) Notwithstanding the making of a return order or transfer order, the debtor may at any time before the goods enter the possession of the creditor, on payment of the balance of the total price and the fulfilment of any other necessary conditions, claim the goods ordered to be returned to the creditor.

(5) When, in pursuance of a time order or under this section, the total price of goods under a regulated hire-purchase agreement or regulated conditional sale agreement is paid and any other necessary conditions are fulfilled, the creditor's title to the goods vests in the debtor.

(6) If, in contravention of a return order or transfer order, any goods to which the order relates are not returned to the creditor, the court, on the application of the creditor, may –

(a)   revoke so much of the order as relates to those goods, and

(b)   order the debtor to pay the creditor the unpaid portion of so much of the total price as is referable to those goods.

(7)   For the purposes of this section, the part of the total price referable to any goods is the part assigned to those goods by the agreement or (if no such assignment is made) the part determined by the court to be reasonable.

134 Evidence of adverse detention in hire-purchase etc. cases

(1)   Where goods are comprised in a regulated hire-purchase agreement, regulated conditional sale agreement or regulated consumer hire agreement, and the creditor or owner –

(a)   brings an action or makes an application to enforce a right to recover possession of the goods from the debtor or hirer, and

(b)   proves that a demand for the delivery of the goods was included in the default notice under section 88(5), or that, after the right to recover possession of the goods accrued but before the action was begun or the application was made, he made a request in writing to the debtor or hirer to surrender the goods,

then, for the purposes of the claim of the creditor or owner to recover possession of the goods, the possession of them by the debtor or hirer shall be deemed to be adverse to the creditor or owner.

(2)   In subsection (1) 'the debtor or hirer' includes a person in possession of the goods at any time between the debtor's or hirer's death and the grant of probate or administration, or (in Scotland) confirmation.

(3)   Nothing in this section affects a claim for damages for conversion or (in Scotland) for delict.

Supplemental provisions as to orders

135 Power to impose conditions, or suspend operation of order

(1)   If it considers it just to do so, the court may in an order made by it in relation to a regulated agreement include provisions –

(a)   making the operation of any term of the order conditional on the doing of specified acts by any party to the proceedings;

(b)   suspending the operation of any term of the order either –

(i)   until such time as the court subsequently directs, or

(ii)   until the occurrence of a specified act or omission.

(2)   The court shall not suspend the operation of a term requiring the delivery up of goods by any person unless satisfied that the goods are in his possession or control.

(3)   In the case of a consumer hire agreement, the court shall not so use its powers under subsection (1)(b) as to extend the period for which, under the terms of the agreement, the hirer is entitled to possession of the goods to which the agreement relates.

(4)   On the application of any person affected by a provision included under subsection (1), the court may vary the provision.

136 Power to vary agreements and securities

The court may in an order made by it under this Act include such provision as it considers just for amending any agreement or security in consequence of a term of the order.

Extortionate credit bargains

137–140 . . .

Unfair relationships

140A Unfair relationships between creditors and debtors

(1) The court may make an order under section 140B in connection with a credit agreement if it determines that the relationship between the creditor and the debtor arising out of the agreement (or the agreement taken with any related agreement) is unfair to the debtor because of one or more of the following –

    (a) any of the terms of the agreement or of any related agreement;

    (b) the way in which the creditor has exercised or enforced any of his rights under the agreement or any related agreement;

    (c) any other thing done (or not done) by, or on behalf of, the creditor (either before or after the making of the agreement or any related agreement).

(2) In deciding whether to make a determination under this section the court shall have regard to all matters it thinks relevant (including matters relating to the creditor and matters relating to the debtor).

(3) For the purposes of this section the court shall (except to the extent that it is not appropriate to do so) treat anything done (or not done) by, or on behalf of, or in relation to, an associate or a former associate of the creditor as if done (or not done) by, or on behalf of, or in relation to, the creditor.

(4) A determination may be made under this section in relation to a relationship notwithstanding that the relationship may have ended.

(5) An order under section 140B shall not be made in connection with a credit agreement which is an exempt agreement by virtue of section 16(6C).

140B Powers of court in relation to unfair relationships

(1) An order under this section in connection with a credit agreement may do one or more of the following –

    (a) require the creditor, or any associate or former associate of his, to repay (in whole or in part) any sum paid by the debtor or by a surety by virtue of the agreement or any related agreement (whether paid to the creditor, the associate or the former associate or to any other person);

    (b) require the creditor, or any associate or former associate of his, to do or not to do (or to cease doing) anything specified in the order in connection with the agreement or any related agreement;

    (c) reduce or discharge any sum payable by the debtor or by a surety by virtue of the agreement or any related agreement;

    (d) direct the return to a surety of any property provided by him for the purposes of a security;

    (e) otherwise set aside (in whole or in part) any duty imposed on the debtor or on a surety by virtue of the agreement or any related agreement;

    (f) alter the terms of the agreement or of any related agreement;

    (g) direct accounts to be taken, or (in Scotland) an accounting to be made, between any persons.

(2) An order under this section may be made in connection with a credit agreement only –

    (a) on an application made by the debtor or by a surety;

    (b) at the instance of the debtor or a surety in any proceedings in any court to which the debtor and the creditor are parties, being proceedings to enforce the agreement or any related agreement; or

(c) at the instance of the debtor or a surety in any other proceedings in any court where the amount paid or payable under the agreement or any related agreement is relevant.

(3) An order under this section may be made notwithstanding that its effect is to place on the creditor, or any associate or former associate of his, a burden in respect of an advantage enjoyed by another person.

(4) An application under subsection (2)(a) may only be made –

(a) in England and Wales, to the county court;
(b) in Scotland, to the sheriff court;
(c) in Northern Ireland, to the High Court (subject to subsection (6)).

(5) In Scotland such an application may be made in the sheriff court for the district in which the debtor or surety resides or carries on business.

(6) In Northern Ireland such an application may be made to the county court if the credit agreement is an agreement under which the creditor provides the debtor with –

(a) fixed-sum credit not exceeding £15,000; or
(b) running-account credit on which the credit limit does not exceed £15,000.

(7) Without prejudice to any provision which may be made by rules of court made in relation to county courts in Northern Ireland, such rules may provide that an application made by virtue of subsection (6) may be made in the county court for the division in which the debtor or surety resides or carries on business.

(8) A party to any proceedings mentioned in subsection (2) shall be entitled, in accordance with rules of court, to have any person who might be the subject of an order under this section made a party to the proceedings.

(9) If, in any such proceedings, the debtor or a surety alleges that the relationship between the creditor and the debtor is unfair to the debtor, it is for the creditor to prove to the contrary.

140C Interpretation of ss. 140A and 140B

(1) In this section and in sections 140A and 140B 'credit agreement' means any agreement between an individual (the 'debtor') and any other person (the 'creditor') by which the creditor provides the debtor with credit of any amount.

(2) References in this section and in sections 140A and 140B to the creditor or to the debtor under a credit agreement include –

(a) references to the person to whom his rights and duties under the agreement have passed by assignment or operation of law;
(b) where two or more persons are the creditor or the debtor, references to any one or more of those persons.

(3) The definition of 'court' in section 189(1) does not apply for the purposes of sections 140A and 140B.

(4) References in sections 140A and 140B to an agreement related to a credit agreement (the 'main agreement') are references to –

(a) a credit agreement consolidated by the main agreement;
(b) a linked transaction in relation to the main agreement or to a credit agreement within paragraph (a);
(c) a security provided in relation to the main agreement, to a credit agreement within paragraph (a) or to a linked transaction within paragraph (b).

(5) In the case of a credit agreement which is not a regulated consumer credit agreement, for the purposes of subsection (4) a transaction shall be treated as being a linked transaction in relation to that agreement if it would have been such a transaction had that agreement been a regulated consumer credit agreement.

(6) For the purposes of this section and section 140B the definitions of 'security' and 'surety' in section 189(1) apply (with any appropriate changes) in relation to –

(a) a credit agreement which is not a consumer credit agreement as if it were a consumer credit agreement; and

(b) a transaction which is a linked transaction by virtue of subsection (5).

(7) For the purposes of this section a credit agreement (the 'earlier agreement') is consolidated by another credit agreement (the 'later agreement') if –

(a) the later agreement is entered into by the debtor (in whole or in part) for purposes connected with debts owed by virtue of the earlier agreement; and

(b) at any time prior to the later agreement being entered into the parties to the earlier agreement included –

(i)   the debtor under the later agreement; and

(ii) the creditor under the later agreement or an associate or a former associate of his.

(8) Further, if the later agreement is itself consolidated by another credit agreement (whether by virtue of this subsection or subsection (7)), then the earlier agreement is consolidated by that other agreement as well.

140D Advice and information

The advice and information published by the OFT under section 229 of the Enterprise Act 2002 shall indicate how the OFT expects sections 140A to 140C of this Act to interact with Part 8 of that Act.

Miscellaneous

141 Jurisdiction and parties

(1) In England and Wales, the county court shall have jurisdiction to hear and determine –

(a) any action by the creditor or owner to enforce a regulated agreement or any security relating to it;

(b) any action to enforce any linked transaction against the debtor or hirer or his relative;

and such an action shall not be brought in any other court.

(2) Where an action or application is brought in the High Court which, by virtue of this Act, ought to have been brought in the county court it shall not be treated as improperly brought, but shall be transferred to the county court.

(3) . . .

(3B) . . .

(4) In Northern Ireland the county court shall have jurisdiction to hear and determine any action or application falling within subsection (1).

(5) Except as may be provided by rules of court, all the parties to a regulated agreement, and any surety, shall be made parties to any proceedings relating to the agreement.

142 Power to declare rights of parties

(1) Where under any provision of this Act a thing can be done by a creditor or owner on an enforcement order only, and either –

(a) the court dismisses (except on technical grounds only) an application for an enforcement order, or

(b) where no such application has been made or such an application has been dismissed on technical grounds only, an interested party applies to the court for a declaration under this subsection, the court may if it thinks just make a declaration that the creditor or owner is not entitled to do that thing, and thereafter no application for an enforcement order in respect of it shall be entertained.

(2) Where –

(a) a regulated agreement or linked transaction is cancelled under section 69(1), or becomes subject to section 69(2), or

(b) a regulated agreement is terminated under section 91, and an interested party applies to the court for a declaration under this subsection,

the court may make a declaration to that effect.

Northern Ireland

143 Jurisdiction of county court in Northern Ireland

Without prejudice to any provision which may be made by rules of court made in relation to county courts in Northern Ireland such rules may provide –

(a) that any action or application such as is mentioned in section 141(4) which is brought against the debtor or hirer in the county court may be brought in the county court for the division in which the debtor or hirer resided or carried on business at the date on which he last made a payment under the regulated agreement;

(b) that an application by a debtor or hirer or any surety under section 129(1)(b) or (ba), 132(1) or 142(1)(b) which is brought in the county court may be brought in the county court for the division in which the debtor, or, as the case may be, the hirer or surety resides or carries on business;

(c) for service of process on persons outside Northern Ireland.

144 Appeal from county court in Northern Ireland

Any person dissatisfied –

(a) with an order, whether adverse to him or in his favour, made by a county court in Northern Ireland in the exercise of any jurisdiction conferred by this Act, or

(b) with the dismissal or refusal by such a county court of any action or application instituted by him under the provisions of this Act,

shall be entitled to appeal from the order or from the dismissal or refusal as if the order, dismissal or refusal had been made in exercise of the jurisdiction conferred by Part III of the County Courts (Northern Ireland) Order 1980 and the appeal brought under Part VI of that Order and Articles 61 and 62 of that Order shall apply accordingly.

PART X   ANCILLARY CREDIT BUSINESS

Definitions

145 Types of ancillary credit business

(1) An ancillary credit business is any business so far as it comprises or relates to –

(a) credit brokerage,

(b) debt-adjusting,

(c) debt-counselling,

(d) debt-collecting,

(da) debt administration,

(db) the provision of credit information services, or

(e) the operation of a credit reference agency.

(2) Subject to section 146(5) and (5A), credit brokerage is the effecting of introductions –

    (a) of individuals desiring to obtain credit –

        (i) to persons carrying on businesses to which this sub-paragraph applies, or

        (ii) in the case of an individual desiring to obtain credit to finance the acquisition or provision of a dwelling occupied or to be occupied by himself or his relative, to any person carrying on a business in the course of which he provides credit secured on land, or

    (b) of individuals desiring to obtain goods on hire to persons carrying on businesses to which this paragraph applies, or

    (c) of individuals desiring to obtain credit, or to obtain goods on hire, to other credit-brokers.

(3) Subsection (2)(a)(i) applies to –

    (a) a consumer credit business;

    (b) a business which comprises or relates to consumer credit agreements being, otherwise than by virtue of section 16(5)(a), exempt agreements;

    (c) a business which comprises or relates to unregulated agreements where –

        (i) the law applicable to the agreement is the law of a country outside the United Kingdom, and

        (ii) if the law applicable to the agreement were the law of a part of the United Kingdom it would be a regulated consumer credit agreement.

(4) Subsection (2)(b) applies to –

    (a) a consumer hire business;

    (aa) a business which comprises or relates to consumer hire agreements being, otherwise than by virtue of section 16(6), exempt agreements;

    (b) a business which comprises or relates to unregulated agreements where –

        (i) the law applicable to the agreement is the law of a country outside the United Kingdom, and

        (ii) if the law applicable to the agreement were the law of a part of the United Kingdom it would be a regulated consumer hire agreement.

(5) Subject to section 146(5B) and (6), debt-adjusting is, in relation to debts due under consumer credit agreements or consumer hire agreements, –

    (a) negotiating with the creditor or owner, on behalf of the debtor or hirer, terms for the discharge of a debt, or

    (b) taking over, in return for payments by the debtor or hirer, his obligation to discharge a debt, or

    (c) any similar activity concerned with the liquidation of a debt.

(6) Subject to section 146(5C) and (6), debt-counselling is the giving of advice to debtors or hirers about the liquidation of debts due under consumer credit agreements or consumer hire agreements.

(7) Subject to section 146(6), debt-collecting is the taking of steps to procure payment of debts due under consumer credit agreements or consumer hire agreements.

(7A) Subject to section 146(7), debt administration is the taking of steps –

    (a) to perform duties under a consumer credit agreement or a consumer hire agreement on behalf of the creditor or owner, or

    (b) to exercise or to enforce rights under such an agreement on behalf of the creditor or owner,

so far as the taking of such steps is not debt-collecting.

(7B) A person provides credit information services if –

    (a) he takes any steps mentioned in subsection (7C) on behalf of an individual; or

    (b) he gives advice to an individual in relation to the taking of any such steps.

(7C) Those steps are steps taken with a view –

    (a) to ascertaining whether a credit information agency (other than that person himself if he is one) holds information relevant to the financial standing of an individual;

    (b) to ascertaining the contents of such information held by such an agency;

    (c) to securing the correction of, the omission of anything from, or the making of any other kind of modification of, such information so held; or

    (d) to securing that such an agency which holds such information –

        (i)   stops holding it; or

        (ii) does not provide it to another person.

(7D) In subsection (7C) 'credit information agency' means –

    (a) a person carrying on a consumer credit business or a consumer hire business;

    (b) a person carrying on a business so far as it comprises or relates to credit brokerage, debt-adjusting, debt-counselling, debt-collecting, debt administration or the operation of a credit reference agency;

    (c) a person carrying on a business which would be a consumer credit business except that it comprises or relates to consumer credit agreements being, otherwise than by virtue of section 16(5)(a), exempt agreements; or

    (d) a person carrying on a business which would be a consumer hire business except that it comprises or relates to consumer hire agreements being, otherwise than by virtue of section 16(6), exempt agreements.

(8) A credit reference agency is a person carrying on a business comprising the furnishing of persons with information relevant to the financial standing of individuals, being information collected by the agency for that purpose.

146 Exceptions from section 145

(1) A barrister or advocate acting in that capacity is not to be treated as doing so in the course of any ancillary credit business.

(2) A solicitor engaging in contentious business (as defined in section 87(1) of the Solicitors Act 1974) is not to be treated as doing so in the course of any ancillary credit business.

(3) A solicitor within the meaning of the Solicitors (Scotland) Act 1933 engaging in business done in or for the purposes of proceedings before a court or before an arbiter is not to be treated as doing so in the course of any ancillary credit business.

(4) A solicitor in Northern Ireland engaging in contentious business (as defined in Article 3(2) of the Solicitors (Northern Ireland) Order 1976, is not to be treated as doing so in the course of any ancillary credit business.

(5) For the purposes of section 145(2), introductions effected by an individual by canvassing off trade premises either debtor-creditor-supplier agreements falling within section 12(a) or regulated consumer hire agreements shall be disregarded if –

    (a) the introductions are not effected by him in the capacity of an employee, and

    (b) he does not by any other method effect introductions falling within section 145(2).

(5A) It is not credit brokerage for a person to effect the introduction of an individual desiring to obtain credit if the introduction is made –

    (a) to an authorised person, within the meaning of the 2000 Act, who has permission under that Act to enter as lender into relevant agreements; or

    (b) to a qualifying broker,

with a view to that individual obtaining credit under a relevant agreement.

(5B) It is not debt-adjusting for a person to carry on an activity mentioned in paragraph (a), (b) or (c) of section 145(5) if –

    (a) the debt in question is due under a relevant agreement; and

(b) that activity is a regulated activity for the purposes of the 2000 Act.

(5C) It is not debt-counselling for a person to give advice to debtors about the liquidation of debts if –

(a) the debt in question is due under a relevant agreement; and

(b) giving that advice is a regulated activity for the purposes of the 2000 Act.

(5D) In this section –

'the 2000 Act' means the Financial Services and Markets Act 2000;

'relevant agreement' means an agreement which is secured by a land mortgage, where entering into that agreement as lender is a regulated activity for the purposes of the 2000 Act;

'qualifying broker' means a person who may effect introductions of the kind mentioned in subsection (5A) without contravening the general prohibition, within the meaning of section 19 of the 2000 Act,

and references to 'regulated activities' and the definition of 'qualifying broker' must be read with –

(a) section 22 of the 2000 Act (regulated activities: power to specify classes of activity and categories of investment);

(b) any order for the time being in force under that section; and

(c) Schedule 2 to that Act.

(6) It is not debt-adjusting, debt-counselling or debt-collecting for a person to do anything in relation to a debt arising under an agreement if any of the following conditions is satisfied –

(aa) that he is the creditor or owner under the agreement, or

(c) that he is the supplier in relation to the agreement, or

(d) that he is a credit-broker who has acquired the business of the person who was the supplier in relation to the agreement, or

(e) that he is a person prevented by subsection (5) from being treated as a credit-broker, and the agreement was made in consequence of an introduction (whether made by him or another person) which, under subsection (5), is to be disregarded.

(7) It is not debt administration for a person to take steps to perform duties, or to exercise or enforce rights, under an agreement on behalf of the creditor or owner if any of the conditions mentioned in subsection (6)(aa) to (e) is satisfied in relation to that person.

Licensing

147 Application of Part III

(1) . . .

(2) Without prejudice to the generality of section 26, regulations under that section may include provisions regulating the collection and dissemination of information by credit reference agencies.

148 Agreement for services of unlicensed trader

(1) An agreement for the services of a person carrying on an ancillary credit business (the 'trader'), if made when the trader was unlicensed, is enforceable against the other party (the 'customer') only where the OFT has made an order under subsection (2) which applies to the agreement.

(2) The trader or his successor in title may apply to the OFT for an order that agreements within subsection (1) are to be treated as if made when the trader was licensed.

(3) Unless the OFT determines to make an order under subsection (2) in accordance with the application, it shall, before determining the application, by notice –

(a) inform the trader, giving its reasons, that, as the case may be, it is minded to refuse the application, or to grant it in terms different from those applied for, describing them, and

(b) invite the trader to submit to the OFT representations in support of his application in accordance with section 34.

(4) In determining whether or not to make an order under subsection (2) in respect of any period the OFT shall consider, in addition to any other relevant factors, –

(a) how far, if at all, customers under agreements made by the trader during that period were prejudiced by the trader's conduct,

(b) whether or not the OFT would have been likely to grant a licence covering that period on an application by the trader, and

(c) the degree of culpability for the failure to obtain a licence.

(5) If the OFT thinks fit, it may in an order under subsection (2) –

(a) limit the order to specified agreements, or agreements of a specified description or made at a specified time;

(b) make the order conditional on the doing of specified acts by the trader.

(6) This section does not apply to an agreement made by a consumer credit EEA firm unless at the time it was made that firm was precluded from entering into it as a result of –

(a) a consumer credit prohibition imposed under section 203 of the Financial Services and Markets Act 2000; or

(b) a restriction imposed on the firm under section 204 of that Act.

149 Regulated agreements made on introductions by unlicensed credit-broker

(1) A regulated agreement made by a debtor or hirer who, for the purpose of making that agreement, was introduced to the creditor or owner by an unlicensed credit-broker is enforceable against the debtor or hirer only where –

(a) on the application of the credit-broker, the OFT has made an order under section 148(2) in respect of a period including the time when the introduction was made, and the order does not (whether in general terms or specifically) exclude the application of this paragraph to the regulated agreement, or

(b) the OFT has made an order under subsection (2) which applies to the agreement.

(2) Where during any period individuals were introduced to a person carrying on a consumer credit business or consumer hire business by an unlicensed credit-broker for the purpose of making regulated agreements with the person carrying on that business, that person or his successor in title may apply to the OFT for an order that regulated agreements so made are to be treated as if the credit-broker had been licensed at the time of the introduction.

(3) Unless the OFT determines to make an order under subsection (2) in accordance with the application, it shall, before determining the application, by notice –

(a) inform the applicant, giving its reasons, that, as the case may be, it is minded to refuse the application, or to grant it in terms different from those applied for, describing them, and

(b) invite the applicant to submit to the OFT representations in support of his application in accordance with section 34.

(4) In determining whether or not to make an order under subsection (2) the OFT shall consider, in addition to any other relevant factors –

(a) how far, if at all, debtors or hirers under regulated agreements to which the application relates were prejudiced by the credit-broker's conduct, and

(b) the degree of culpability of the applicant in facilitating the carrying on by the credit-broker of his business when unlicensed.

(5) If the OFT thinks fit, it may in an order under subsection (2) –

(a) limit the order to specified agreements, or agreements of a specified description or made at a specified time;

(b) make the order conditional on the doing of specified acts by the applicant.

(6) For the purposes of this section, 'unlicensed credit-broker' does not include a consumer credit EEA firm unless at the time the introduction was made that firm was precluded from making it as a result of –

(a) a consumer credit prohibition imposed under section 203 of the Financial Services and Markets Act 2000; or

(b) a restriction imposed on the firm under section 204 of that Act.

150 . . .

Seeking business

151 Advertisements

(1) Sections 44 to 47 apply to an advertisement published for the purposes of a business of credit brokerage carried on by any person, whether it advertises the services of that person or the services of persons to whom he effects introductions, as they apply to an advertisement to which Part IV applies.

(2) Sections 44, 46 and 47 apply to an advertisement, published for the purposes of a business carried on by the advertiser, indicating that he is willing to advise on debts, to engage in transactions concerned with the liquidation of debts or to provide credit information services, as they apply to an advertisement to which Part IV applies.

(2A) An advertisement does not fall within subsection (1) or (2) in so far as it is a communication of an invitation or inducement to engage in investment activity within the meaning of section 21 of the Financial Services and Markets Act 2000, other than an exempt generic communication (as defined in section 43(3B)).

(3) The Secretary of State may by order provide that an advertisement published for the purposes of a business of credit brokerage, debt-adjusting, debt-counselling or the provision of credit information services shall not fall within subsection (1) or (2) if it is of a description specified in the order.

(4) An advertisement (other than one for credit information services) does not fall within subsection (2) if it indicates that the advertiser is not willing to act in relation to consumer credit agreements and consumer hire agreements.

(5) In subsections (1) and (3) 'credit brokerage' includes the effecting of introductions of individuals desiring to obtain credit to any person carrying on a business in the course of which he provides credit secured on land.

152 Application of sections 52 to 54 to credit brokerage etc

(1) Sections 52 to 54 apply to a business of credit brokerage, debt-adjusting, debt-counselling or the provision of credit information services as they apply to a consumer credit business.

(2) In their application to a business of credit brokerage, sections 52 and 53 shall apply to the giving of quotations and information about the business of any person to whom the credit-broker effects introductions as well as to the giving of quotations and information about his own business.

153 Definition of canvassing off trade premises (agreements for ancillary credit services)

(1) An individual (the 'canvasser') canvasses off trade premises the services of a person carrying on an ancillary credit business if he solicits the entry of another individual

(the 'consumer') into an agreement for the provision to the consumer of those services by making oral representations to the consumer, or any other individual, during a visit by the canvasser to any place (not excluded by subsection (2)) where the consumer, or that other individual, as the case may be, is, being a visit –

(a) carried out for the purpose of making such oral representations to individuals who are at that place, but

(b) not carried out in response to a request made on a previous occasion.

(2) A place is excluded from subsection (1) if it is a place where (whether on a permanent or temporary basis) –

(a) the ancillary credit business is carried on, or

(b) any business is carried on by the canvasser or the person whose employee or agent the canvasser is, or by the consumer.

154 Prohibition of canvassing certain ancillary credit services off trade premises

It is an offence to canvass off trade premises the services of a person carrying on a business of credit brokerage, debt-adjusting, debt-counselling or the provision of credit information services.

155 Right to recover brokerage fees

(1) Subject to subsection (2A), the excess over £5 of a fee or commission for his services charged by a credit-broker to an individual to whom this subsection applies shall cease to be payable or, as the case may be, shall be recoverable by the individual if the introduction does not result in his entering into a relevant agreement within the six months following the introduction (disregarding any agreement which is cancelled under section 69(1) or becomes subject to section 69(2)).

(2) Subsection (1) applies to an individual who sought an introduction for a purpose which would have been fulfilled by his entry into –

(a) a regulated agreement, or

(b) in the case of an individual such as is referred to in section 145(2)(a)(ii), an agreement for credit secured on land, or

(c) an agreement such as is referred to in section 145(3)(b) or (c) or (4)(b).

(2A) But subsection (1) does not apply where –

(a) the fee or commission relates to the effecting of an introduction of a kind mentioned in section 146(5A); and

(b) the person charging that fee or commission is an authorised person or an appointed representative, within the meaning of the Financial Services and Markets Act 2000.

(3) An agreement is a relevant agreement for the purposes of subsection (1) in relation to an individual if it is an agreement such as is referred to in subsection (2) in relation to that individual.

(4) In the case of an individual desiring to obtain credit under a consumer credit agreement, any sum payable or paid by him to a credit-broker otherwise than as a fee or commission for the credit-broker's services shall for the purposes of subsection (1) be treated as such a fee or commission if it enters, or would enter, into the total charge for credit.

Entry into agreements

156 Entry into agreements

Regulations may make provision, in relation to agreements entered into in the course of a business of credit brokerage, debt-adjusting, debt-counselling or the provision of credit information services, corresponding, with such modifications as the Secretary of State thinks fit, to the provision which is or may be made by or under sections 55, 60, 61, 62, 63, 65, 127, 179 or 180 in relation to agreements to which those sections apply.

Credit reference agencies

157 Duty to disclose name etc of agency

(1) A creditor, owner or negotiator, within the prescribed period after receiving a request in writing to that effect from the debtor or hirer, shall give him notice of the name and address of any credit reference agency from which the creditor, owner or negotiator has, during the antecedent negotiations, applied for information about his financial standing.

(2) Subsection (1) does not apply to a request received more than 28 days after the termination of the antecedent negotiations, whether on the making of the regulated agreement or otherwise.

(3) If the creditor, owner or negotiator fails to comply with subsection (1) he commits an offence.

158 Duty of agency to disclose filed information

(1) A credit reference agency, within the prescribed period after receiving,

    (a) a request in writing to that effect from a consumer,

    (b) such particulars as the agency may reasonably require to enable them to identify the file, and

    (c) a fee of £2,

shall give the consumer a copy of the file relating to it kept by the agency.

(2) When giving a copy of the file under subsection (1), the agency shall also give the consumer a statement in the prescribed form of the consumer's rights under section 159.

(3) If the agency does not keep a file relating to the consumer it shall give the consumer notice of that fact, but need not return any money paid.

(4) If the agency contravenes any provision of this section it commits an offence.

(4A) In this section 'consumer' means –

    (a) a partnership consisting of two or three persons not all of whom are bodies corporate; or

    (b) an unincorporated body of persons which does not consist entirely of bodies corporate and is not a partnership.

(5) In this Act 'file', in relation to an individual, means all the information about him kept by a credit reference agency, regardless of how the information is stored and 'copy of the file', as respects information not in plain English, means a transcript reduced into plain English.

159 Correction of wrong information

(1) Any individual (the 'objector') given –

    (a) information under section 7 of the Data Protection Act 1998 by a credit reference agency, or

    (b) information under section 158,

who considers that an entry in his file is incorrect, and that if it is not corrected he is likely to be prejudiced, may give notice to the agency requiring it either to remove the entry from the file or amend it.

(2) Within 28 days after receiving a notice under subsection (1), the agency shall by notice inform the objector that it has –

    (a) removed the entry from the file, or

(b) amended the entry, or

(c) taken no action,

and if the notice states that the agency has amended the entry it shall include a copy of the file so far as it comprises the amended entry.

(3) Within 28 days after receiving a notice under subsection (2) or, where no such notice was given, within 28 days after the expiry of the period mentioned in subsection (2), the objector may, unless he has been informed by the agency that it has removed the entry from his file, serve a further notice on the agency requiring it to add to the file an accompanying notice of correction (not exceeding 200 words) drawn up by the objector and include a copy of it when furnishing information included in or based on that entry.

(4) Within 28 days after receiving a notice under subsection (3), the agency, unless it intends to apply to the the relevant authority under subsection (5), shall by notice inform the objector that it has received the notice under subsection (3) and intends to comply with it.

(5) If –

(a) the objector has not received a notice under subsection (4) within the time required, or

(b) it appears to the agency that it would be improper for it to publish a notice of correction because it is incorrect, or unjustly defames any person, or is frivolous or scandalous, or is for any other reason unsuitable,

the objector or, as the case may be, the agency may, in the prescribed manner and on payment of the specified fee, apply to the the relevant authority, who may make such order on the application as he thinks fit.

(6) If a person to whom an order under this section is directed fails to comply with it within the period specified in the order he commits an offence.

(7) The Information Commissioner may vary or revoke any order made by him under this section.

(8) In this section 'the relevant authority' means –

(a) where the objector is a partnership or other unincorporated body of persons, the OFT, and

(b) in any other case, the Information Commissioner.

160 Alternative procedure for business consumers

(1) The OFT, on an application made by a credit reference agency, may direct that this section shall apply to the agency if it is satisfied –

(a) that compliance with section 158 in the case of consumers who carry on a business would adversely affect the service provided to its customers by the agency, and

(b) that, having regard to the methods employed by the agency and to any other relevant factors, it is probable that consumers carrying on a business would not be prejudiced by the making of the direction.

(2) Where an agency to which this section applies receives a request, particulars and a fee under section 158(1) from a consumer who carries on a business, and section 158(3) does not apply, the agency, instead of complying with section 158, may elect to deal with the matter under the following subsections.

(3) Instead of giving the consumer a copy of the file, the agency shall within the prescribed period give notice to the consumer that it is proceeding under this section, and by notice give the consumer such information included in or based on entries in the file as the OFT may direct, together with a statement in the prescribed form of the consumer's rights under subsections (4) and (5).

(4) If within 28 days after receiving the information given to the consumer under subsection (3), or such longer period as the OFT may allow, the consumer –

(a) gives notice to the OFT that the consumer is dissatisfied with the information, and

(b) satisfies the OFT that the consumer has taken such steps in relation to the agency as may be reasonable with a view to removing the cause of the consumer's dissatisfaction, and

(c) pays the OFT the specified fee,

the OFT may direct the agency to give the OFT a copy of the file, and the OFT may disclose to the consumer such of the information on the file as the OFT thinks fit.

(5) Section 159 applies with any necessary modifications to information given to the consumer under this section as it applies to information given under section 158.

(6) If an agency making an election under subsection (2) fails to comply with subsection (3) or (4) it commits an offence.

(7) In this section 'consumer' has the same meaning as in section 158.

PART XI   ENFORCEMENT OF ACT

161 Enforcement authorities

(1) The following authorities ('enforcement authorities') have a duty to enforce this Act and regulations made under it –

(a) the OFT,

(b) in Great Britain, the local weights and measures authority,

(c) in Northern Ireland, the Department of Commerce for Northern Ireland.

(2) . . .

(3) Every local weights and measures authority shall, whenever the OFT requires, report to it in such form and with such particulars as it requires on the exercise of their functions under this Act.

(4)–(6) . . .

162 Powers of entry and inspection

(1) A duly authorised officer of an enforcement authority, at all reasonable hours and on production, if required, of his credentials, may –

(a) in order to ascertain whether a breach of any provision of or under this Act has been committed, inspect any goods and enter any premises (other than premises used only as a dwelling);

(b) if he has reasonable cause to suspect that a breach of any provision of or under this Act has been committed, in order to ascertain whether it has been committed, require any person –

(i) carrying on, or employed in connection with, a business to produce any documents relating to it; or

(ii) having control of any information relating to a business to provide him with that information;

(c) if he has reasonable cause to believe that a breach of any provision of or under this Act has been committed, seize and detain any goods in order to ascertain (by testing or otherwise) whether such a breach has been committed;

(d) seize and detain any goods, or documents which he has reason to believe may be required as evidence in proceedings for an offence under this Act;

(e) for the purpose of exercising his powers under this subsection to seize goods, or documents, but only if and to the extent that it is reasonably necessary for securing that the provisions of this Act and of any regulations made under it are duly observed, require any person having authority to do so to break open any container and, if that person does not comply, break it open himself.

(2) An officer seizing goods, or documents in exercise of his powers under this section shall not do so without informing the person he seizes them from.

(3) If a justice of the peace, on sworn information in writing, or, in Scotland, a sheriff or a magistrate or justice of the peace, on evidence on oath, –

   (a) is satisfied that there is reasonable ground to believe either –

      (i) that any goods, or documents which a duly authorised officer has power to inspect under this section are on any premises and their inspection is likely to disclose evidence of a breach of any provision of or under this Act; or

      (ii) that a breach of any provision of or under this Act has been, is being or is about to be committed on any premises; and

   (b) is also satisfied either –

      (i) that admission to the premises has been or is likely to be refused and that notice of intention to apply for a warrant under this subsection has been given to the occupier; or

      (ii) that an application for admission, or the giving of such a notice, would defeat the object of the entry or that the premises are unoccupied or that the occupier is temporarily absent and it might defeat the object of the entry to wait for his return,

the justice or, as the case may be, the sheriff or magistrate may by warrant under his hand, which shall continue in force for a period of one month, authorise an officer of an enforcement authority to enter the premises (by force if need be).

(4) An officer entering premises by virtue of this section may take such other persons and equipment with him as he thinks necessary; and on leaving premises entered by virtue of a warrant under subsection (3) shall, if they are unoccupied or the occupier is temporarily absent, leave them as effectively secured against trespassers as he found them.

(5) Regulations may provide that, in cases described by the regulations, an officer of a local weights and measures authority is not to be taken to be duly authorised for the purposes of this section unless he is authorised by the OFT.

(6) A person who is not a duly authorised officer of an enforcement authority, but purports to act as such under this section, commits an offence.

(7) . . .

(8) References in this section to a breach of any provision of or under this Act do not include references to –

   (a) a failure to comply with a requirement imposed under section 33A or 33B;

   (b) a failure to comply with section 36A; or

   (c) a failure in relation to which the OFT can apply for an order under section 36E.

163 Compensation for loss

(1) Where, in exercising his powers under section 162, an officer of an enforcement authority seizes and detains goods and their owner suffers loss by reason of –

   (a) that seizure, or

   (b) the loss, damage or deterioration of the goods during detention,

then, unless the owner is convicted of an offence under this Act committed in relation to the goods, the authority shall compensate him for the loss so suffered.

(2) Any dispute as to the right to or amount of any compensation under subsection (1) shall be determined by arbitration.

164 Power to make test purchases etc

(1) An enforcement authority may –

   (a) make, or authorise any of their officers to make on their behalf, such purchases of goods; and

(b) authorise any of their officers to procure the provision of such services or facilities or to enter into such agreements or other transactions,

as may appear to them expedient for determining whether any provisions made by or under this Act are being complied with.

(2) Any act done by an officer authorised to do it under subsection (1) shall be treated for the purposes of this Act as done by him as an individual on his own behalf.

(3) Any goods seized by an officer under this Act may be tested, and in the event of such a test he shall inform the person mentioned in section 162(2) of the test results.

(4) Where any test leads to proceedings under this Act, the enforcement authority shall –

(a) if the goods were purchased, inform the person they were purchased from of the test results, and

(b) allow any person against whom the proceedings are taken to have the goods tested on his behalf if it is reasonably practicable to do so.

165 Obstruction of authorised officers

(1) Any person who –

(a) wilfully obstructs an officer of an enforcement authority acting in pursuance of this Act; or

(b) wilfully fails to comply with any requirement properly made to him by such an officer under section 162; or

(c) without reasonable cause fails to give such an officer (so acting) other assistance or information he may reasonably require in performing his functions under this Act,

commits an offence.

(1A) A failure to give assistance or information shall not constitute an offence under subsection (1)(c) if it is also –

(a) a failure to comply with a requirement imposed under section 33A or 33B;

(b) a failure to comply with section 36A; or

(c) a failure in relation to which the OFT can apply for an order under section 36E.

(2) If any person, in giving such information as is mentioned in subsection (1)(c), makes any statement which he knows to be false, he commits an offence.

(3) Nothing in this section requires a person to answer any question or give any information if to do so might incriminate that person or (where that person is married or a civil partner) the spouse or civil partner of that person.

166 Notification of convictions and judgments to OFT

Where a person is convicted of an offence or has a judgment given against him by or before any court in the United Kingdom and it appears to the court –

(a) having regard to the functions of the OFT under this Act, that the conviction or judgment should be brought to the OFT's attention, and

(b) that it may not be brought to its attention unless arrangements for that purpose are made by the court,

the court may make such arrangements notwithstanding that the proceedings have been finally disposed of.

167 Penalties

(1) An offence under a provision of this Act specified in column 1 of Schedule 1 is triable in the mode or modes indicated in column 3, and on conviction is punishable as indicated in column 4 (where a period of time indicates the maximum term of imprisonment, and a monetary amount indicates the maximum fine, for the offence in question).

(2) A person who contravenes any regulations made under section 44, 52, 53, or 112, or made under section 26 by virtue of section 54, commits an offence.

168 Defences

(1) In any proceedings for an offence under this Act it is a defence for the person charged to prove –

    (a) that his act or omission was due to a mistake, or to reliance on information supplied to him, or to an act or omission by another person, or to an accident or some other cause beyond his control, and

    (b) that he took all reasonable precautions and exercised all due diligence to avoid such an act or omission by himself or any person under his control.

(2) If in any case the defence provided by subsection (1) involves the allegation that the act or omission was due to an act or omission by another person or to reliance on information supplied by another person, the person charged shall not, without leave of the court, be entitled to rely on that defence unless, within a period ending seven clear days before the hearing, he has served on the prosecutor a notice giving such information identifying or assisting in the identification of that other person as was then in his possession.

169 Offences by bodies corporate

Where at any time a body corporate commits an offence under this Act with the consent or connivance of, or because of neglect by, any individual, the individual commits the like offence if at that time –

    (a) he is a director, manager, secretary or similar officer of the body corporate, or

    (b) he is purporting to act as such an officer, or

    (c) the body corporate is managed by its members, of whom he is one.

170 No further sanctions for breach of Act

(1) A breach of any requirement made (otherwise than by any court) by or under this Act shall incur no civil or criminal sanction as being such a breach, except to the extent (if any) expressly provided by or under this Act.

(2) In exercising its functions under this Act the OFT may take account of any matter appearing to it to constitute a breach of a requirement made by or under this Act, whether or not any sanction for that breach is provided by or under this Act and, if it is so provided, whether or not proceedings have been brought in respect of the breach.

(3) Subsection (1) does not prevent the grant of an injunction, or the making of an order of certiorari, mandamus or prohibition or as respects Scotland the grant of an interdict or of an order under section 91 of the Court of Session Act 1868 (order for specific performance of statutory duty).

171 Onus of proof in various proceedings

(1) If an agreement contains a term signifying that in the opinion of the parties section 10(3)(b)(iii) does not apply to the agreement, it shall be taken not to apply unless the contrary is proved.

(2) It shall be assumed in any proceedings, unless the contrary is proved, that when a person initiated a transaction as mentioned in section 19(1)(c) he knew the principal agreement had been made, or contemplated that it might be made.

(3) Regulations under section 44 or 52 may make provision as to the onus of proof in any proceedings to enforce the regulations.

(4) In proceedings brought by the creditor under a credit-token agreement –

    (a) it is for the creditor to prove that the credit-token was lawfully supplied to the debtor, and was accepted by him, and

(b) if the debtor alleges that any use made of the credit-token was not authorised by him, it is for the creditor to prove either –

    (i)   that the use was so authorised, or

    (ii)   that the use occurred before the creditor had been given notice under section 84(3).

(5) In proceedings under section 50(1) in respect of a document received by a minor at any school or other educational establishment for minors, it is for the person sending it to him at that establishment to prove that he did not know or suspect it to be such an establishment.

(6) In proceedings under section 119(1) it is for the pawnee to prove that he had reasonable cause to refuse to allow the pawn to be redeemed.

(7) . . .

172 Statements by creditor or owner to be binding

(1) A statement by a creditor or owner is binding on him if given under –

section 77(1),
section 78(1),
section 79(1),
section 97(1),
section 107(1)(c),
section 108(1)(c), or
section 109(1)(c).

(2) Where a trader –

(a) gives a customer a notice in compliance with section 103(1)(b), or

(b) gives a customer a notice under section 103(1) asserting that the customer is not indebted to him under an agreement,

the notice is binding on the trader.

(3) Where in proceedings before any court –

(a) it is sought to rely on a statement or notice given as mentioned in subsection (1) or (2), and

(b) the statement or notice is shown to be incorrect,

the court may direct such relief (if any) to be given to the creditor or owner from the operation of subsection (1) or (2) as appears to the court to be just.

173 Contracting-out forbidden

(1) A term contained in a regulated agreement or linked transaction, or in any other agreement relating to an actual or prospective regulated agreement or linked transaction, is void if, and to the extent that, it is inconsistent with a provision for the protection of the debtor or hirer or his relative or any surety contained in this Act or in any regulation made under this Act.

(2) Where a provision specifies the duty or liability of the debtor or hirer or his relative or any surety in certain circumstances, a term is inconsistent with that provision if it purports to impose, directly or indirectly, an additional duty or liability on him in those circumstances.

(3) Notwithstanding subsection (1), a provision of this Act under which a thing may be done in relation to any person on an order of the court or the OFT only shall not be taken to prevent its being done at any time with that person's consent given at that time, but the refusal of such consent shall not give rise to any liability.

PART XII   SUPPLEMENTAL

General

174 . . .

. . .

174A Powers to require provision of information or documents etc.

(1) Every power conferred on a relevant authority by or under this Act (however expressed) to require the provision or production of information or documents includes the power –

(a) to require information to be provided or produced in such form as the authority may specify, including, in relation to information recorded otherwise than in a legible form, in a legible form;

(b) to take copies of, or extracts from, any documents provided or produced by virtue of the exercise of the power;

(c) to require the person who is required to provide or produce any information or document by virtue of the exercise of the power –

(i)   to state, to the best of his knowledge and belief, where the information or document is;

(ii) to give an explanation of the information or document;

(iii) to secure that any information provided or produced, whether in a document or otherwise, is verified in such manner as may be specified by the authority;

(iv) to secure that any document provided or produced is authenticated in such manner as may be so specified;

(d) to specify a time at or by which a requirement imposed by virtue of paragraph (c) must be complied with.

(2) Every power conferred on a relevant authority by or under this Act (however expressed) to inspect or to seize documents at any premises includes the power to take copies of, or extracts from, any documents inspected or seized by virtue of the exercise of the power.

(3) But a relevant authority has no power under this Act –

(a) to require another person to provide or to produce,

(b) to seize from another person, or

(c) to require another person to give access to premises for the purposes of the inspection of,

any information or document which the other person would be entitled to refuse to provide or produce in proceedings in the High Court on the grounds of legal professional privilege or (in Scotland) in proceedings in the Court of Session on the grounds of confidentiality of communications.

(4) In subsection (3) 'communications' means –

(a) communications between a professional legal adviser and his client;

(b) communications made in connection with or in contemplation of legal proceedings and for the purposes of those proceedings.

(5) In this section 'relevant authority' means –

(a) the OFT or an enforcement authority (other than the OFT);

(b) an officer of the OFT or of an enforcement authority (other than the OFT).

175 Duty of persons deemed to be agents

Where under this Act a person is deemed to receive a notice or payment as agent of the creditor or owner under a regulated agreement, he shall be deemed to be under a contractual duty to the creditor or owner to transmit the notice, or remit the payment, to him forthwith.

176 Service of documents

(1) A document to be served under this Act by one person ('the server') on another person ('the subject') is to be treated as properly served on the subject if dealt with as mentioned in the following subsections.

(2) The document may be delivered or sent by an appropriate method to the subject, or addressed to him by name and left at his proper address.

(3) For the purposes of this Act, a document sent by post to, or left at, the address last known to the server as the address of a person shall be treated as sent by post to, or left at, his proper address.

(4) Where the document is to be served on the subject as being the person having any interest in land, and it is not practicable after reasonable inquiry to ascertain the subject's name or address, the document may be served by –

    (a) addressing it to the subject by the description of the person having that interest in the land (naming it), and

    (b) delivering the document to some responsible person on the land or affixing it, or a copy of it, in a conspicuous position on the land.

(5) Where a document to be served on the subject as being a debtor, hirer or surety, or as having any other capacity relevant for the purposes of this Act, is served at any time on another person who –

    (a) is the person last known to the server as having that capacity, but

    (b) before that time had ceased to have it,

    the document shall be treated as having been served at that time on the subject.

(6) Anything done to a document in relation to a person who (whether to the knowledge of the server or not) has died shall be treated for the purposes of subsection (5) as service of the document on that person if it would have been so treated had he not died.

(7) The following enactments shall not be construed as authorising service on the Public Trustee (in England and Wales) or the Probate Judge (in Northern Ireland) of any document which is to be served under this Act –
section 9 of the Administration of Estates Act 1925;
section 3 of the Administration of Estates Act (Northern Ireland) 1955.

(8) References in the preceding subsections to the serving of a document on a person include the giving of the document to that person.

176A Electronic transmission of documents

(1) A document is transmitted in accordance with this subsection if –

    (a) the person to whom it is transmitted agrees that it may be delivered to him by being transmitted to a particular electronic address in a particular electronic form,

    (b) it is transmitted to that address in that form, and

    (c) the form in which the document is transmitted is such that any information in the document which is addressed to the person to whom the document is transmitted is capable of being stored for future reference for an appropriate period in a way which allows the information to be reproduced without change.

(2) A document transmitted in accordance with subsection (1) shall, unless the contrary is proved, be treated for the purposes of this Act, except section 69, as having been

delivered on the working day immediately following the day on which it is transmitted.

(3) In this section, 'electronic address' includes any number or address used for the purposes of receiving electronic communications.

177 Saving for registered charges

(1) Nothing in this Act affects the rights of a proprietor of a registered charge (within the meaning of the Land Registration Act 2002), who –

    (a) became the proprietor under a transfer for valuable consideration without notice of any defect in the title arising (apart from this section) by virtue of this Act, or

    (b) derives title from such a proprietor.

(2) Nothing in this Act affects the operation of section 104 of the Law of Property Act 1925 (protection of purchaser where mortgagee exercises power of sale).

(3) Subsection (1) does not apply to a proprietor carrying on a consumer credit business, a consumer hire business or a business of debt-collecting or debt administration.

(4) Where, by virtue of subsection (1), a land mortgage is enforced which apart from this section would be treated as never having effect, the original creditor or owner shall be liable to indemnify the debtor or hirer against any loss thereby suffered by him.

(5) In the application of this section to Scotland for subsections (1) to (3) there shall be substituted the following subsections –

    '(1) Nothing in this Act affects the rights of a creditor in a heritable security who –

        (a) became the creditor under a transfer for value without notice of any defect in the title arising (apart from this section) by virtue of this Act; or

        (b) derives title from such a creditor.

    (2) Nothing in this Act affects the operation of section 41 of the Conveyancing (Scotland) Act 1924 (protection of purchasers), or of that section as applied to standard securities by section 32 of the Conveyancing and Feudal Reform (Scotland) Act 1970.

    (3) Subsection (1) does not apply to a creditor carrying on a consumer credit business, a consumer hire business or a business of debt-collecting or debt administration.'.

(6) In the application of this section to Northern Ireland –

    (a) any reference to the proprietor of a registered charge (within the meaning of the Land Registration Act 2002) shall be construed as a reference to the registered owner of a charge under the Local Registration of Title (Ireland) Act 1891 or Part IV of the Land Registration Act (Northern Ireland) 1970, and

    (b) for the reference to section 104 of the Law of Property Act 1925 there shall be substituted a reference to section 21 of the Conveyancing and Law of Property Act 1881 and section 5 of the Conveyancing Act 1911.

178 Local Acts

The Secretary of State or the Department of Commerce for Northern Ireland may by order make such amendments or repeals of any provision of any local Act as appears to the Secretary of State or, as the case may be, the Department, necessary or expedient in consequence of the replacement by this Act of the enactments relating to pawnbrokers and moneylenders.

Regulations, orders, etc

179 Power to prescribe form etc of secondary documents

(1) Regulations may be made as to the form and content of credit-cards, trading-checks, receipts, vouchers and other documents or things issued by creditors, owners or

suppliers under or in connection with regulated agreements or by other persons in connection with linked transactions, and may in particular –

(a) require specified information to be included in the prescribed manner in documents, and other specified material to be excluded;

(b) contain requirements to ensure that specified information is clearly brought to the attention of the debtor or hirer, or his relative, and that one part of a document is not given insufficient or excessive prominence compared with another.

(2) If a person issues any document or thing in contravention of regulations under subsection (1) then, as from the time of the contravention but without prejudice to anything done before it, this Act shall apply as if the regulated agreement had been improperly executed by reason of a contravention of regulations under section 60(1).

180 Power to prescribe form etc of copies

(1) Regulations may be made as to the form and content of documents to be issued as copies of any executed agreement, security instrument or other document referred to in this Act, and may in particular –

(a) require specified information to be included in the prescribed manner in any copy, and contain requirements to ensure that such information is clearly brought to the attention of a reader of the copy;

(b) authorise the omission from a copy of certain material contained in the original, or the inclusion of such material in condensed form.

(2) A duty imposed by any provision of this Act (except section 35) to supply a copy of any document –

(a) is not satisfied unless the copy supplied is in the prescribed form and conforms to the prescribed requirements;

(b) is not infringed by the omission of any material, or its inclusion in condensed form, if that is authorised by regulations;

and references in this Act to copies shall be construed accordingly.

(3) Regulations may provide that a duty imposed by this Act to supply a copy of a document referred to in an unexecuted agreement or an executed agreement shall not apply to documents of a kind specified in the regulations.

181 Power to alter monetary limits etc

(1) The Secretary of State may by order made by statutory instrument amend, or further amend, any of the following provisions of this Act so as to reduce or increase a sum mentioned in that provision, namely, sections 16B(1), 17(1), 43(3)(a), 70(6), 75(3)(b), 77(1), 78(1), 79(1), 84(1), 101(7)(a), 107(1), 108(1), 109(1), 110(1), 118(1)(b), 120(1)(a), 140B(6), 155(1) and 158(1).

(2) An order under subsection (1) amending section 16B(1), 17(1), 39A(3), 75(3)(b) or 140B(6) shall be of no effect unless a draft of the order has been laid before and approved by each House of Parliament.

182 Regulations and orders

(1) Any power of the Secretary of State to make regulations or orders under this Act, except the power conferred by sections 2(1)(a), 181 and 192, shall be exercisable by statutory instrument subject to annulment in pursuance of a resolution of either House of Parliament.

(1A) The power of the Lord Chancellor to make rules under section 40A(3) shall be exercisable by statutory instrument subject to annulment in pursuance of a resolution of either House of Parliament.

(2) Where a power to make regulations or orders or rules is exercisable by the Secretary of State or by the Lord Chancellor by virtue of this Act, regulations or orders or rules made in the exercise of that power may –

 (a) make different provision in relation to different cases or classes of case, and
 (b) exclude certain cases or classes of case, and
 (c) contain such transitional provisions as the person making them thinks fit.

(3) Regulations may provide that specified expressions, when used as described by the regulations, are to be given the prescribed meaning, notwithstanding that another meaning is intended by the person using them.

(4) Any power conferred on the Secretary of State by this Act to make orders includes power to vary or revoke an order so made.

183 Determinations etc. by OFT

(1) The OFT may vary or revoke any determination made, or direction given, by it under this Act.

(2) Subsection (1) does not apply to –

 (a) a determination to issue, renew or vary a licence;
 (b) a determination to extend a period under section 28B or to refuse to extend a period under that section;
 (c) a determination to end a suspension under section 33;
 (d) a determination to make an order under section 40(2), 148(2) or 149(2);
 (e) a determination mentioned in column 1 of the Table in section 41.

Interpretation

184 Associates

(1) A person is an associate of an individual if that person is –

 (a) the individual's husband or wife or civil partner,
 (b) a relative of –

  (i)   the individual, or
  (ii) the individual's husband or wife or civil partner, or

 (c) the husband or wife or civil partner of a relative of –

  (i)   the individual, or
  (ii) the individual's husband or wife or civil partner.

(2) A person is an associate of any person with whom he is in partnership, and of the husband or wife or civil partner or a relative of any individual with whom he is in partnership.

(3) A body corporate is an associate of another body corporate –

 (a) if the same person is a controller of both, or a person is a controller of one and persons who are his associates, or he and persons who are his associates, are the controllers of the other; or
 (b) if a group of two or more persons is a controller of each company, and the groups either consist of the same persons or could be regarded as consisting of the same persons by treating (in one or more cases) a member of either group as replaced by a person of whom he is an associate.

(4) A body corporate is an associate of another person if that person is a controller of it or if that person and persons who are his associates together are controllers of it.

(5) In this section 'relative' means brother, sister, uncle, aunt, nephew, niece, lineal ancestor or lineal descendant, . . . references to a husband or wife include a former husband or wife and a reputed husband or wife, and references to a civil partner include a former civil partner and a reputed civil partner; and for the purposes of this subsection

a relationship shall be established as if any illegitimate child, step-child or adopted child of a person were the legitimate child of the relationship in question.

185 Agreement with more than one debtor or hirer

(1) Where an actual or prospective regulated agreement has two or more debtors or hirers (not being a partnership or an unincorporated body of persons) –

    (a) anything required by or under this Act to be done to or in relation to the debtor or hirer shall be done to or in relation to each of them; and

    (b) anything done under this Act by or on behalf of one of them shall have effect as if done by or on behalf of all of them.

(2) Notwithstanding subsection (1)(a), where credit is provided under an agreement to two or more debtors jointly, in performing his duties –

    (a) in the case of fixed-sum credit, under section 77A, or

    (b) in the case of running-account credit, under section 78(4), the creditor need not give statements to any debtor who has signed and given to him a notice (a 'dispensing notice') authorising him not to comply in the debtor's case with section 77A or (as the case may be) 78(4).

(2A) A dispensing notice given by a debtor is operative from when it is given to the creditor until it is revoked by a further notice given to the creditor by the debtor.

(2B) But subsection (2) does not apply if (apart from this subsection) dispensing notices would be operative in relation to all of the debtors to whom the credit is provided.

(2C) Any dispensing notices operative in relation to an agreement shall cease to have effect if any of the debtors dies.

(2D) A dispensing notice which is operative in relation to an agreement shall be operative also in relation to any subsequent agreement which, in relation to the earlier agreement, is a modifying agreement.

(3) Subsection (1)(b) does not apply for the purposes of section 61(1)(a).

(4) Where a regulated agreement has two or more debtors or hirers (not being a partnership or an unincorporated body of persons), section 86 applies to the death of any of them.

(5) An agreement for the provision of credit, or the bailment or (in Scotland) the hiring of goods, to two or more persons jointly where –

    (a) one or more of those persons is an individual, and

    (b) one or more of them is not an individual,

is a consumer credit agreement or consumer hire agreement if it would have been one had they all been individuals; and each person within paragraph (b) shall accordingly be included among the debtors or hirers under the agreement.

(6) Where subsection (5) applies, references in this Act to the signing of any document by the debtor or hirer shall be construed in relation to a body corporate within paragraph (b) of that subsection as referring to a signing on behalf of the body corporate.

186 Agreement with more than one creditor or owner

Where an actual or prospective regulated agreement has two or more creditors or owners, anything required by or under this Act to be done to, or in relation to, or by, the creditor or owner shall be effective if done to, or in relation to, or by, any one of them.

187 Arrangements between creditor and supplier

(1) A consumer credit agreement shall be treated as entered into under pre-existing arrangements between a creditor and a supplier if it is entered into in accordance with, or in furtherance of, arrangements previously made between persons mentioned in subsection (4)(a), (b) or (c).

(2) A consumer credit agreement shall be treated as entered into in contemplation of future arrangements between a creditor and a supplier if it is entered into in the

expectation that arrangements will subsequently be made between persons mentioned in subsection (4)(a), (b) or (c) for the supply of cash, goods and services (or any of them) to be financed by the consumer credit agreement.

(3)   Arrangements shall be disregarded for the purposes of subsection (1) or (2) if –

(a)   they are arrangements for the making, in specified circumstances, of payments to the supplier by the creditor, and

(b)   the creditor holds himself out as willing to make, in such circumstances, payments of the kind to suppliers generally.

(3A) Arrangements shall also be disregarded for the purposes of subsections (1) and (2) if they are arrangements for the electronic transfer of funds from a current account at a bank within the meaning of the Bankers' Books Evidence Act 1879.

(4)   The persons referred to in subsections (1) and (2) are –

(a)   the creditor and the supplier;

(b)   one of them and an associate of the other's;

(c)   an associate of one and an associate of the other's.

(5)   Where the creditor is an associate of the supplier's, the consumer credit agreement shall be treated, unless the contrary is proved, as entered into under pre-existing arrangements between the creditor and the supplier.

187A Definition of 'default sum'

(1)   In this Act 'default sum' means, in relation to the debtor or hirer under a regulated agreement, a sum (other than a sum of interest) which is payable by him under the agreement in connection with a breach of the agreement by him.

(2)   But a sum is not a default sum in relation to the debtor or hirer simply because, as a consequence of his breach of the agreement, he is required to pay it earlier than he would otherwise have had to.

188 Examples of use of new terminology

(1)   Schedule 2 shall have effect for illustrating the use of terminology employed in this Act.

(2)   The examples given in Schedule 2 are not exhaustive.

(3)   In the case of conflict between Schedule 2 and any other provision of this Act, that other provision shall prevail.

(4)   The Secretary of State may by order amend Schedule 2 by adding further examples or in any other way.

189 Definitions

(1)   In this Act, unless the context otherwise requires –

'advertisement' includes every form of advertising, whether in a publication, by television or radio, by display of notices, signs, labels, showcards or goods, by distribution of samples, circulars, catalogues, price lists or other material, by exhibition of pictures, models or films, or in any other way, and references to the publishing of advertisements shall be construed accordingly;

'advertiser' in relation to an advertisement, means any person indicated by the advertisement as willing to enter into transactions to which the advertisement relates;

'ancillary credit business' has the meaning given by section 145(1);

'antecedent negotiations' has the meaning given by section 56;

'appeal period' means the period beginning on the first day on which an appeal to the Tribunal may be brought and ending on the last day on which it may be brought or, if it is brought, ending on its final determination, or abandonment;

'appropriate method' means –

(a)   post, or

(b)   transmission in the form of an electronic communication in accordance with section 176A(1);

'assignment', in relation to Scotland, means assignation;

'associate' shall be construed in accordance with section 184;

. . .

'bill of sale' has the meaning given by section 4 of the Bills of Sale Act 1878 or, for Northern Ireland, by section 4 of the Bills of Sale (Ireland) Act 1879;

'building society' means a building society within the meaning of the Building Societies Act 1986;

'business' includes profession or trade, and references to a business apply subject to subsection (2);

'cancellable agreement' means a regulated agreement which, by virtue of section 67, may be cancelled by the debtor or hirer;

'canvass' shall be construed in accordance with sections 48 and 153;

'cash' includes money in any form;

'charity' means as respects England and Wales a charity registered under the Charities Act 1993 or an exempt charity (within the meaning of that Act), as respects Northern Ireland an institution or other organisation established for charitable purposes only ('organisation' including any persons administering a trust and 'charitable' being construed in the same way as if it were contained in the Income Tax Acts) and as respects Scotland a body entered in the Scottish Charity Register;

'conditional sale agreement' means an agreement for the sale of goods or land under which the purchase price or part of it is payable by instalments, and the property in the goods or land is to remain in the seller (notwithstanding that the buyer is to be in possession of the goods or land) until such conditions as to the payment of instalments or otherwise as may be specified in the agreement are fulfilled;

'consumer credit agreement' has the meaning given by section 8, and includes a consumer credit agreement which is cancelled under section 69(1), or becomes subject to section 69(2), so far as the agreement remains in force;

'consumer credit business' means any business being carried on by a person so far as it comprises or relates to –

(a)   the provision of credit by him, or

(b)   otherwise his being a creditor,

under regulated consumer credit agreements;

'consumer hire agreement' has the meaning given by section 15;

'consumer hire business' means any business being carried on by a person so far as it comprises or relates to –

(a)   the bailment or (in Scotland) the hiring of goods by him, or

(b)   otherwise his being an owner,

under regulated consumer hire agreements;

'controller', in relation to a body corporate, means a person –

(a)   in accordance with whose directions or instructions the directors of the body corporate or of another body corporate which is its controller (or any of them) are accustomed to act, or

(b)   who, either alone or with any associate or associates, is entitled to exercise or control the exercise of, one third or more of the voting power at any general meeting of the body corporate or of another body corporate which is its controller;

'copy' shall be construed in accordance with section 180;

. . .

'court' means in relation to England and Wales the county court, in relation to Scotland the sheriff court and in relation to Northern Ireland the High Court or the county court;

'credit' shall be construed in accordance with section 9;

'credit-broker' means a person carrying on a business of credit brokerage;

'credit brokerage' has the meaning given by section 145(2);

'credit information services' has the meaning given by section 145(7B).

'credit limit' has the meaning given by section 10(2);

'creditor' means the person providing credit under a consumer credit agreement or the person to whom his rights and duties under the agreement have passed by assignment or operation of law, and in relation to a prospective consumer credit agreement, includes the prospective creditor;

'credit reference agency' has the meaning given by section 145(8);

'credit-sale agreement' means an agreement for the sale of goods, under which the purchase price or part of it is payable by instalments, but which is not a conditional sale agreement;

'credit-token' has the meaning given by section 14(1);

'credit-token agreement' means a regulated agreement for the provision of credit in connection with the use of a credit-token;

'debt-adjusting' has the meaning given by section 145(5);

'debt administration' has the meaning given by section 145(7A);

'debt-collecting' has the meaning given by section 145(7);

'debt-counselling' has the meaning given by section 145(6);

'debtor' means the individual receiving credit under a consumer credit agreement or the person to whom his rights and duties under the agreement have passed by assignment or operation of law, and in relation to a prospective consumer credit agreement includes the prospective debtor;

'debtor-creditor agreement' has the meaning given by section 13;

'debtor-creditor-supplier agreement' has the meaning given by section 12;

'default notice' has the meaning given by section 87(1);

'default sum' has the meaning given by section 187A;

'deposit' means (except in section 16(10) and 25(1B)) any sum payable by a debtor or hirer by way of deposit or down-payment, or credited or to be credited to him on account of any deposit or down-payment, whether the sum is to be or has been paid to the creditor or owner or any other person, or is to be or has been discharged by a payment of money or a transfer or delivery of goods or by any other means;

'documents' includes information recorded in any form;

. . .

'electric line' has the meaning given by the Electricity Act 1989 or, for Northern Ireland, the Electricity (Northern Ireland) Order 1992;

'electronic communication' means an electronic communication within the meaning of the Electronic Communications Act 2000 (c 7);

'embodies' and related words shall be construed in accordance with subsection (4);

'enforcement authority' has the meaning given by section 161(1);

'enforcement order' means an order under section 65(1), 105(7)(a) or (b), 111(2) or 124(1) or (2);

'executed agreement' means a document, signed by or on behalf of the parties, embodying the terms of a regulated agreement, or such of them as have been reduced to writing;

'exempt agreement' means an agreement specified in or under section 16, 16A or 16B;

'finance' means to finance wholly or partly and 'financed' and 'refinanced' shall be construed accordingly;

'file' and 'copy of the file' have the meanings given by section 158(5);

'fixed-sum credit' has the meaning given by section 10(1)(b);

'friendly society' means a society registered or treated as registered under the Friendly Societies Act 1974 or the Friendly Societies Act 1992 . . .;

'future arrangements' shall be construed in accordance with section 187;

'general notice' means a notice published by the OFT at a time and in a manner appearing to it suitable for securing that the notice is seen within a reasonable time by persons likely to be affected by it;

'give', means, deliver or send by an appropriate method to;

'goods' has the meaning given by section 61(1) of the Sale of Goods Act 1979;

'group licence' has the meaning given by section 22(1)(b);

'High Court' means Her Majesty's High Court of Justice, or the Court of Session in Scotland or the High Court of Justice in Northern Ireland;

'hire-purchase agreement' means an agreement, other than a conditional sale agreement, under which –

(a) goods are bailed or (in Scotland) hired in return for periodical payments by the person to whom they are bailed or hired, and

(b) the property in the goods will pass to that person if the terms of the agreement are complied with and one or more of the following occurs –

(i) the exercise of an option to purchase by that person,

(ii) the doing of any other specified act by any party to the agreement,

(iii) the happening of any other specified event;

'hirer' means the individual to whom goods are bailed or (in Scotland) hired under a consumer hire agreement, or the person to whom his rights and duties under the agreement have passed by assignment or operation of law, and in relation to a prospective consumer hire agreement includes the prospective hirer;

'individual' includes –

(a) a partnership consisting of two or three persons not all of whom are bodies corporate; and

(b) an unincorporated body of persons which does not consist entirely of bodies corporate and is not a partnership;

'installation' means –

(a) the installing of any electric line or any gas or water pipe,

(b) the fixing of goods to the premises where they are to be used, and the alteration of premises to enable goods to be used on them,

(c) where it is reasonably necessary that goods should be constructed or erected on the premises where they are to be used, any work carried out for the purpose of constructing or erecting them on those premises;

. . .

'judgment' includes an order or decree made by any court;

'land', includes an interest in land, and in relation to Scotland includes heritable subjects of whatever description;

'land improvement company' means an improvement company as defined by section 7 of the Improvement of Land Act 1899;

'land mortgage' includes any security charged on land;

'licence' means a licence under Part III;

'licensed', in relation to any act, means authorised by a licence to do the act or cause or permit another person to do it;

'licensee', in the case of a group licence, includes any person covered by the licence;

'linked transaction' has the meaning given by section 19(1);

'local authority', in relation to England . . ., means . . . a county council, a London borough council, a district council, the Common Council of the City of London, or the Council of Isles of Scilly, in relation to Wales means a county council or a county borough council, and in relation to Scotland, means a council constituted under section 2 of the Local Government etc (Scotland) Act 1994, and, in relation to Northern Ireland, means a district council;

. . .

'modifying agreement' has the meaning given by section 82(2);

'mortgage', in relation to Scotland, includes any heritable security;

'multiple agreement' has the meaning given by section 18(1);

'negotiator' has the meaning given by section 56(1);

'non-commercial agreement' means a consumer credit agreement or a consumer hire agreement not made by the creditor or owner in the course of a business carried on by him;

'notice' means notice in writing;

'notice of cancellation' has the meaning given by section 69(1);

'OFT' means the Office of Fair Trading;

'owner' means a person who bails or (in Scotland) hires out goods under a consumer hire agreement or the person to whom his rights and duties under the agreement have passed by assignment or operation of law, and in relation to a prospective consumer hire agreement, includes the prospective bailor or persons from whom the goods are to be hired;

'pawn' means any article subject to a pledge;

'pawn-receipt' has the meaning given by section 114;

'pawnee' and 'pawnor' include any person to whom the rights and duties of the original pawnee or the original pawnor, as the case may be, have passed by assignment or operation of law;

'payment' includes tender;

. . .

'pledge' means the pawnee's rights over an article taken in pawn;

'prescribed' means prescribed by regulations made by the Secretary of State;

'pre-existing arrangements' shall be construed in accordance with section 187;

'principal agreement' has the meaning given by section 19(1);

'protected goods' has the meaning given by section 90(7);

'quotation' has the meaning given by section 52(1)(a);

'redemption period' has the meaning given by section 116(3);

'register' means the register kept by the OFT under section 35;

'regulated agreement' means a consumer credit agreement, or consumer hire agreement, other than an exempt agreement, and 'regulated' and 'unregulated' shall be construed accordingly;

'regulations' means regulations made by the Secretary of State;

'relative', except in section 184, means a person who is an associate by virtue of section 184(1);

'representation' includes any condition or warranty, and any other statement or undertaking, whether oral or in writing;

'restricted-use credit agreement' and 'restricted-use credit' have the meanings given by section 11(1);

'rules of court', in relation to Northern Ireland means, in relation to the High Court, rules made under section 7 of the Northern Ireland Act 1962, and, in relation to any other court, rules made by the authority having for the time being power to make rules regulating the practice and procedure in that court;

'running-account credit' shall be construed in accordance with section 10;

'security', in relation to an actual or prospective consumer credit agreement or consumer hire agreement, or any linked transaction, means a mortgage, charge, pledge, bond, debenture, indemnity, guarantee, bill, note or other right provided by the debtor or hirer, or at his request (express or implied), to secure the carrying out of the obligations of the debtor or hirer under the agreement;

'security instrument' has the meaning given by section 105(2);

'serve on' means deliver or send by an appropriate method to;

'signed' shall be construed in accordance with subsection (3);

'small agreement' has the meaning given by section 17(1), and 'small' in relation to an agreement within any category shall be construed accordingly;

'specified fee' shall be construed in accordance with section 2(4) and (5);

'standard licence' has the meaning given by section 22(1)(a);

'supplier' has the meaning given by section 11(1)(b) or 12(c) or 13(c) or, in relation to an agreement falling within section 11(1)(a), means the creditor, and includes a person to whom the rights and duties of a supplier (as so defined) have passed by assignment or operation of law, or (in relation to a prospective agreement) the prospective supplier;

'surety' means the person by whom any security is provided, or the person to whom his rights and duties in relation to the security have passed by assignment or operation of law;

'technical grounds' shall be construed in accordance with subsection (5);

'time order' has the meaning given by section 129(1);

'total charge for credit' means a sum calculated in accordance with regulations under section 20(1);

'total price' means the total sum payable by the debtor under a hire-purchase agreement or a conditional sale agreement, including any sum payable on the exercise of an option to purchase, but excluding any sum payable as a penalty or as compensation or damages for a breach of the agreement;

'the Tribunal' means the Consumer Credit Appeals Tribunal;

'unexecuted agreement' means a document embodying the terms of a prospective regulated agreement, or such of them as it is intended to reduce to writing;

'unlicensed' means without a licence but applies only in relation to acts for which a licence is required;

'unrestricted-use credit agreement' and 'unrestricted-use credit' have the meanings given by section 11(2);

'working day' means any day other than –

    (a)   Saturday or Sunday,

    (b)   Christmas Day or Good Friday,

    (c)   a bank holiday within the meaning given by section 1 of the Banking and Financial Dealings Act 1971.

(1A) In sections 36E(3), 70(4), 73(4) and 75(2) and paragraphs 14 and 15 of Schedule A1 'costs', in relation to proceedings in Scotland, means expenses.

(2) A person is not to be treated as carrying on a particular type of business merely because occasionally he enters into transactions belonging to a business of that type.

(3) Any provision of this Act requiring a document to be signed is complied with by a body corporate if the document is sealed by that body. This subsection does not apply to Scotland.

(4) A document embodies a provision if the provision is set out either in the document itself or in another document referred to in it.

(5) An application dismissed by the court or the OFT shall, if the court or the OFT (as the case may be) so certifies, be taken to be dismissed on technical grounds only.

(6) Except in so far as the context otherwise requires, any reference in this Act to an enactment shall be construed as a reference to that enactment as amended by or under any other enactment, including this Act.

(7) In this Act, except where otherwise indicated –

    (a)   a reference to a numbered Part, section or Schedule is a reference to the Part or section of, or the Schedule to, this Act so numbered, and

    (b)   a reference in a section to a numbered subsection is a reference to the subsection of that section so numbered, and

    (c)   a reference in a section, subsection or Schedule to a numbered paragraph is a reference to the paragraph of that section, subsection or Schedule so numbered.

189A Meaning of 'consumer credit EEA firm'

In this Act 'consumer credit EEA firm' means an EEA firm falling within sub-paragraph (a), (b) or (c) of paragraph 5 of Schedule 3 to the Financial Services and Markets Act 2000 carrying on, or seeking to carry on, consumer credit business, consumer hire business or ancillary credit business for which a licence would be required under this Act but for paragraph 15(3) of Schedule 3 to the Financial Services and Markets Act 2000.

Miscellaneous

190 Financial provisions

(1) There shall be defrayed out of money provided by Parliament –

    (a) all expenses incurred by the Secretary of State in consequence of the provisions of this Act;

    (b) any expenses incurred in consequence of those provisions by any other Minister of the Crown or Government department;

    (c) any increase attributable to this Act in the sums payable out of money so provided under the Superannuation Act 1972 or the Fair Trading Act 1973.

(2) Any fees, charges, penalties or other sums received by the OFT under this Act shall be paid into the Consolidated Fund.

191 Special provisions as to Northern Ireland

(1) The OFT may make arrangements with the Department of Commerce for Northern Ireland for the Department, on the OFT's behalf, –

    (a) to receive applications notices, charges and fees;

    (b) to maintain, and make available for inspection and copying, copies of entries in the register; and

    (c) to provide certified copies of entries in the register,

to the extent that seems to the OFT desirable for the convenience of persons in Northern Ireland.

(2) The OFT shall give general notice of any arrangements made under subsection (1).

(3) Nothing in this Act shall authorise any Northern Ireland department to incur any expenses attributable to the provisions of this Act until provision has been made for those expenses to be defrayed out of money appropriated for the purpose.

(4) The power of the Department of Commerce for Northern Ireland to make an order under section 178 shall be exercisable by statutory rule for the purposes of the Statutory Rules (Northern Ireland) Order 1979, and any such order shall be subject to negative resolution within the meaning of the Interpretation Act (Northern Ireland) 1954 as if it were a statutory instrument within the meaning of that Act.

(5) In this Act 'enactment' includes an enactment of the Parliament of Northern Ireland or the Northern Ireland Assembly, and 'Act' shall be construed in a corresponding manner; and (without prejudice to section 189(6)) any reference in this Act to such an enactment shall include a reference to any enactment re-enacting it with or without modifications.

(6) Section 38 of the Interpretation Act 1889 (effect of repeals) shall have the same operation in relation to any repeal by this Act of an enactment of the Parliament of Northern Ireland as it has in relation to the repeal of an Act of the Parliament of the United Kingdom, references in that section of the Act of 1889 to Acts and enactments being construed accordingly.

192 Transitional and commencement provisions, amendments and repeals

(1) The provisions of Schedule 3 shall have effect for the purposes of this Act.

(2) The appointment of a day for the purposes of any provision of Schedule 3 shall be

effected by an order of the Secretary of State made by statutory instrument; and any such order shall include a provision amending Schedule 3 so as to insert an express reference to the day appointed.

(3) Subject to subsection (4) –

(a) the enactments specified in Schedule 4 shall have effect subject to the amendments specified in that Schedule (being minor amendments or amendments consequential on the preceding provisions of this Act), and

(b) the enactments specified in Schedule 5 are hereby repealed to the extent shown in column 3 of that Schedule.

(4) The Secretary of State shall by order made by statutory instrument provide for the coming into operation of the amendments contained in Schedule 4 and the repeals contained in Schedule 5, and those amendments and repeals shall have effect only as provided by an order so made.

193 Short title and extent

(1) This Act may be cited as the Consumer Credit Act 1974.

(2) This Act extends to Northern Ireland.

SCHEDULES

SCHEDULE A1   THE CONSUMER CREDIT APPEALS TRIBUNAL

PART 1   INTERPRETATION

1   In this Schedule –

'the Deputy President' means the Deputy President of the Consumer Credit Appeals Tribunal;

'lay panel' means the panel established under paragraph 3(3);

'panel of chairmen' means the panel established under paragraph 3(1);

'party' means, in relation to an appeal, the appellant or the OFT;

'the President' means the President of the Consumer Credit Appeals Tribunal;

'rules' means rules under section 40A(3) of this Act;

'specified' means specified by rules.

PART 2   THE TRIBUNAL

The President and the Deputy President

2   (1)   The Lord Chancellor shall appoint one of the members of the panel of chairmen to preside over the discharge of the Tribunal's functions.

(2)   The person so appointed shall be known as the President of the Consumer Credit Appeals Tribunal.

(3)   The Lord Chancellor may appoint one of the members of the panel of chairmen to be the Deputy President of the Consumer Credit Appeals Tribunal.

(4)   The Deputy President shall have such functions in relation to the Tribunal as the President may assign to him.

(5)   If the President or the Deputy President ceases to be a member of the panel of chairmen, he shall also cease to be the President or (as the case may be) the Deputy President.

(6)   The functions of the President may, if he is absent or is otherwise unable to act, be discharged –

(a)   by the Deputy President; or

(b)   if there is no Deputy President or he too is absent or otherwise unable to act, by a person appointed for that purpose from the panel of chairmen by the Lord Chancellor.

Panels

3   (1)   The Lord Chancellor shall appoint a panel of persons for the purpose of serving as chairmen of the Tribunal.

(2)   A person shall not be appointed to the panel of chairmen unless he –

(a)   has a seven year general qualification within the meaning of section 71 of the Courts and Legal Services Act 1990;

(b)   is an advocate or solicitor in Scotland of at least seven years' standing; or

(c)   is a member of the Bar of Northern Ireland, or a solicitor of the Supreme Court of Northern Ireland, of at least seven years' standing.

(3)   The Lord Chancellor shall also appoint a panel of persons who appear to him to be qualified by experience or otherwise to deal with appeals of the kind that may be made to the Tribunal.

Terms of office etc.

4   (1)   Each member of the panel of chairmen or the lay panel shall hold and vacate office in accordance with the terms of his appointment.

(2)   The Lord Chancellor may remove a member of either panel from office on the ground of incapacity or misbehaviour.

(3)   A member of either panel –

(a)   may at any time resign office by notice in writing to the Lord Chancellor;

(b)   is eligible for re-appointment if he ceases to hold office.

Remuneration and allowances

5   The Lord Chancellor may pay to a person in respect of his service –

(a)   as the President or the Deputy President,

(b)   as a member of the Tribunal, or

(c)   as a person appointed under paragraph 7(4),

such remuneration and allowances as the Lord Chancellor may determine.

Staff and costs

6   (1)   The Lord Chancellor may appoint such staff for the Tribunal as he may determine.

(2)   The Lord Chancellor shall defray –

(a)   the remuneration of the Tribunal's staff; and

(b)   such other costs of the Tribunal as he may determine.

PART 3   CONSTITUTION OF THE TRIBUNAL

7   (1)   On an appeal to the Tribunal, the persons to act as members of the Tribunal for the purposes of the appeal shall be selected from the panel of chairmen or the lay panel.

(2)   The selection shall be in accordance with arrangements made by the President for the purposes of this paragraph.

(3)   Those arrangements shall provide for at least one member to be a person selected from the panel of chairmen.

(4)   If it appears to the Tribunal that a matter before it involves a question of fact of special difficulty, it may appoint one or more experts to provide assistance.

PART 4   TRIBUNAL POWERS AND PROCEDURE

Sittings

8   The Tribunal shall sit at such times and in such places as the Lord Chancellor may direct.

Evidence

9   (1)   Subject to sub-paragraph (2), the Tribunal may, on an appeal, consider any evidence that it thinks relevant, whether or not it was available to the OFT at the time it made the determination appealed against.

(2) Rules may make provision restricting the evidence that the Tribunal may consider on an appeal in specified circumstances.

Rules on procedure

10   Rules may include, amongst other things, provision –

(a)   about the withdrawal of appeals;

(b)   about persons who may appear on behalf of a party to an appeal;

(c)   about how an appeal is to be dealt with if a person acting as member of the Tribunal in respect of the appeal becomes unable to act;

(d)   setting time limits in relation to anything that is to be done for the purposes of an appeal or for such limits to be set by the Tribunal or a member of the panel of chairmen;

(e)   for time limits (including the period specified for the purposes of section 41(1) of this Act) to be extended by the Tribunal or a member of the panel of chairmen;

(f)   conferring powers on the Tribunal or a member of the panel of chairmen to give such directions to the parties to an appeal as it or he thinks fit for purposes connected with the conduct and disposal of the appeal;

(g)   about the holding of hearings by the Tribunal or a member of the panel of chairmen (including for such hearings to be held in private);

(h)   placing restrictions on the disclosure of information and documents or for such restrictions to be imposed by the Tribunal or a member of the panel of chairmen;

(i)   about the consequences of a failure to comply with a requirement imposed by or under any rule (including for the immediate dismissal or allowing of an appeal if the Tribunal or a member of the panel of chairmen thinks fit);

(j)   for proceedings on different appeals (including appeals with different appellants) to take place concurrently;

(k)   for the suspension of determinations of the OFT;

(l)   for the suspension of decisions of the Tribunal;

(m)   for the Tribunal to reconsider its decision disposing of an appeal where it has reason to believe that the decision was wrongly made because of an administrative error made by a member of its staff.

Council on Tribunals

11   A member of the Council on Tribunals or of its Scottish Committee shall be entitled –

(a)   to attend any hearing held by the Tribunal or a member of the panel of chairmen whether or not it is held in public; and

(b)   to attend any deliberations of the Tribunal in relation to an appeal.

Disposal of appeals

12   (1)   The Tribunal shall decide an appeal by reference to the grounds of appeal set out in the notice of appeal.

(2)   In disposing of an appeal the Tribunal may do one or more of the following –

(a)   confirm the determination appealed against;

(b)   quash that determination;

(c)   vary that determination;

(d) remit the matter to the OFT for reconsideration and determination in accordance with the directions (if any) given to it by the Tribunal;

(e) give the OFT directions for the purpose of giving effect to its decision.

(3) In the case of an appeal against a determination to impose a penalty, the Tribunal –

(a) has no power by virtue of sub-paragraph (2)(c) to increase the penalty;

(b) may extend the period within which the penalty is to be paid (including in cases where that period has already ended).

(4) Sub-paragraph (3) does not affect –

(a) the Tribunal's power to give directions to the OFT under subparagraph (2)(d); or

(b) what the OFT can do where a matter is remitted to it under subparagraph (2)(d).

(5) Where the Tribunal remits a matter to the OFT, it may direct that the requirements of section 34 of this Act are not to apply, or are only to apply to a specified extent, in relation to the OFT's reconsideration of the matter.

(6) Subject to sub-paragraphs (7) and (8), where the Tribunal remits an application to the OFT, section 6(1) and (3) to (9) of this Act shall apply as if the application had not been previously determined by the OFT.

(7) In the case of a general notice which came into effect after the determination appealed against was made but before the application was remitted, the applicant shall provide any information or document which he is required to provide under section 6(6) within –

(a) the period of 28 days beginning with the day on which the application was remitted; or

(b) such longer period as the OFT may allow.

(8) In the case of –

(a) any information or document which was superseded,

(b) any change in circumstances which occurred, or

(c) any error or omission of which the applicant became aware,

after the determination appealed against was made but before the application was remitted, any notification that is required to be given by the applicant under section 6(7) shall be given within the period of 28 days beginning with the day on which the application was remitted.

Decisions of the Tribunal

13 (1) A decision of the Tribunal may be taken by majority.

(2) A decision of the Tribunal disposing of an appeal shall –

(a) state whether it was unanimous or taken by majority; and

(b) be recorded in a document which –

(i) contains a statement of the reasons for the decision and any other specified information; and

(ii) is signed and dated by a member of the panel of chairmen.

(3) Where the Tribunal disposes of an appeal it shall –

(a) send to each party to the appeal a copy of the document mentioned in sub-paragraph (2)(b); and

(b) publish that document in such manner as it thinks fit.

(4) The Tribunal may exclude from what it publishes under sub-paragraph (3)(b) information of a specified description.

Costs

14 (1) Where the Tribunal disposes of an appeal and –

    (a) it decides that the OFT was wrong to make the determination appealed against, or

    (b) during the course of the appeal the OFT accepted that it was wrong to make that determination,

it may order the OFT to pay to the appellant the whole or a part of the costs incurred by the appellant in relation to the appeal.

  (2) In determining whether to make such an order, and the terms of such an order, the Tribunal shall have regard to whether it was unreasonable for the OFT to make the determination appealed against.

15 Where –

    (a) the Tribunal disposes of an appeal or an appeal is withdrawn before the Tribunal disposes of it, and

    (b) the Tribunal thinks that a party to the appeal acted vexatiously, frivolously or unreasonably in bringing the appeal or otherwise in relation to the appeal,

it may order that party to pay to the other party the whole or a part of the costs incurred by the other party in relation to the appeal.

16 An order of the Tribunal under paragraph 14 or 15 may be enforced –

    (a) as if it were an order of the county court; or

    (b) in Scotland, as if it were an interlocutor of the Court of Session.

SCHEDULE 1   PROSECUTION AND PUNISHMENT OF OFFENCES

Section 167

1 Section	2 Offence	3 Mode of prosecution	4 Imprisonment or fine
7	Knowingly or recklessly giving false information to OFT.	(a) Summarily.	The prescribed sum.
		(b) On indictment.	2 years or a fine or both.
39(1)	Engaging in activities requiring a licence when not a licensee.	(a) Summarily.	The prescribed sum.
		(b) On indictment.	2 years or a fine or both.
39(2)	Carrying on business under a name not specified in licence.	(a) Summarily.	The prescribed sum.
		(b) On indictment.	2 years or a fine or both.
39(3)	Failure to notify changes in registered particulars.	(a) Summarily.	The prescribed sum.
		(b) On indictment.	2 years or a fine or both.
45	Advertising credit where goods etc not available for cash.	(a) Summarily.	The prescribed sum.
		(b) On indictment.	2 years or a fine or both.

1 Section	2 Offence	3 Mode of prosecution	4 Imprisonment or fine
46(1)	False or misleading advertisements.	(a) Summarily.	The prescribed sum.
		(b) On indictment.	2 years or a fine or both.
47(1)	Advertising infringements.	(a) Summarily.	The prescribed sum.
		(b) On indictment.	2 years or a fine or both.
49(1)	Canvassing debtor-creditor agreements off trade premises.	(a) Summarily.	The prescribed sum.
		(b) On indictment.	1 year or a fine or both.
49(2)	Soliciting debtor-creditor agreements during visits made in response to previous oral requests.	(a) Summarily.	The prescribed sum.
		(b) On indictment.	1 year or a fine or both.
50(1)	Sending circulars to minors.	(a) Summarily.	The prescribed sum.
		(b) On indictment.	1 year or a fine or both.
51(1)	Supplying unsolicited credit-tokens.	(a) Summarily.	The prescribed sum.
		(b) On indictment.	2 years or a fine or both.
77(4)	Failure of creditor under fixed-sum credit agreement to supply copies of documents etc.	Summarily.	Level 4 on the standard scale.
78(6)	Failure of creditor under running-account credit agreement to supply copies of documents etc.	Summarily.	Level 4 on the standard scale.
79(3)	Failure of owner under consumer hire agreement to supply copies of documents etc.	Summarily.	Level 4 on the standard scale.
80(2)	Failure to tell creditor or owner whereabouts of goods.	Summarily.	Level 3 on the standard scale.
85(2)	Failure of creditor to supply copy of credit-token agreement.	Summarily.	Level 4 on the standard scale.
97(3)	Failure to supply debtor with statement of amount required to discharge agreement.	Summarily.	Level 3 on the standard scale.
103(5)	Failure to deliver notice relating to discharge of agreements.	Summarily.	Level 3 on the standard scale.
107(4)	Failure of creditor to give information to surety under fixed-sum credit agreement.	Summarily.	Level 4 on the standard scale.

1 Section	2 Offence	3 Mode of prosecution	4 Imprisonment or fine
108(4)	Failure of creditor to give information to surety under running-account credit agreement.	Summarily.	Level 4 on the standard scale.
109(3)	Failure of owner to give information to surety under consumer hire agreement.	Summarily.	Level 4 on the standard scale.
110(3)	Failure of creditor or owner to supply a copy of any security instrument to debtor or hirer.	Summarily.	Level 4 on the standard scale.
114(2)	Taking pledges from minors.	(a) Summarily. (b) On indictment.	The prescribed sum. 1 year or a fine or both.
115	Failure to supply copies of a pledge agreement or pawn-receipt.	Summarily.	Level 4 on the standard scale.
119(1)	Unreasonable refusal to allow pawn to be redeemed.	Summarily.	Level 4 on the standard scale.
154	Canvassing ancillary credit services off trade premises.	(a) Summarily. (b) On indictment.	The prescribed sum. 1 year or a fine or both.
157(3)	Refusal to give name etc of credit reference agency.	Summarily.	Level 4 on the standard scale.
158(4)	Failure of credit reference agency to disclose filed information.	Summarily.	Level 4 on the standard scale.
159(6)	Failure of credit reference agency to correct information.	Summarily.	Level 4 on the standard scale.
160(6)	Failure of credit reference agency to comply with section 160(3) or (4).	Summarily.	Level 4 on the standard scale.
162(6)	Impersonation of enforcement authority officers.	(a) Summarily. (b) On indictment.	The prescribed sum. 2 years or a fine or both.
165(1)	Obstruction of enforcement authority officers.	Summarily.	Level 4 on the standard scale.
165(2)	Giving false information to enforcement authority officers.	(a) Summarily. (b) On indictment.	The prescribed sum. 2 years or a fine or both.
167(2)	Contravention of regulations under section 44, 52, 53, 54 or 112.	(a) Summarily. (b) On indictment.	The prescribed sum. 2 years or a fine or both.
174(5)	Wrongful disclosure of information.	(a) Summarily. (b) On indictment.	The prescribed sum. 2 years or a fine or both.

SCHEDULE 2   EXAMPLES OF USE OF NEW TERMINOLOGY

Section 188(1)

PART I   LIST OF TERMS

Term	Defined in section	Illustrated by example(s)
Advertisement	189(1)	2
Advertiser	189(1)	2
Antecedent negotiations	56	1, 2, 3, 4
Cancellable agreement	67	4
Consumer credit agreement	8	5, 6, 7, 15, 19, 21
Consumer hire agreement	15	20, 24
Credit	9	16, 19, 21
Credit-broker	189(1)	2
Credit limit	10(2)	6, 7, 19, 22, 23
Creditor	189(1)	1, 2, 3, 4
Credit-sale agreement	189(1)	5
Credit-token	14	3, 14, 16
Credit-token agreement	14	3, 14, 16, 22
Debtor-creditor agreement	13	8, 16, 17, 18
Debtor-creditor-supplier agreement	12	8, 16
Fixed-sum credit	10	9, 10, 17, 23
Hire-purchase agreement	189(1)	10
Individual	189(1)	19, 24
Linked transaction	19	11
Modifying agreement	82(2)	24
Multiple agreement	18	16, 18
Negotiator	56(1)	1, 2, 3, 4
. . .	. . .	. . .
Pre-existing arrangements	187	8, 21
Restricted-use credit	11	10, 12, 13, 14, 16
Running-account credit	10	15, 16, 18, 23
Small agreement	17	16, 17, 22
Supplier	189(1)	3, 14
Total charge for credit	20	5, 10
Total price	189(1)	10
Unrestricted-use credit	11	8, 12, 16, 17, 18

PART II   EXAMPLES

Example 1

Facts. Correspondence passes between an employee of a moneylending company (writing on behalf of the company) and an individual about the terms on which the company would grant him a loan under a regulated agreement.
Analysis. The correspondence constitutes antecedent negotiations falling within section 56(1)(a), the moneylending company being both creditor and negotiator.

Example 2

Facts. Representations are made about goods in a poster displayed by a shopkeeper near the goods, the goods being selected by a customer who has read the poster and then sold by the shopkeeper to a finance company introduced by him (with whom he has a business relationship). The goods are disposed of by the finance company to the customer under a regulated hire-purchase agreement.

Analysis. The representations in the poster constitute antecedent negotiations falling within section 56(1)(b), the shopkeeper being the credit-broker and negotiator and the finance company being the creditor. The poster is an advertisement and the shopkeeper is the advertiser.

Example 3

Facts. Discussions take place between a shopkeeper and a customer about goods the customer wishes to buy using a credit-card issued by the D Bank under a regulated agreement.

Analysis. The discussions constitute antecedent negotiations falling within section 56(1)(c), the shopkeeper being the supplier and negotiator and the D Bank the creditor. The credit-card is a credit-token as defined in section 14(1), and the regulated agreement under which it was issued is a credit-token agreement as defined in section 14(2).

Example 4

Facts. Discussions take place and correspondence passes between a secondhand car dealer and a customer about a car, which is then sold by the dealer to the customer under a regulated conditional sale agreement. Subsequently, on a revocation of that agreement by consent, the car is resold by the dealer to a finance company introduced by him (with whom he has a business relationship), who in turn dispose of it to the same customer under a regulated hire-purchase agreement.

Analysis. The discussions and correspondence constitute antecedent negotiations in relation both to the conditional sale agreement and the hire-purchase agreement. They fall under section 56(1)(a) in relation to the conditional sale agreement, the dealer being the creditor and the negotiator. In relation to the hire-purchase agreement they fall within section 56(1)(b), the dealer continuing to be treated as the negotiator but the finance company now being the creditor. Both agreements are cancellable if the discussions took place when the individual conducting the negotiations (whether the 'negotiator' or his employee or agent) was in the presence of the debtor, unless the unexecuted agreement was signed by the debtor at trade premises (as defined in section 67(b)). If the discussions all took place by telephone however, or the unexecuted agreement was signed by the debtor on trade premises (as so defined) the agreements are not cancellable.

Example 5

Facts. E agrees to sell to F (an individual) an item of furniture in return for 24 monthly instalments of £10 payable in arrears. The property in the goods passes to F immediately.

Analysis. This is a credit-sale agreement (see definition of 'credit-sale agreement' in section 189(1)). The credit provided amounts to £240 less the amount which, according to regulations made under section 20(1), constitutes the total charge for credit. (This amount is required to be deducted by section 9(4)). Accordingly the agreement falls within section 8(2) and is a consumer credit agreement.

Example 6

Facts. The G Bank grants H (an individual) an unlimited overdraft, with an increased rate of interest on so much of any debit balance as exceeds £2,000.

Analysis. Although the overdraft purports to be unlimited, the stipulation for increased interest above £2,000 brings the agreement within section 10(3)(b)(ii) and it is a consumer credit agreement.

Example 7

Facts. J is an individual who owns a small shop which usually carries a stock worth about £1,000. K makes a stocking agreement under which he undertakes to provide on short-term credit the stock needed from time to time by J without any specified limit.

Analysis. Although the agreement appears to provide unlimited credit, it is probable, having regard to the stock usually carried by J, that his indebtedness to K will not at any time rise above £5,000. Accordingly the agreement falls within section 10(3)(b)(iii) and is a consumer credit agreement.

Example 8

Facts. U, a moneylender, lends £500 to V (an individual) knowing he intends to use it to buy office equipment from W. W introduced V to U, it being his practice to introduce customers needing finance to him. Sometimes U gives W a commission for this and sometimes not. U pays the £500 direct to V.

Analysis. Although this appears to fall under section 11(1)(b), it is excluded by section 11(3) and is therefore (by section 11(2)) an unrestricted-use credit agreement. Whether it is a debtor-creditor agreement (by section 13(c)) or a debtor-creditor-supplier agreement (by section 12(c)) depends on whether the previous dealings between U and W amount to 'pre-existing arrangements', that is whether the agreement can be taken to have been entered into 'in accordance with, or in furtherance of' arrangements previously made between U and W, as laid down in section 187(1).

Example 9

Facts. A agrees to lend B (an individual) £4,500 in nine monthly instalments of £500.

Analysis. This is a cash loan and is a form of credit (see section 9 and definition of 'cash' in section 189(1)). Accordingly it falls within section 10(1)(b) and is fixed-sum credit amounting to £4,500.

Example 10

Facts. C (in England) agrees to bail goods to D (an individual) in return for periodical payments. The agreement provides for the property in the goods to pass to D on payment of a total of £7,500 and the exercise by D of an option to purchase. The sum of £7,500 includes a down-payment of £1,000. It also includes an amount which, according to regulations made under section 20(1), constitutes a total charge for credit of £1,500.

Analysis. This is a hire-purchase agreement with a deposit of £1,000 and a total price of £7,500 (see definitions of 'hire-purchase agreement', 'deposit' and 'total price' in section 189(1)). By section 9(3), it is taken to provide credit amounting to £7,500 − (£1,500 + £1,000), which equals £5,000. Under section 8(2), the agreement is therefore a consumer credit agreement, and under sections 9(3) and 11(1) it is a restricted-use credit agreement for fixed-sum credit. A similar result would follow if the agreement by C had been a hiring agreement in Scotland.

Example 11

Facts. X (an individual) borrows £500 from Y (Finance). As a condition of the granting of the loan X is required –

    (a) to execute a second mortgage on his house in favour of Y (Finance), and

    (b) to take out a policy of insurance on his life with Y (Insurances).

In accordance with the loan agreement, the policy is charged to Y (Finance) as collateral security for the loan. The two companies are associates within the meaning of section 184(3).

Analysis. The second mortgage is a transaction for the provision of security and accordingly does not fall within section 19(1), but the taking out of the insurance policy is a linked transaction falling within section 19(1)(a). The charging of the policy is a separate transaction (made between different parties) for the provision of security and again is excluded from section 19(1). The only linked transaction is therefore the taking out of the insurance policy. If X had not been required by the loan agreement to take out the policy, but it had been done at the suggestion of Y (Finance) to induce them to enter into the loan agreement, it would have been a linked transaction under section 19(1)(c)(i) by virtue of section 19(2)(a).

Example 12

Facts. The N Bank agrees to lend O (an individual) £2,000 to buy a car from P. To make sure the loan is used as intended, the N Bank stipulates that the money must be paid by it direct to P.

Analysis. The agreement is a consumer credit agreement by virtue of section 8(2). Since it falls within section 11(1)(b), it is a restricted-use credit agreement, P being the supplier. If the N Bank had not stipulated for direct payment to the supplier, section 11(3) would have operated and made the agreement into one for unrestricted-use credit.

Example 13

Facts. Q, a debt-adjuster, agrees to pay off debts owed by R (an individual) to various moneylenders. For this purpose the agreement provides for the making of a loan by Q to R in return for R's agreeing to repay the loan by instalments with interest. The loan money is not paid over to R but retained by Q and used to pay off the moneylenders.

Analysis. This is an agreement to refinance existing indebtedness of the debtor's, and if the loan by Q does not exceed £5,000 is a restricted-use credit agreement falling within section 11(1)(c).

Example 14

Facts. On payment of £1, S issues to T (an individual) a trading check under which T can spend up to £20 at any shop which has agreed, or in future agrees, to accept S's trading checks.

Analysis. The trading check is a credit-token falling within section 14(1)(b). The credit-token agreement is a restricted-use credit agreement within section 11(1)(b), any shop in which the credit-token is used being the 'supplier'. The fact that further shops may be added after the issue of the credit-token is irrelevant in view of section 11(4).

Example 15

Facts. A retailer, L, agrees with M (an individual) to open an account in M's name and, in return for M's promise to pay a specified minimum sum into the account each month and to pay a monthly charge for credit, agrees to allow to be debited to the account, in respect of purchases made by M from L, such sums as will not increase the debit balance at any time beyond the credit limit, defined in the agreement as a given multiple of the specified minimum sum.

Analysis. This arrangement provides credit falling within the definition of running-account credit in section 10(1)(a). Provided the credit limit is not over £5,000, the agreement falls within section 8(2) and is a consumer credit agreement for running-account credit.

Example 16

Facts. Under an unsecured agreement, A (Credit), an associate of the A Bank, issues to B (an individual) a credit-card for use in obtaining cash on credit from A (Credit), to be paid by branches of the A Bank (acting as agent of A (Credit)), or goods or cash from suppliers or banks who have agreed to honour credit-cards issued by A (Credit). The credit limit is £30.

Analysis. This is a credit-token agreement falling within section 14(1)(a) and (b). It is a regulated consumer credit agreement for running-account credit. Since the credit limit does not exceed £30, the agreement is a small agreement. So far as the agreement relates to goods it is a debtor-creditor-supplier agreement within section 12(b), since it provides restricted-use credit under section 11(1)(b). So far as it relates to cash it is a debtor-creditor agreement within section 13(c) and the credit it provides is unrestricted-use credit. This is therefore a multiple agreement. In that the whole agreement falls within several of the categories of agreement mentioned in this Act, it is, by section 18(3), to be treated as an agreement in each of those categories. So far as it is a debtor-creditor-supplier agreement providing restricted-use credit it is, by section 18(2), to be treated as a separate agreement; and similarly so far as it is a debtor-creditor agreement providing unrestricted-used credit. (See also Example 22.)

Example 17

Facts. The manager of the C Bank agrees orally with D (an individual) to open a current account in D's name. Nothing is said about overdraft facilities. After maintaining the account in credit for some weeks, D draws a cheque in favour of E for an amount exceeding D's credit balance by £20. E presents the cheque and the Bank pay it.

Analysis. In drawing the cheque D, by implication, requests the Bank to grant him an overdraft of £20 on its usual terms as to interest and other charges. In deciding to honour the cheque, the Bank by implication accepts the offer. This constitutes a regulated small consumer credit agreement for unrestricted-use, fixed-sum credit. It is a debtor-creditor agreement, and falls within section 74(1)(b) if covered by a determination under section 74(3). (Compare Example 18.)

Example 18

Facts. F (an individual) has had a current account with the G Bank for many years. Although usually in credit, the account has been allowed by the Bank to become overdrawn from time to time. The maximum such overdraft has been is about £1,000. No explicit agreement has ever been made about overdraft facilities. Now, with a credit balance of £500, F draws a cheque for £1,300.

Analysis. It might well be held that the agreement with F (express or implied) under which the Bank operate his account includes an implied term giving him the right to overdraft facilities up to say £1,000. If so, the agreement is a regulated consumer credit agreement for unrestricted-use, running-account credit. It is a debtor-creditor agreement, and falls within section 74(1)(b) if covered by a direction under section 74(3). It is also a multiple agreement, part of which (i.e. the part not dealing with the overdraft), as referred to in section 18(1)(a), falls within a category of agreement not mentioned in this Act. (Compare Example 17.)

Example 19

Facts. H (a finance house) agrees with J (a partnership of individuals) to open an unsecured loan account in J's name on which the debit balance is not to exceed £7,000 (having regard to payments into the account made from time to time by J). Interest is to be payable in advance on this sum, with provision for yearly adjustments. H is entitled to debit the account with interest, a 'setting-up' charge, and other charges. Before J has an opportunity to draw on the account it is initially debited with £2,250 for advance interest and other charges.

Analysis. This is a personal running-account credit agreement (see sections 8(1) and 10(1)(a), and definition of 'individual' in section 189(1)). By section 10(2) the credit limit is £7,000. By section 9(4) however the initial debit of £2,250, and any other charges later debited to the account by H, are not to be treated as credit even though time is allowed for their payment. Effect is given to this by section 10(3). Although the credit limit of £7,000 exceeds the amount (£5,000) specified in section 8(2) as the maximum for a consumer credit agreement, so that the agreement is not within section 10(3)(a), it is caught by section 10(3)(b)(i). At the beginning J can effectively draw (as credit) no more than £4,750, so the agreement is a consumer credit agreement.

Example 20

Facts. K (in England) agrees with L (an individual) to bail goods to L for a period of three years certain at £2,000 a year, payable quarterly. The agreement contains no provision for the passing of the property in the goods to L.

Analysis. This is not a hire-purchase agreement (see paragraph (b) of the definition of that term in section 189(1)) and is capable of subsisting for more than three months. Paragraphs (a) and (b) of section 15(1) are therefore satisfied, but paragraph (c) is not. The payments by L must exceed £5,000 if he conforms to the agreement. It is true that under section 101 L has a right to terminate the agreement on giving K three months' notice expiring not earlier than eighteen months after the making of the agreement, but that section applies only where the agreement is a regulated consumer hire agreement apart from the section (see subsection (1)). So the agreement is not a consumer hire agreement, though it would be if the hire charge were say £1,500 a year, or there were a 'break' clause in it operable by either party before the hire charges exceeded £5,000. A similar result would follow if the agreement by K had been a hiring agreement in Scotland.

Example 21

Facts. The P Bank decides to issue cheque cards to its customers under a scheme whereby the Bank undertakes to honour cheques of up to £30 in every case where the payee has taken the cheque in reliance on the cheque card, whether the customer has funds in his account or not. The P Bank writes to the major retailers advising them of this scheme and also publicises it by advertising. The Bank issues a cheque card to Q (an individual), who uses it to pay by cheque for goods costing £20 bought by Q from R, a major retailer. At the time, Q has £500 in his account at the P Bank.

Analysis. The agreement under which the cheque card is issued to Q is a consumer credit agreement even though at all relevant times Q has more than £30 in his account. This is because Q is free to draw out his whole balance and then use the cheque card, in which case the Bank has bound itself to honour the cheque. In other words the cheque card agreement provides Q with credit, whether he avails himself of it or not. Since the amount of the credit is not subject to any express limit, the cheque card can be used any number of times. It may be presumed however that section 10(3)(b)(iii) will apply. The agreement is an unrestricted-use debtor-creditor agreement (by section 13(c)). Although the P Bank wrote to R informing R of the P Bank's willingness to honour any cheque taken by R in reliance on a cheque card, this does not constitute pre-existing arrangements as mentioned in section 13(c) because section 187(3) operates to prevent it. The agreement is not a credit-token agreement within section 14(1)(b) because payment by the P Bank to R, would be a payment of the cheque and not a payment for the goods.

Example 22

Facts. The facts are as in Example 16. On one occasion B uses the credit-card in a way which increases his debit balance with A (Credit) to £40. A (Credit) writes to B agreeing to allow the excess on that occasion only, but stating that it must be paid off within one month.

Analysis. In exceeding his credit limit B, by implication, requests A (Credit) to allow him a temporary excess (compare Example 17). A (Credit) is thus faced by B's action with the choice of treating it as a breach of contract or granting his implied request. He does the latter. If he had done the former, B would be treated as taking credit to which he was not entitled (section 14(3)) and, subject to the terms of his contract with A (Credit), would be liable to damages for breach of contract. As it is, the agreement to allow the excess varies the original credit-token agreement by adding a new term. Under section 10(2), the new term is to be disregarded in arriving at the credit limit, so that the credit-token agreement at no time ceases to be a small agreement. By section 82(2) the later agreement is deemed to revoke the original agreement and contain provisions reproducing the combined effect of the two agreements. By section 82(4), this later agreement is exempted from Part V (except section 56).

Example 23

Facts. Under an oral agreement made on 10th January, X (an individual) has an overdraft on his current account at the Y Bank with a credit limit of £100. On 15th February, when his overdraft stands at £90, X draws a cheque for £5. It is the first time that X has exceeded his credit limit, and on 16th February the bank honours the cheque.

Analysis. The agreement of 10th January is a consumer credit agreement for running-account credit. The agreement of 15th-16th February varies the earlier agreement by adding a term allowing the credit limit to be exceeded merely temporarily. By section 82(2) the later agreement is deemed to revoke the earlier agreement and reproduce the combined effect of the two agreements. By section 82(4), Part V of this Act (except section 56) does not apply to the later agreement. By section 18(5), a term allowing a merely temporary excess over the credit limit is not to be treated as a separate agreement, or as providing fixed-sum credit. The whole of the £115 owed to the Bank by X on 16th February is therefore running-account credit.

Example 24

Facts. On 1st March 1975 Z (in England) enters into an agreement with A (an unincorporated body of persons) to bail to A equipment consisting of two components (component

P and component Q). The agreement is not a hire-purchase agreement and is for a fixed term of 3 years, so paragraphs (a) and (b) of section 15(1) are both satisfied. The rental is payable monthly at a rate of £2,400 a year, but the agreement provides that this is to be reduced to £1,200 a year for the remainder of the agreement if at any time during its currency A returns component Q to the owner Z. On 5th May 1976 A is incorporated as A Ltd., taking over A's assets and liabilities. On 1st March 1977, A Ltd. returns component Q. On 1st January 1978, Z and A Ltd. agree to extend the earlier agreement by one year, increasing the rental for the final year by £250 to £1,450.

Analysis. When entered into on 1st March 1975, the agreement is a consumer hire agreement. A falls within the definition of 'individual' in section 189(1) and if A returns component Q before 1st May 1976 the total rental will not exceed £5,000 (see section 15(1)(c)). When this date is passed without component Q having been returned it is obvious that the total rental must now exceed £5,000. Does this mean that the agreement then ceases to be a consumer hire agreement? The answer is no, because there has been no change in the terms of the agreement, and without such a change the agreement cannot move from one category to the other. Similarly, the fact that A's rights and duties under the agreement pass to a body corporate on 5th May 1976 does not cause the agreement to cease to be a consumer hire agreement (see the definition of 'hirer' in section 189(1)).

The effect of the modifying agreement of 1st January 1978 is governed by section 82(2), which requires it to be treated as containing provisions reproducing the combined effect of the two actual agreements, that is to say as providing that –

(a) obligations outstanding on 1st January 1978 are to be treated as outstanding under the modifying agreement;
(b) the modifying agreement applies at the old rate of hire for the months of January and February 1978, and
(c) for the year beginning 1st March 1978 A Ltd. will be the bailee of component P at a rental of £1,450.

The total rental under the modifying agreement is £1,850. Accordingly the modifying agreement is a regulated agreement. Even if the total rental under the modifying agreement exceeded £5,000 it would still be regulated because of the provisions of section 82(3).

SCHEDULE 3   TRANSITIONAL AND COMMENCEMENT PROVISIONS

Section 192(1)

Note. Except as otherwise mentioned in this Schedule, the provisions of this Act come into operation on its passing, that is on 31st July 1974.

PART II OF ACT   CREDIT AGREEMENTS, HIRE AGREEMENTS AND LINKED TRANSACTIONS

Regulated agreements

1   (1) An agreement made before 1st April 1977 is not a regulated agreement within the meaning of this Act.

(2) In this Act 'prospective regulated agreement' does not include a prospective agreement which, if made as expected, would be made before the day appointed for the purposes of this paragraph.

Linked transactions

2   A transaction may be a linked transaction in relation to a regulated agreement or prospective regulated agreement even though the transaction was entered into before the day appointed for the purposes of paragraph 1.

3   Section 19(3) applies only to transactions entered into on or after 19th May 1985.

Total charge for credit

4   Section 20 applies to consumer credit agreements whenever made.

PART III OF ACT   LICENSING OF CREDIT AND HIRE BUSINESS

Businesses needing a licence

5   (1) Section 21 does not apply to the carrying on of any description of consumer credit business or consumer hire business –

    (a) before 31st July 1989 in the case of a consumer credit business which is carried on by an individual and in the course of which only the following regulated consumer credit agreements (excluding agreements made before that date) are made, namely –

        (i)   agreements for fixed-sum credit not exceeding £30, and

        (ii) agreements for running-account credit where the credit limit does not exceed that amount;

    (b) before 1st October 1977 in the case of any other description of consumer credit business; and

    (c) before 1st October 1977 in the case of any consumer hire business.

(2) Where the person carrying on a consumer credit business or consumer hire business applies for a licence –

    (a) before 31st July 1989 in the case of a consumer credit business to which sub-paragraph (1)(a) above applies, or

    (b) before 1st October 1977 in the case of any other description of consumer credit business or in the case of any consumer hire business,

he shall be deemed to have been granted on 31st July 1989 or 1st October 1977, as the case may be, a licence covering that business and continuing in force until the licence applied for is granted or, if the application is refused, until the end of the appeal period.

The register

6   Sections 35 and 36 come into operation on 2nd February 1976.

Enforcement of agreements made by unlicensed trader

7   Section 40 does not apply to a regulated agreement made in the course of any business before the day specified or referred to in paragraph 5(1) in relation to the description of business in question.

PART IV OF ACT   SEEKING BUSINESS

Advertisements

8   Part IV does not apply to any advertisement published before 6th October 1980.

Canvassing

9   Section 49 comes into operation on 1st October 1977.

Circulars to minors

10   Section 50 comes into operation on 1st July 1977.

Unsolicited credit-tokens

11   (1)   Section 51(1) does not apply to the giving of a credit-token before 1st July 1977.
       (2)   In section 51(3), 'agreement' means an agreement whenever made.

PART V OF ACT   ENTRY INTO CREDIT OR HIRE AGREEMENT

Antecedent negotiations

12   (1)   Section 56 applies to negotiations in relation to an actual or prospective regulated agreement where the negotiations begin after 16th May 1977.
       (2)   In section 56(3), 'agreement', where it first occurs, means an agreement whenever made.

General

13   Sections 57 to 59, 61 to 65 and 67 to 73 come into operation on 19th May 1985.
14   Section 66 comes into operation on 19th May 1985.

PART VI OF ACT   MATTERS ARISING DURING CURRENCY OF CREDIT OR HIRE AGREEMENTS

Liability of creditor for breaches by supplier

15   Section 75 comes into operation on 1st July 1977 but only in relation to regulated agreements made on or after that day.

Duty to give notice

16   (1)   Section 76 comes into operation on 19th May 1985.
       (2)   Section 76 applies to an agreement made before 19th May 1985 where the agreement would have been a regulated agreement if made on that day.

Duty to give information

17 (1) Sections 77 to 80 come into operation on 19th May 1985.

(2) Sections 77 to 79 apply to an agreement made before 19th May 1985 where the agreement would have been a regulated agreement if made on that day.

Appropriation of payments

18 Section 81 comes into operation on 19th May 1985.

Variation of agreements

19 Section 82 comes into operation on 1st April 1977.

Misuse of credit facilities

20 (1) Sections 83 and 84 come into operation on 19th May 1985.

(2) Subject to sub-paragraph (4), section 83 applies to an agreement made before 19th May 1985 where the agreement would have been a regulated consumer credit agreement if made on that day.

(3) Subject to sub-paragraph (4), section 84 applies to an agreement made before 19th May 1985 where the agreement would have been a credit-token agreement if made on that day.

(4) Sections 83 and 84 do not apply to losses arising before 19th May 1985.

(5) Section 84(4) shall be taken to be satisfied in relation to an agreement made before 19th May 1985 if, within 28 days after that day, the creditor gives notice to the debtor of the name, address and telephone number of a person stated in that notice to be the person to whom notice is to be given under section 84(3).

Duty on issue of new credit-tokens

21 (1) Section 85 comes into operation on 19th May 1985.

(2) Section 85 applies to an agreement made before 19th May 1985 where the agreement would have been a regulated agreement if made on that day.

Death of debtor or hirer

22 (1) Section 86 comes into operation on 19th May 1985.

(2) Section 86 applies to an agreement made before 19th May 1985 where the agreement would have been a regulated agreement if made on that day.

PART VII OF ACT   DEFAULT AND TERMINATION

Default notices

23 Sections 87 to 89 come into operation on 19th May 1985.

Retaking of goods and land

24 Sections 90 and 91 come into operation on 19th May 1985.

25   Section 92 comes into operation on 19th May 1985.

Interest on default

26   Section 93 comes into operation on 19th May 1985.

Early payment by debtor

27   Sections 94 to 97 come into operation on 19th May 1985.

Termination of agreements

28   Section 98 comes into operation on 19th May 1985.
28   Section 99 comes into operation on 19th May 1985.
30   Section 100 comes into operation on 19th May 1985.
31   Section 101 comes into operation on 19th May 1985.
32   Section 102 comes into operation on 19th May 1985.
33   Section 103 comes into operation on 19th May 1985.
34   Section 104 comes into operation on 19th May 1985.

Old agreements

35   Part VII (except sections 90, 91, 93 and 99 to 102 and 104) applies to an agreement made before 19th May 1985 where the agreement would have been a regulated agreement if made on that day.

PART VIII OF ACT   SECURITY

General

36   Section 105 comes into operation on 19th May 1985.
37   (1)   Sections 107 to 110 come into operation on 19th May 1985.
       (2)   Sections 107 to 110 apply to an agreement made before 19th May 1985 where the agreement would have been a regulated agreement if made on that day.
38   (1)   Section 111 comes into operation on 19th May 1985.
       (2)   Section 111 applies to an agreement made before 19th May 1985 where the agreement would have been a regulated agreement if made on that day.

Pledges

39   Sections 114 to 122 come into operation on 19th May 1985 but only in respect of articles taken in pawn under a regulated consumer credit agreement.

Negotiable instruments

40   Sections 123 to 125 come into operation on 19th May 1985.

Land mortgages

41   Section 126 comes into operation on 19th May 1985.

PART IX OF ACT   JUDICIAL CONTROL

42   Sections 137 to 140 (extortionate credit bargains) come into operation on 16th May 1977, and apply to agreements and transactions whenever made.

43   Subject to paragraph 42, Part IX comes into operation on 19th May 1985.

PART X OF ACT   ANCILLARY CREDIT BUSINESSES

Licensing

44   (1)   Section 21(1) does not apply (by virtue of section 147(1)) to the carrying on of any ancillary credit business before 3rd August 1976 in the case of any business so far as it comprises or relates to –

(a)   debt-adjusting,
(b)   debt-counselling,
(c)   debt-collecting, or
(d)   the operation of a credit reference agency.

(1A) Section 21(1) does not apply (by virtue of section 147(1)) to the carrying on of any ancillary credit business before 1st July 1978 so far as it comprises or relates to credit brokerage, not being a business which is carried on by an individual and in the course of which introductions are effected only of individuals desiring to obtain credit –

(a)   under debtor-creditor-supplier agreements which fall within section 12(a) and where, in the case of any such agreement –

(i)   the person carrying on the business would be willing to sell the goods which are the subject of the agreement to the debtor under a transaction not financed by credit, and
(ii)   the amount of credit does not exceed £30; and

(b)   under debtor-creditor-supplier agreements which fall within section 12(b) or (c) and where, in the case of any such agreement –

(i)   the person carrying on the business is the supplier,
(ii)   the creditor is a person referred to in section 145(2)(a)(i), and
(iii)   the amount of credit or, in the case of an agreement for running-account credit, the credit limit does not exceed £30.

(1B) Section 21(1) does not apply (by virtue of section 147(1)) to the carrying on of any ancillary credit business before the day appointed for the purposes of this paragraph in the case of any description of ancillary credit business in relation to which no day is appointed under the foregoing provisions of this paragraph.

(2)   Where the person carrying on an ancillary credit business applies for a licence before –

(a)   3rd August 1976 in the case of an ancillary credit business of a description to which subparagraph (1) above applies;
(b)   1st July 1978 in the case of an ancillary credit business of a description to which subparagraph (1A) above applies; or
(c)   the day appointed for the purposes of this paragraph in the case of an ancillary credit business to which subparagraph (1B) above applies,

he shall be deemed to have been granted on 3rd August 1976, 1st July 1978 or the day so appointed, as the case may be, a licence covering the description of ancillary credit business in question and continuing in force until the licence applied for is granted or, if the application is refused, until the end of the appeal period.

Enforcement of agreements made by unlicensed trader

45   Section 148(1) does not apply to an agreement made in the course of any business before 3rd August 1976 in the case of any business so far as it comprises or relates to –

(a) debt-adjusting,
(b) debt-counselling,
(c) debt-collecting, or
(d) the operation of a credit reference agency,

or before 1st July 1978 in the case of an ancillary credit business of a description to which subparagraph (1A) of paragraph 44 applies or before the day appointed for the purposes of that paragraph in the case of an ancillary credit business to which subparagraph (1B) of that paragraph applies.

Introductions by unlicensed credit-broker

46   Section 149 does not apply to a regulated agreement made on an introduction effected in the course of any business if the introduction was effected before 1st July 1978 in the case of an ancillary credit business to which subparagraph (1A) of paragraph 44 applies or before the day appointed for the purposes of that paragraph in the case of an ancillary credit business to which subparagraph (1B) of that paragraph applies.

Advertisements

47   Subsections (1) and (2) of section 151 do not apply to any advertisement published before 6th October 1980.

Credit reference agencies

48   Sections 157 and 158 do not apply to a request received before 16th May 1977.

PART XII OF ACT   SUPPLEMENTAL

Interpretation

49   (1) In the case of an agreement –
(a) which was made before 19th May 1985, and
(b) to which (by virtue of paragraph 17(2)) section 78(4) applies,

section 185(2) shall have effect as respects a notice given before that day in relation to the agreement (whether given before or after the passing of this Act) as it would have effect if section 78(4) had been in operation when the notice was given.

(2) Paragraph (1) applies to an agreement made on or after 19th May 1985 to provide credit on a current account opened before that day as it applies to an agreement made before that day.

50

. . .

SCHEDULE 4   MINOR AND CONSEQUENTIAL AMENDMENTS

Section 192

PART I   UNITED KINGDOM

1–27

. . .

28

. . .

29–37

. . .

PART II   NORTHERN IRELAND

38–51

. . .

INDEX

Execution of Documents

A Practical Guide

Mark Anderson and Victor Warner

This practical and user-friendly book provides all of the tools required to execute the more commonly encountered legal documents, including:

- deeds
- contracts
- powers of attorney
- documents used in litigation.

A step-by-step guide to the correct procedure is provided for each type of document, together with a commentary on the underlying legal principles.

Fully up-to-date, the book considers the introduction of electronic signatures and the Law Commission's proposals for changes to the execution of documents by corporations. It also features a helpful range of execution clauses and signature blocks. The book will be invaluable to any practitioner conducting commercial or property transactions or private client work.

Available from Marston Book Services:
Tel. 01235 465 656.

1 85328 980 9
416 pages
£39.95
January 2005

The Law Society

Freedom of Information Handbook

General Editors: Peter Carey and Marcus Turle

The Freedom of Information Handbook offers a straightforward and authoritative overview of the law. It is accessible and practical, providing:

• full coverage of the Codes of Practice for public authorities, model publication schemes and important secondary legislation
• explanations of the practical consequences of the law
• a clear and user-friendly narrative.

Written by a team of leading experts in the freedom of information field, the book is indispensable for public bodies' legal officers and departments, freedom of information officers and those new to the area. It is equally suitable for solicitors advising clients with commercial or contractual interests affected by the Freedom of Information Act.

Available from Marston Book Services:
Tel. 01235 465 656.

1 85328 968 X
360 pages
£69.95
January 2006

The Law Society

Pensions Act 2004

A Guide to the New Law

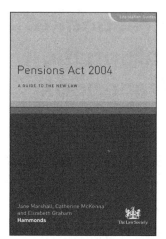

Jane Marshall, Catherine McKenna and Elizabeth Graham

Written by an experienced team of specialist lawyers, this practical and concise guide provides a clear and complete overview of the provisions of this important new Act, which is reproduced in full for ease of reference.

The far-reaching financial and regulatory changes are covered in detail, concentrating on their practical effects. Each chapter looks at a key area of pensions law putting the provisions of the Act in the relevant context, for example:

• trustee responsibilities
• funding and investments
• winding up and insolvency
• amending pension schemes
• the Pension Protection Fund.

Available from Marston Book Services:
Tel. 01235 465 656.

1 85328 923 X
568 pages
£44.95
April 2005

The Law Society